The Sexual Face of Violence
Rapists on Rape

The Sexual Face of Violence

Rapists on Rape

LLOYD VOGELMAN

 Ravan Press. Johannesburg

Published by Ravan Press (Pty) Ltd
PO Box 31134, Braamfontein,
Johannesburg, 2017
South Africa

First published 1990
Second impression 1991
ISBN 0 86975 396 7

Cover design by Jeffrey Lok
Cover painting by Deborah Bell
Typeset in 10/12 Plantin by Industrial Graphics
Printed by Galvin and Sales, Cape Town
(7528)

To
Nathan and Ida
For their support and holding
For being dynamic and able to laugh
And most of all for being my loving parents.

Acknowledgements

There are many people I wish to acknowledge and thank. All of them have in some way helped to make this study possible.

Firstly, I wish to thank the men who participated in this study. Their honesty and expressiveness will hopefully contribute to a more humane way of relating between the sexes.

Many thanks also go to:

Jackie Cock, who has been an inspiration and who has always been, both in this and other work, a source of never-ending encouragement. Her insights were invaluable.

Clive Fullager, for his useful questions and his patience in allowing me to discuss through issues with him.

My editor, Orenna Krut, who was superb not only because she explained the basics of the English language to me, but because she took an avid interest in the work which went beyond her job description and provided me with many new ideas.

For their time and support I thank Lydia Levin, for sharing her knowledge, for posing sometimes unanswerable questions and for spending so much of her time proof-reading; my wife, Jane Barrett, for giving me so much love and so much of the energy needed to complete this work; Terry Shakinovsky, my dear friend, for her assistance and support; and Leo and Hilda Shakinovsky, who gave of their hospitality during the initial writing phase.

Thanks go too to my parents, for always reminding me that I had not finished the study, and for helping wherever they could. And to my mother, more particularly, who helped with some of the typing and with the press clips. I also gratefully acknowledge Jenny Lewis, who spent hours transcribing and typing the interviews; the ultra-responsible Vicki Moore, who typed much of the initial draft; and Graeme Simpson, my friend and colleague, for buying me ice-creams when I most needed them.

And finally, my thanks go to Glenn Moss for making the publication of this work possible, and to Jill Huber for her assistance in those numerous last minute tasks.

Contents

Preface

This is an important and pioneering study. Vogelman explodes many of the myths about rape as an infrequent act of uncontrollable sexual aggression perpetrated by strangers in public places. He does so in a series of remarkable interviews with a group of men, including rapists, in which he explores their experiences, feelings and attitudes.

Vogelman locates these responses in the particular social context of contemporary South Africa. The ways in which gender relations in this society operate to privilege men and subordinate women is a neglected area of research. Vogelman shows how rape emerges from a culture which involves the domination and objectification of women. He analyses how rape, as an act of sexual violence, reflects the masculine role as dominant, powerful, tough and controlling. He points to what he calls a 'rape culture' in which rape is often not acknowledged as a crime and its victims are frequently blamed and held responsible for their own violation.

Rape is a component of the 'war culture' that dominates contemporary South Africa. This involves a set of meanings and practices which accepts violence as a legitimate solution to conflict. The scale and intensity of political violence is a distinguishing feature of contemporary South Africa. Almost four thousand people have died in incidents of political violence since 1984. This violence is classified very differently by different people. It is variously termed 'terrorism,' or 'criminality', or actions of 'war'. If terrorism means acts of violence that impact on power relations in society by spreading fear and intimidation, then rape is clearly a terrorist weapon. If war is defined by the scale and intensity of political violence, then perhaps there is a hidden war being waged against women in our society. Vogelman quotes sources which estimate that over one thousand women are raped daily in South Africa. This would suggest that almost two million women have been raped here since 1984. Clearly the most common form of direct physical violence in our society is this violence by men against women. The effect of such widespread sexual violence is intimidation and restrictions on women's freedom and mobility generally. In this way rape is a crime that affects the behaviour of all women, making all women its victims.

In this book Vogelman exposes rape as both a cause and a consequence of women's subordination. He is an unusual writer to do so in at least two senses. Firstly, he is a man with a deep commitment to feminist analysis and practice. Secondly, he is a social scientist who cares deeply and passionately about the subjects of his study. His book is a fine example of committed social exploration. It is accessible, linking social structure and individual experience and providing us with a fresh and deepened understanding of our social world. The writer's own insight, sympathy and compassion emerges very clearly from his text. He is clearly concerned with achieving gender equality; a situation where men and women can experience more free and loving relationships and enjoy the full range of human alternatives. Hopefully his book will contribute towards reaching this goal.

Jacklyn Cock
October, 1989

Chapter One

Introduction

In present day South African society, every woman is a potential rape victim. This susceptibility means many women are haunted by fear of rape. They inhibit their movement, restrict their behaviour and modify their dress – all in the interest of eluding the rapist's grasp. The frightening effects rape has on women's lives and its increasing occurrence make an understanding of the crime and its perpetrators of utmost importance. Achieving such an understanding requires exposing some of the sexual and rape myths that have helped protect the rapist and men's dominant position in society. Contrary to public opinion, the rapist is not always an uninhibited, aggressive psychopath, a psychotic, an imbecile or a sex maniac who lurks in dark alleys. He is, in most cases, a friend, an acquaintance, a date, a father or a husband. The rapist is usually what society calls the 'normal man'. It is the societal context and the motivations and feelings of these 'normal men' that are of primary concern in this book.

My decision to research rape and the rapist arose largely from the high incidence of rape in South Africa. In 1988, there were officially 19 368 rape cases.[1] Official annual figures for rape in the 1980s record between fifteen and sixteen thousand cases, nine thousand prosecutions and five thousand convictions.[2] It is estimated, therefore, that only fifty to fifty-five percent of prosecutions lead to conviction.[3] Unofficially it is estimated that three hundred and ninety thousand rapes are committed annually in South Africa.[4] This would mean on average that over one thousand women are raped daily in South Africa – almost one every one and a half minutes.[5] The high incidence of rape in South Africa is also reflected in a four hundred percent increase in telephone calls to rape crisis centres from 1983 to 1984.[6] Figures for reported rapes from 1986 to 1987 showed an increase of 14,7%.

Yet in spite of the high incidence of rape, information on the rapist's thoughts, drives and feelings before, during and after his crime is minimal. Part of the motivation for this research is to add to the body of knowledge about the rapist. It is hoped that by providing more insight into rape and the rapist, rape as a crime will be taken more seriously and social practitioners will be able to use the information to help decrease the incidence of rape.

A further reason for concentrating on the rapist himself arose from an earlier piece of research entitled 'The Client: A Study of Sexism and Prostitution'.[7] The research was generally different from other work on prostitution in that it attempted to develop an understanding of the client, the prostitute and prostitution, not by the normal procedure of looking at the prostitute, but by studying the client. What became apparent during the research was the paucity of work done on male sexuality and male sex offenders in South Africa.

Researching the rapist has been a difficult task. The prison authorities refused to co-operate and thus most subjects were found through my own initiative. Because rapists held by institutions were not available to me, and because others outside of institutions feared legal punishment if they admitted to rape, the recruitment of subjects was an arduous endeavour and the sample size remained small. The paucity of academic research on the rapist meant fewer studies to learn from and therefore increased likelihood of interpretive errors.

In the light of the above, this work should be seen largely as an exploratory study. It aims to investigate and examine the causes, nature and consequences of the rapist's behaviours. The study does not claim to offer definitive answers about the rapist. But it does seek to show that despite research difficulties, work on the rapist can be informative and can help to bring to light a number of issues pertinent to sexuality and violence.

Definition of rape

Legally, rape has been separated into two different forms: statutory rape and forcible rape. Statutory rape laws apply to the man who engages in sexual intercourse with a female under the age of consent, even if she participates willingly.[8]

Forcible rape 'consists of intentional unlawful sexual intercourse with a woman without her consent'.[9] Intercourse is defined as any degree of penetration by the male genital organ into the woman's vulva or labia.[10] The rapist does not necessarily have to achieve orgasm or ejaculate. Forcible rape is the type of rape which is considered in this book.

Other factors pertinent to the legal definition of rape are:

(a) The age of the rapist – if he is below fourteen years of age he is not considered capable of committing the offence. This is currently under parliamentary review.
(b) His relationship to the woman – at present a husband cannot be found guilty of raping his wife. He can only be found guilty of assisting others to do so.
(c) The sex of the rapist and the victim – the rapist can only be a man and the victim, a woman.[11]

Brownmiller's definition of American law on rape is similar to the South African definition:

> The perpetration of an act of sexual intercourse with a female, not one's wife, against her will and consent, whether her will is overcome by force or fear resulting from the threat of force, or by drugs or intoxicants; or when, because of mental deficiency, she is incapable of exercising rational judgement; or when she is below an arbitrary 'age of consent'.[12]

Both the South African and American legal definitions of rape are inadequate. Limiting rape to penetration of the vagina by the penis ignores other forms of sexual contact which may violate the victim's body and psyche. The result is that acts such as oral and anal intercourse and penetration using objects – in which rapists freely engage – are not included in the definition of rape.

Contrary to contemporary practice, the victim's sexual history, her prior sexual relations with the offender and whether she engaged in foreplay should not be regarded as significant factors in considering her consent to sexual intercourse. Furthermore, consent to sex should be considered in relation to husbands as well. Such a re-definition would constitute a rejection of the assumption that the marriage contract entails a woman giving consent to any sexual approach a husband chooses to make, even if it involves violence.

An additional problem in the legal definition is that rape is deemed an act committed exclusively by men against women. Consequently, male rape victims are not protected by the law and female offenders are not liable for prosecution.

These reasons make it imperative that an alternative definition be formulated. One preferred definition favoured by feminists such as Brownmiller, Burgess and Holmstroom and Medea and Thompson is that rape is any sexual intimacy forced on one person by another.[13] According to this definition of rape, it is feasible for a man to be a victim of rape and for his rapist to be either a man or a woman. However, because such situations are rare in comparison to incidents involving a male rapist and a female victim, homosexual and female rapists will not be studied here. It should be noted that although the preferred definition encapsulates all forms of forced sexual intimacy, all the rapists in the present study committed rapes in which penetration occurred.

Rape offences differ widely. Some involve acts of extreme physical force; others are characterised by manipulation and threat of force. It would therefore be more academically rigorous to avoid generalised analyses of rape offences and rapists. However, because the vast number of unreported rapes and the difficulty in gaining access to rapists make for small research sample sizes, this becomes an unfeasible task. Nevertheless, this study will not posit a prototype of a typical rape offender as Brownmiller has done. She defines the typical rape offender as young, probably black, suffering under harsh socio-economic conditions and dedicated to a subculture of violence.[14] Since this study is confined to working class 'coloured' rapists, it can neither endorse nor detract from the validity of Brownmiller's prototype. Nor does the scope of this study imply that white middle class men seldom rape. I was in fact able to interview three white rapists but did not include the material since a primary purpose of this study was to employ a comparative analysis without too many contaminating variables. The inclusion of white rapists from a different class background and different geographical regions would have increased the already numerous methodological problems of this work.

Chapter outline

An understanding of the rapist requires an exploration of his social context, since this is a primary cause of his behaviour. Chapter 2 locates rape within the context of the social control of women in society. The subordination of women is conducive to their continued subjection to rape, while rape in turn acts in concert with other social mechanisms of control to confine women to acceptable, subordinate gender role behaviour. Rape reflects the masculine social and sexual role – domineering, powerful and controlling.

Male domination is propped up by the ideology of sex roles. Chapter 3 pursues the relationship between sex roles and rape, focusing on certain psychological contributions to this issue. Emphasis on psychology derives from the social influence of the discipline and from the importance of psychological factors as a source of rape.

Chapters 4 and 5 examine rape-promoting factors. These factors have been divided between two different chapters so as to distinguish between those with a greater sexual orientation and those with less. While all rape-promoting factors are, in the final analysis, interrelated, such an academic division serves to emphasise the importance of the sexual dynamic in rape. Rape is not merely an act of violence – it is an act of sexual violence. Chapter 5, with its focus on economic exploitation, racial oppression, social violence and masculinity, illustrates the close relationship between rape and the social relations and structures dominant in our society.

Chapter 6 narrows the focus from the rapist's motivations to his experience of rape. An examination of his feelings and thoughts about and during the rape assists a more complete discovery of his personality. Again, power, domination and conquest are important features.

The aftermath of the rape experience, examined in Chapter 7, further unfolds the rapist's character, this time unveiling his rationalisations, the lenient treatment he sometimes receives from the police and courts and the likelihood that he will rape again.

Psychological framework

Analysing the rapist requires a specific psychological framework. Very broadly, psychology has three analytical approaches to the study of human behaviour. The first is primarily concerned with internal processes, the second concentrates on external factors and the third emphasises the dynamic interaction between the two.

Many psychologists focusing on internal factors tend to be interested in physiological psychology. Considerable attention is devoted to the workings of the brain,[15] the nervous system and the hormonal system.[16] Traditional psychoanalysts and some of the more orthodox object relation theorists (such as Melanie Klein) also fall into this category. While these psychologists take cognisance of social factors, they stress the internal traits and drives of the individual.

Psychologists concentrating on external factors are generally from the behaviourist school. They argue that factors external to the individual largely determine his or her behaviour. B.F. Skinner, for example, writes: 'The problems we face are not to be found in men and women but in the world in which they live, especially in those social environments we call cultures.'[17]

The framework adopted by this study is based on the third broad analytical approach, described as an interactionist approach.[18] While postulating the overwhelming importance of social factors in determining behaviour, the interactionist approach recognises the role of internal psychic processes and traits. It is important to note that while much of the argument in this book relies on the view that external factors are primary in contributing to the execution of rape, this does not mean that individuals are determined wholly by their environment, nor that they are entirely at its mercy. They are able to change their social world. This means that rape, like other forms of violence, need not forever occupy such a prominent part of the annual crime calender: rape is a social problem and social solutions may help decrease its incidence.

An interactionist research approach stresses the individual's experience rather than relying exclusively on quantitative analysis. The dangers of drawing conclusions purely on the basis of quantitative data are outlined by Fischer:

Although scores can be helpful in classifying people into general categories and in making related decisions about them, they do not assist in understanding the individual in his particular situation or in making concrete suggestions about that person's actual life.[19]

While the quantitative approach and positivism have helped to provide much needed rigour to psychology, one of their major inadequacies is the assumption that in order for psychological knowledge to be legitimate, it must be based on experimentation or variations of the methods used by the natural sciences.[20] The method favoured in this study is the phenomenological method. This method requires that the subject give a comprehensive account of his or her perceptions. Value is placed on human experience and there is an attempt to preserve the unity of a person's life.[21] This method postulates that in the interests of academic clarity, the sociological, psychological, physiological and experimental aspects of a person's life can be differentiated. Differentiation exists in order to put things in an easily understandable form and to ensure sensitivity to the particular complexities of issues; it is not used because factors exist independently. This is the motivation for chapters and sub-sections of the book being divided up as they have been.

Phenomenology holds that facts do not exist in a vacuum and are not autonomous. Facts require interpretation by the researcher. To ensure coherent interpretation and to allow facts to further knowledge of, in this case, the rapist's behaviour, data must be placed within a theoretical framework. Without theory, research remains an anarchic collection of unrelated facts and untranslatable meanings. It is for this reason that qualitative and quantitative data are linked in this book with interpretations and theoretical formulations.

Together with an interactionist theory of human behaviour, feminism, and more specifically (on occasion) socialist feminism, has been used to help build a framework of analysis. While socialist feminism is a political position, it also provides valuable insights into the functioning of society and the individuals who inhabit it. Briefly, socialist feminism stresses the interconnection between economic structures and women's oppression and the political nature of sexuality.[22] Socialist feminists such as Rowbotham and Zaretsky interpret the social factors influencing human behaviour very differently from behavioural psychologists, who are primarily concerned with environmental influences.[23] Behavioural psychologists are content to see these environmental factors as merely extant; they are not particularly interested in exploring the reasons for the existence of these factors or the forms they take. Socialist feminists argue that any study of sexuality or rape must take into account economic control of resources and male domination in both the private and public spheres of life. Central to this investigation is a crucial tenet of socialist feminism: namely that the various components of society – the economic, political and social – are all integrated. Interpersonal relations, domestic life, sexuality and social issues are all seen as reinforcing and sustaining the status quo.[24] By extension, rape and male violence are factors which help to perpetuate patriarchal oppression.[25]

In order for an interactionist and feminist theory to make a greater contribution to the transformation of social relations, more knowledge about the rapist and his experience is required.

Review of research on rapists

The world of academia has until recently told us little about rape, and even less about rapists.[26] This is despite the fact that the subject of rape has been widely reported on in other forms of media including novels, movies, newspapers and pornographic material.

There are many reasons why rape has received scant attention by researchers in the past. Perhaps the most important, suggested by Clark and Lewis, is that a crime only attracts attention when the actual and potential victims have sufficient resources and power to summons such attention.[27] It is no coincidence that the increasing attention paid to rape is historically linked to the growth of the feminist movement in the late 1960s.

Some of the most compelling insights into rape were first aired in feminist publications at this time.[28] Most were articles dealing with the feelings and reactions of the victim and often included angry attacks on official and public attitudes towards rape and rape victims.[29] The 1970s and 1980s saw more comprehensive reports on the rape victim's ordeal.[30] Throughout this period, however, the men responsible for making women victims of rape were, to a large extent, ignored.

Many researchers studying the rapist have avoided speaking to or interviewing him, and instead have tried to understand him theoretically, from a knowledge of patriarchy, sex roles and the victim's account of her experience. Gaining information about the rapist from the victim is problematic, because her experience of the rape is very different from his. In her fear and intense concentration on saving her life, the victim may not be able to assess accurately the rapist's emotions. Most importantly, she may be unaware of the factors responsible for her assailant's behaviour.

When studies do provide data on the rapist, it is often empirical.[31] Amir obtained his data through official records.[32] He provides many figures and percentages, descriptions of the rapist's demographic profile, the probability of the rapist repeating offences, the type of victim he prefers and the setting where he is likely to commit the rape. The facts gathered by Amir are not, however, used to their full potential because they are not sufficiently illustrated by a thorough explanation and interpretation of the rapist's motivations, attitudes and behaviour. Nevertheless, as Brownmiller and Paske note, Amir's work on the rapist was pioneering and its 'single most important contribution was to place the rapist squarely within the subculture of violence'.[33]

Research on rapists available in South Africa has been conducted primarily in Western countries.[34] To date, there has been no comprehensive study of the rapist in South Africa. The present study, therefore, has had to rely on data from overseas. This raises the inevitable question of generalisability, but it appears that there are more similarities than differences between urban South African and Western sex role behaviour and rape patterns.[35] The unique features of the South African rapist, if there are any, can only be ascertained once there is a large body of data from which to draw. The need for specifically South African research has, in part, provided motivation for the present study.

Research into rapists has to overcome complex methodological problems. Fremont remarks: 'No one really knows what most rapists are like. There is no satisfactory way to conduct a study of rapists, no way of obtaining a statistically valid cross-section.'[36] Other psychological and sociological research also makes detailed reference to theoretical, statistical and methodological inadequacies in rape research.[37]

Sample sizes are often very small because of difficulties in obtaining subjects.[38] In this study, for example, access to subjects was hampered by the prison authorities' refusal to allow interviews with prisoners; rapists often did not live at the address which appeared on the court records; and some rapists who had not been charged were afraid to be interviewed because rape is punishable by law. It is expected that studies based on police or other institutional records would accumulate a larger sample than those conducted independently at state institutions. Since a sample should adequately represent 'the universe or frame in which one is trying to draw a conclusion',[39] studies (like this one) using smaller samples should draw attention to their weakness rather than attempt to present full-scale demographic details and profiles. A study which fails to recognise the problem with its small sample is that of Ennis.[40] He uses a sample of thirteen rape victims and projects data concerning their age, race and socio-economic status on to a population figure of ten thousand.

There is a lack of control groups in most research on rapists.[41] Consequently, a fundamental basis of analysis – the comparison of two or more samples with the aim of seeking similarities and differences between them – is missing.[42] A control group has therefore been included in this study.

Another problem common to rape research is sample selection. The rapists studied are normally convicted men.[43] This is because researchers can generally only gain access to rapists through prisons and mental institutions. Since the arrest and conviction of rapists is disproportionately low in relation to the actual incidence of the crime, and the majority of detected rapists are from working class backgrounds, it could be argued that samples of convicted rapists are unrepresentative of the rapist population.[44]

Research relying on rapists found through police records also has sample difficulties because these rapists, like those who are convicted, have been detected. Furthermore, police records are not always reliable. Katz and Mazur describe the inadequacies of police information:

> Police practices of juggling statistics, failure to record reported cases, careless record keeping, and reclassifying cases as unfounded and thus dropping them from the . . . crime count add to distortion . . . in investigations based on police records.[45]

Court and social agency samples have similar limitations to the above samples as they too deal only with detected rapists. Four of the rapists in the present study sample were located through court records, while the rest were all undetected. One advantage of dealing with the undetected rapist is that because he has not been institutionalised or faced legal sanction, his attitudes or behaviour since the rape may not have changed significantly.

Follow-up research procedures could, potentially, investigate changes in the rapist's psyche and cognition from the time of the rape to a later period, but this was not the aim of the present study.

Bias is a further problem in researching rapists. Work done solely through records relies absolutely on data prepared by others, and no information is gleaned from the rapist himself. Research which studies rapists purely on the basis of clinical observations encounters the obstacle of non-standardisation of information, since not all the rapists are asked the same questions.[46] The use of questionnaires may also pose problems as there is always the possibility of fraudulent answers. This study has attempted to overcome some of these limitations through using the focused interview. This does not mean, however, that the above limitations do not apply here. They do. The class background of the rapists interviewed makes them unrepresentative of the rapist population as a whole, for example, and fraudulent answers may have been given during the interview.

The picture of research, however, is not totally gloomy. Levine and Koenig's *Why Men Rape* provides useful data about rapists' lives and their understanding of their crime.[47] Interviews were conducted with convicted rapists in which they described their childhood and their motivations, feelings and attitudes during and after the rape. Included in the rapists' accounts is information about the relationship between sex roles and rape as well as details of both their and the victims' experiences.

Fremont's 'Rapists Speak for Themselves' does what the title suggests: it records rapists' personal descriptions of their rape experiences.[48] In addition, Fremont presents an interpretation of the personality of each rapist. Themes drawn from the interviews include the rapist's insecurity, his hatred, his power, his desire to humiliate and his objectification of women. Fremont recognises the limitations of his study, pointing out that his sample cannot be regarded as stereotypical because his respondents, unlike other rapists, answered his advertisements in newspapers and radio talk shows. He goes on to say that while it is impossible to know what most rapists are like, he is prepared to make one generalisation: most rapists are unable to perceive women as people.

Also available are numerous articles or single chapters of books that deal with the rapist.[49] Authors worth noting include Alder, Melani and Fodaski and Selkin. The problem common to these studies is the brevity of information provided about the rapist himself. This is partly because in some studies the rapist is not the major focus. One work which deserves comment is Katz and

Mazur's chapter 'The Stranger or the Man Next Door: Who is the Rapist?' in their book *Understanding the Rape Victim. A Synthesis of Research Findings.*[50] The authors refer to numerous studies in their attempt to give a demographic profile of the rapist. Empirical findings are interspersed with and illuminated by some insightful interpretations. Some of their findings are detailed in Chapter 6.

An extensive understanding of rapists would aid the development of treatment programmes for rape offenders. Such knowledge is also important for those involved in feminist struggle: in order to achieve sexual equality and liberation, it is crucial to know what the men who inhibit it are thinking so that, where opportunity permits, they can be treated or challenged.

Method: Subjects

The subjects were twenty-seven coloured men. Coloured men were chosen as a result of both socio-political and circumstantial factors. As has been stated, the prison authorities' refusal to allow me to interview rape prisoners meant that the information provided in court records was one of the few means available of gaining access to rapists.

The majority of names in the court records were categorised according to three racial groups: coloured, African and white. To make comparisons between the individual subjects more rigourous, it was important that subjects be drawn from one geographical locality. The Group Areas Act in South Africa has meant that particular racial groups are assigned to specific geographical areas. Thus the study focuses on one racial group.

Language difficulties with African men were seen as a potential problem in the interview, particularly because the inclusion of interpreters would have destroyed confidentiality.

Although three white rapists were interviewed, tracing white subjects proved difficult as, unlike coloured subjects, many of them no longer resided at the address listed for them in the court records. Greater mobility among whites may be attributed, in part, to greater access to jobs and housing in the white community.

The choice of the twenty-seven men was further determined by their fitting into three groups: rapists, physically violent men and non-violent men. There were nine men in each group. Briefly, these groups allowed for a study of why some men are only physically rather than sexually aggressive, while the choice of non-violent men was primarily based on the need to have a control group for the purpose of comparison.

The following were the criteria for membership of each group:

The Rape group: The commital of a violent act by a man whereby a woman is coerced into having sexual intercourse with him alone.

As has been discussed, the act of rape is broader than implied by this definition, but the necessity of a standardised behaviour for research purposes required the adoption of this definition. All other forms of rape will be prefixed by a description of their particular nature, for example, verbal rape, gang rape.

The Physically Violent group: The commital of a physically violent act against a woman. This act has no explicit sexual component.

Members of this group had, however, committed physical violence against both men and women.

The Non-Violent group: Men who have never committed an act of sexual or physical violence.

Subjects from the first two groups were found by using three major methods:

(a) Some of the subjects who had faced prosecution in court were traced through information disclosed in court records, such as names, addresses of family and accused and projected date of release.
(b) Contacts in the community supplied information about men who had been involved in rape or physical violence (refer to Chapter 6 for advantages of interviewing non-convicted rapists).
(c) In the course of interviewing men who were selected as part of the control group, four admitted to raping after being asked.

All subjects were chosen randomly from the same geographical area, Riverlea.

Four subjects in the Rape group had been convicted of rape, while in the Physically Violent group, only two subjects had been convicted for assault.[51] Only one of the subjects, a member of the Physically Violent group, had committed murder.

The problem of non-convicted rapists and physically violent men giving fictional accounts of their crimes was considered, but did not appear to arise. In the interviews there was a logic and consistency to their descriptions of their own violence. All interviewees, especially rapists, were initially cautious when describing their crime. This may have reflected either embarrassment about their crime or fear that they may be reported to the police. The possibility that people might pretend to have engaged in rape and physical violence in order to be interviewed and gain financial remuneration was ruled out by prospective interviewees being informed from the outset that no payment would be made for their time.

It should be noted that the main methodological and sample difficulties that face researchers studying rapists make the possibility of attaining a simple random sample – one in which all members of a population have an equal chance of being selected – highly unlikely.[52]

Method: Ethics

I initially set out to interview only convicted rapists. At the same time, I was attempting to gather a sample of men who had not raped or committed assault. In the process of these interviews, some of these men revealed that they had raped and had not been convicted. This came as a shock to me in the interview.

There could be a variety of reasons for their admission of their crimes. The first is that they expected me to keep my promise of confidentiality. Secondly, they trusted me and felt comfortable with the interviewing style. Their trust was enhanced by the fact that I did not probe into the identifying details of the rape – such as the identity of the victim, the address or specific location of the incident and the identities of any possible witnesses to the crime. On the other hand, the rapists may have been prepared to discuss their crime because they did not see it as something to hide. While my sense was that they did not feel guilty, there was some apprehension about being arrested, and for this reason they showed caution in speaking about the rape.

A number of ethical questions emerge which are important for rape researchers to consider. Should I have attempted to gather sufficient information about the rape in order to report it to the police? Such direct questioning might have led the rapist to terminate the interview. It would also have meant breaking confidentiality and contravening basic research ethics. In South Africa, there is no legal obligation to report unconfirmed crimes. The dilemma is thus purely a moral one. In these situations, is one's ethical responsibility greater to women who are potential rape victims of the rapist interviewed, or to the ethics of research? Rape can result in severe psychological and social disruption, and may even end in loss of life. Can research and ethics be of greater importance than the life of a woman?

Intuitively, my answer is that research can never take precedence. But the answer is not that simple. If there is a common belief that researchers break confidentiality, research in a variety of sensitive areas could be severely compromised. One consequence would be a lack of information beneficial in the struggle to end the perpetration of rape.

Another problem is the victim's privilege of confidentiality. She may not wish to be known – especially if she failed to report the crime – and a researcher acquiring information about her identity is invading a privacy she might rather preserve. Active police involvement would be a still more serious invasion.

The subjects' community

The subjects were all drawn from the coloured township of Riverlea on the south-western border of Johannesburg. It is a small residential area which in 1985 had an offical population of just under twelve thousand people. It is likely that the figure is closer to twenty to twenty-five thousand.

Riverlea is generally divided up into two sections by its inhabitants – the areas below and above the railway line. In the area below the line, there is overcrowding, the houses are of poor quality, there is considerable unemployment and those who are employed usually receive inadequate remuneration, the streets are littered, the incidence of violence is high, teenage pregnancy is not unusual, alcohol and drug abuse is widespread and gangs are prominent in public life. While the rest of the community is not immune from any of these problems, they are less pronounced above the dividing railway line. In fact, in this section of Riverlea there are a number of streets where a strong taste of middle class suburbia is discernable and where the poor social conditions of Extension 1 are entirely absent. Although individuals from the more affluent side of the line were interviewed, they will not be the focus of the study. This investigation has drawn its subjects from the area below the railway line and this sub-community will be given primary attention. Nevertheless, it is important to give the reader some sense of the (1985-6) demography of Riverlea as a whole.

The majority of its residents are between twenty-five and thirty-four years of age. There are few elderly people – officially there are two hundred and eighteen people between sixty-five and seventy-four years of age, and only eighty people over seventy-five. The reasons for this are unclear, but may be related to inadequate socio-economic conditions which result in poor life expectancy.

The working and lower middle class nature of Riverlea is reflected in the low levels of education amongst its residents. Approximately half a percent of its adult population have post-matric academic qualifications, while ten percent have matriculated. The majority of its residents have completed between a standard five and standard eight. This corresponds to the educational standard of the subject sample in this study.

Nearly thirty percent of Riverlea residents were engaged in trade and apprenticeship, quarrying and production work. Approximately ten percent were unemployed. Senior white collar work such as managerial and administrative work accounted for approximately one percent of the work done by the adult population.

Housing below the railway line ranges from extremely poor to adequate. There are approximately two thousand houses and one hundred and fifty flats in Riverlea. Based on official estimates, this means there are approximately six people per house and flat. And considering that most people above the railway line live comfortably, overcrowding in the area below the line is way above the River-lea average. A further index of discrepancies in wealth is that of the seven hundred and eighty-three houses sold in Riverlea by 1986, only three had been sold below the line. In this area houses are mostly rented. House rentals in Riverlea range from approximately thirty to three hundred rands per month.

There are few formal businesses in Riverlea. In 1986 there were officially only ten commercial shops. An informal sector does exist. Individuals working within this sector include mechanics, small-scale vendors, prostitutes, drug pedlars and shebeen owners. Many of the residents seem to do their large-scale and specialised shopping in Johannesburg.

No hospitals exist in Riverlea, but outpatient clinics are provided. Riverlea residents use the Coronationville hospital, the officially designated coloured hospital. This is where the community's rape victims are often treated.

Demographic details of subjects

All the groups tended to have similar educational backgrounds, age levels, marital status and occupations. The Non-Violent group had a slightly higher educational standard than the Rape and Physically Violent groups. Most men in the Non-Violent group had completed standard eight, while those in the Rape and Physically Violent groups had passed standard seven. The average age in the Non-Violent group was 28,7 years, in the Rape group 24,5 years and in the Physically Violent group 24,2 years.

Most subjects in all the groups were unmarried. Of those subjects who reported being single or unmarried, seven were from the Rape group, six from the Physically Violent group and seven from the Non-Violent group. The other subjects in each of these groups were married. None of the subjects was divorced. A small proportion of rapists (twenty-two percent) and physically violent men (thirty-three percent) was married, and over half of the men in each of these groups had children. In the Non-Violent group the two married men both had children.

The occupations of the majority of subjects in each group centred on manual labour. Unemployment was found in each group.

All the subjects, except for one in the Non-Violent group who belongs to the Moslem faith, reported being members of a Christian denomination. Of the total number of subjects, thirty-three percent were Anglican, eighteen percent Ebenezer, fourteen percent Roman Catholic, seven percent N.G. Kerk, seven percent Seventh Day Adventists, seven percent Church of England, three percent Baptists and three percent Methodists.[53]

On the question of language, approximately half of the subjects spoke English fluently, with thirty-seven percent claiming English as their first language. Afrikaans was the first language of close to half, while fifty-nine percent spoke it fluently. Afrikaans-speaking subjects nevertheless showed a high degree of articulateness in English – the language of the interview and questionnaire.

The interviewing procedure

Upon meeting subjects, I informed them that I was conducting a study on men's experience with women and other men, and required their assistance. Assurances of confidentiality were given and the interviewing procedure was described. After permission to interview was granted (which occurred in all the cases), a time was set for transportation to the interviewing venue. On the appointed date, ninety-two percent of all subjects were there at the scheduled time. As no financial payment for their assistance was promised, their punctuality seemed to reveal an interest in the study.

The subjects were then transported by car from Riverlea to the interviewing venue – a small, comfortable room at the School of Psychology, University of the Witwatersrand. The transportation period provided an opportunity to establish some trust with the interviewee.

In the interviewing room, testees were seated at a table, with me sitting beside them. The issue of confidentiality was dealt with once more and questions on the matter were invited. Permission to tape the interview by means of a small tape recorder was requested. This was agreed to by all the interviewees.

Before beginning the interview, some of its features and aims were explained. Subjects were told of its approximate length, that correct or incorrect answers do not exist within an interview situation and that one of the goals of the interview was to glean some information about their behaviour, attitudes and feelings. After completing the interview, subjects were supplied with refreshments and transported back to Riverlea.

Focused interview

The stress placed upon both individual experience and standardised data requires the adoption of a method which will satisfy both criteria. To cater for the uniqueness of each individual, the focused interview was conducted with all subjects.[54] Unlike the standardised interview, where the wording and order of questions are fixed, the focused interview has a less structured form.[55] Questions are prepared, but not all contain the same wording or sequence and sometimes additional questions are included.[56] To engender trust in the interviewer, a common vocabulary with the respondent must be found which corresponds with his or her characteristics and personality. It is for this reason that rephrasing of questions is often necessary. Consequently, when interviewing a rapist who has a low standard of education and uses sexist language littered with profanities, the wording of questions was simple and included words like 'cherry', 'chick', 'shit' and 'fuck'.

Research indicates that to a certain degree, respondents regulate their responses according to the social attributes, attitudes and behaviour of the interviewer.[57] Therefore, in addition to modifications to language used, an attempt was made to reduce class and race differences by dressing in the appropriate manner, speaking in a similar way and by sometimes taking the same position on issues.

A subject's openness and expressiveness had some influence on the directness of questions. Questions would be more direct if the subject was confident. However, if the subject appeared slightly inhibited, information would be ascertained more slowly and in a less direct fashion. This entailed, for instance, participating in the subject's jokes, reassuring him and slowly introducing the next topic of discussion.

Some of the interview questions could be called open-ended questions, for example: 'Why do you think men rape?' Such questions require more of the respondent in terms of remembering, ordering and evaluating his attitudes and experiences.[58]

Bearing the above in mind, the sequence of questions was aimed at reducing the respondent's anxiety and increasing his trust. Non-anxiety-provoking questions (occupation, age, marital status, religion) were asked at the beginning of the interview, followed by the more psychologically demanding questions which required explanations, motivations, descriptions of feelings and so on. Through this technique, it was hoped that the respondent would reveal a greater amount of personal information about himself.

Interviews took between thirty-five and eighty minutes. It appears, from the information obtained, that the style of interviewing had a bearing on the interviewees' relaxation and resultant honesty during the interviews. Many of the respondents expressed their enjoyment of the interview and of having the opportunity to speak about their history, beliefs and experiences. The following are a few of the remarks made by the respondents about their interview.

Two members of the Non-Violent group commented:

> It was good, ek sê. Something special, that's just happened.
> I didn't expect it to happen. It was a good chat between me
> and you.

> I think it was good to speak for a while since I have never
> really spoken to someone like this, the way I did.

Two rapists stated:

> I wanted to do it long ago already. I wanted someone to come
> and talk so I can explain what's happening and how's my
> life. I even told my wife last week that someone will come
> and fetch me to talk.

> It was nice. I got a lot off my shoulders.

A member of the Physically Violent group said:

> I feel very good, it's once in a lifetime.

Data analysis of interviews was similar to the procedure laid out
by Colaizzi.[59] After being transcribed, interviews were studied to
gain an overall impression of the respondent's attitudes and experiences. Exerpts which pertained to the issues under investigation or shed new light on rapists and rape were highlighted. Examining statements entailed, at times, discovering the meaning behind significant statements. This required a knowledge of the subject's social and historical milieu and cognisance of the fact that
the researcher must go beyond what is given in the original data
and at the same time, stay with it.[60]
    Before any of the information from the interviews and the vari-
ous factors inducing men to rape can be elaborated upon (see Chapters 4 and 5), it is necessary to locate rape within a social context.
Men do not rape purely because of their family histories, their psychological make-up, sexist ideology (see Chapter 3) and rape-
encouraging institutions such as prostitution and pornography (see
Chapter 4). They rape also as a result of their social conditions (see
Chapter 5) and women's position in society. Women's traditional
subservience to male needs is expressed within the political, economic, social and sexual spheres of life. A variety of discriminato-

ry and repressive measures keep women trapped in their sexual oppression, and rape can be seen as such a measure. Sexual violence, as will be illustrated in the next chapter, helps guarantee that women remain dependent and under the control of men.

NOTES

1 *The Star,* 19 April 1989.
2 *The Star,* 29 May 1985; *Sunday Star,* 15 January 1989.
3 *Sunday Star,* 15 January 1989.
4 *The Star,* 5 January 1983; Medical Association of South Africa (MASA), no date.
5 *Sunday Star,* 15 January 1989.
6 *The Star,* 6 June 1985.
7 Vogelman, 1981.
8 Criminal Procedure Act 51 of 1977; Katz and Mazur, 1979; Le Grand, 1983; Medea and Thompson, 1972.
9 Hunt, 1982, page 435.
10 Hunt, 1982.
11 Hunt, 1982.
12 Brownmiller, 1975, page 412.
13 Brownmiller, 1975; Burgess and Holmstroom, 1975; Medea and Thompson, 1974, page 12.
14 1975.
15 Craft, 1966; Arieti and Benporad, 1978.
16 Gyermeck, Genther and Fleming, 1967; Vernikos – Daniellis, 1972. All references cited in Lloyd and Archer (1976) and Rohrbaugh (1981).
17 1975, page 42.
18 Zimbardo, 1977.
19 1976, page 412.
20 Colaizzi, 1973.
21 Colaizzi, 1973; Fischer, 1973.
22 Barrett, 1980.
23 Rowbotham, 1973; Zaretsky, 1978.
24 Eisenstein, 1979; Hartmann, 1981.
25 *Masculinity and Violence,* 1982.
26 Clark and Lewis, 1977; Katz and Mazur, 1979.
27 1977.
28 The popular reaction to rape began with an article by Susan Griffin in a magazine called *Ramparts* in 1971. The article, titled 'Rape – The All American Culture', was a powerful attack on beliefs about rape and rape victims.
29 Clark and Lewis, 1977.
30 Bart, 1981; Kanin and Parcell, 1977; Katz and Mazur, 1979; Kilpatrick, Resick and Veronen, 1981.
31 Alder, 1984; Amir, 1971; Schiff, 1969; Van Ness, 1984.
32 1971.
33 Paske, 1982, page 10.
34 Fremont, 1975; Levine and Koenig, 1983; Rada, 1978.
35 MASA, no date; Mayne and Levett, 1977.
36 1975, page 244.
37 Amir, 1971; Deming and Eppy, 1981.

38 Fremont, 1975; Levine, 1983.
39 Lipstein, 1975, page 36.
40 1967.
41 Deming and Eppy, 1981.
42 Zito, 1975.
43 Groth, Longo and McFadin, 1982; Levine and Koenig, 1983.
44 Clark and Lewis, 1977; Levett, 1981; Rada, 1979.
45 1979, page 19.
46 Selkin, 1975.
47 1983.
48 1975.
49 Alder, 1984; Clark and Lewis, 1977; McDonald and Patrick, 1983; Medea and Thompson, 1972; Melani and Fodaksi, 1974; Sailly and Marolla, 1984; Selkin, 1975.
50 1979.
51 No statistics are available for subjects in the Rape group who have been convicted for non-sexual violence.
52 McCall, 1970.
53 These percentages account for ninety-two percent of the subjects. The remaining eight percent is made up of different percentage points and the Moslem subject.
54 Mayntz, et. al., 1976.
55 Kerlinger, 1973.
56 Mayntz, Holm and Hoebner, 1976; Simon, 1979.
57 Mayntz, Holm and Hoebner, 1976.
58 Connell and Kahn, 1957.
59 1978.
60 Colaizzi, 1978, page 59.

Chapter Two

Rape and the social control of women

Rape and the rapist must be examined within the context of patri-archy and the social control of women. This is because it is op-pressive structures and social relations which relegate women to a position of relative powerlessness that contributes substantially to their susceptibility to rape. In addition, rape has wide-ranging social and psychological consequences for women. Rape limits the life opportunities of women.[1] In this way, it serves as a control mechanism, schooling women to confine their actions and attitudes to within the parameters of acceptable gender role behaviour.

Rape, however, is not the only reason women fear deviating from the norm. Other social control mechanisms also effect adherence to behavioural norms. Within the socio-economic sphere, marri-age performs this role. Quick, for example, argues that marriage serves the same function for women as the wage contract serves for men: it helps to secure their livelihood.[2] As Quick puts it:

> Marriage is a contract which is theoretically entered into freely by a man and a woman. However, for a woman, there is lit-tle choice involved – they may choose whom to marry, but they will not willingly remain unmarried. An analogy may be useful. Members of the working class may choose their employers (if they are fortunate enough), but they will not remain unemployed if they can help it, and they cannot be independent since they own no capital.[3]

Women's (often) greater need for marriage, which derives from both social expectations and economic vulnerability (women are usually paid less than men and are retrenched first in recessionary times), puts men in a powerful position.[4] Some feminists argue that if a woman is to marry or remain married, she must comply with the prevailing societal norms of behaviour, even if this means living under extremely unpleasant conditions. Put in its crudest and most extreme terms, the wife provides her husband with domestic and sexual services, is solely responsible for the bearing and rearing of their children and, when possible, adds to the income of the family. In return, she is given financial support, physical protection and social affirmation.[5]

The institution of marriage also reflects the stereotyped perception of women as dependent human beings. A husband is expected to control and direct his wife's actions, because, say Hutter and Williams, a woman is understood to be 'a person with something of a childish incapacity to govern herself and in some need of protection'.[6] With regard to social and economic status, women are, in most cases, accorded recognition in terms of their husbands' achievements and social stature. Within the sexual and reproductive spheres, women are more easily able to develop status independently of their husbands; and it is men's desire to gain exclusive access to women's sexuality that has largely made women's sexual and reproductive capacities so valued.[7] Men's control over these capacities is so marked that it is still legally permissible for a man to rape his wife.

Rape laws attach great importance to the marital and sexual status of women. Many feminist writers argue that courts have often given better treatment to rape victims who have high social status and value – virgins or women under the protection of their fathers, or faithful wives. These women are differentiated from sexually promiscuous or single women who are seen as the property of all men and often receive an unsympathetic hearing from the court.

In South Africa, a woman's social value is also determined by her class and race. Some courts appear to be particularly unsympathetic towards black working class victims. This reflects both class and racial bias. One legal case in which such prejudice seemed to manifest occurred in late 1988. Two policemen found guilty of breaking into the house of a black domestic worker and assaulting her were given a three year sentence which was suspended in full. Commenting on this case and another in which a twenty-three year old white man was given a five year suspended sentence and a three thousand rand fine for beating a black farm labourer to death, Brian

Currin, chair of the organisation 'Lawyers for Human Rights', stated:

> We are very surprised at the leniency of this [with reference to the latter case] sentence. It's this sort of sentence which could lead to black people holding the view that people are not all equal before the law . . . This is a terribly gross violation of a person's [referring to the assault on the black domestic worker] dignity and rights and one wonders what the sentence would have been had a black man committed a similar assault on a white woman.[8]

Within the racial and racist framework of South Africa, the rape of a black working class woman is not seen as a violation of the men who hold power in South African society, the majority of whom are white and middle class. Many of these men are likely to show real concern only if it is 'their' women (women with a similar social background to their own) who have been raped. This displeasure is intensified when the rapist is black. In such cases, the black man is often painted as an uncontrollable animal deserving of the most severe punishment, and the rape is used to confirm and give credence to racist attitudes about blacks being violent and uncivilized.

Rape laws have been described as being more concerned with protecting women's property value for men than with women themselves.[9] The roots of this lie in the early history of rape law. The London Action Rape Group writes that since biblical times, rape laws have generally dealt with rape as a crime against a man's property.[10] In early Hebrew law, fathers sold their virgin daughters into marriage for a fixed sum of money. If a rape was perpetrated against a virgin outside the walls of a city, the rapist had to pay the bride-price to her father and was forced to marry her. Rape committed inside the walls of a city had very different consequences – both the rapist and the victim were stoned to death. The rationale behind this was that if the woman had shouted, she would have been heard and saved.[11]

In Assyrian law, the rape victim's father was permitted to rape the wife of the offender.[12]

Under Anglo Saxon law, if a woman was raped, a sum of money was paid to either her husband or father, depending on who had exclusive rights of control over her. The amount of money paid

was determined by the victim's economic position and her potential value as an object for monogamous marriage. The financial com-
pensation was not given to the victim herself; it was paid to her
husband or father because he was the person believed to have been
wronged.[13]

Le Grand, reflecting on current rape law, states:

> Rape laws bolster, and in turn are bolstered by, a masculine
> pride in the exclusive possession of a sexual object; they fo-
> cus on a male's aggression, based on fear of losing his sexual
> partner, against rapists rather than innocent competitors; rape
> laws help protect the male from a decrease in the 'value' of
> his sexual 'possession' which results from forcible
> violation.[14]

Double standards of morality characterise the arena of human sexuality: certain modes of behaviour are regarded as legitimate for
one sex and not legitimate for the other. The most striking example of this is that sexual promiscuity is encouraged in men as a sign
of virility, and condemned in women as a display of sinful and
shameful behaviour.[15] It is suggested that such notions derive
from women being defined as important male possessions, a definition which may have its origins in women's ability to reproduce
heirs to the family name and fortune.[16] Women who are sexually
promiscuous – and not exclusive possessions – are attributed less
status. They are given derogatory labels such as 'whore' or 'slut'.
In line with the sexual double standard, there are no comparable
derogatory terms for men.[17]

The rape victim also has to face these slurs. She, like the promiscuous woman and the lesbian, has engaged in non-conformist sexual acts. Society doesn't always recognise that she was *forced* to
partake in the act – what is at issue is that she has gone beyond
the limits of 'normal' behaviour.[18] In each of the study's three
groups of subjects, many of the men held the same opinion: they
regarded rape victims as 'fucked', 'not worth marrying' and not
able 'to have a nice clean wedding'.

Men have come to define rape as the worst experience that could
occur in a woman's life. According to Clark and Lewis, this is not
always true.[19] They argue that many women would rather be
raped than suffer death. And while many women feel emotionally
battered and even destroyed after being raped, this does not mean

they will feel that way for the rest of their lives. With time, the pain of the trauma often subsides.

However, being defined as a raped woman in our society and being subjected to the courts' frequently unsympathetic judgements extend the victim's torment way beyond the period of the rape itself, and social control of her may further increase.[20] Her husband may accuse her of consenting to the crime and consequently further limit her freedom outside of the home, especially in developing friendships with other men. She may be accused of not being able to function as a proper mother. Friends and family may feel she has been made alien by her experience, and may become less tolerant of any non-conformist behaviour she displays.[21]

Women may comply with their increased restrictions to the point of indulging in self-restriction, because of their poor sense of self. Women's assessment of their own capabilities is closely linked to the expectations communicated to them by others – men and women.[22] Social pressure of this sort is obviously not unique to women – men also face it – but the pressure is more damaging for women because of their subordinate status. Economically, socially and physically vulnerable, numerous women do not aspire to a life other than that assigned them within a sexist social structure.[23]

Within the realm of social expectations and rules to which both men and women subscribe is the ideology of 'natural' laws of human behaviour. Social norms define certain modes of behaviour as instinctual and therefore proper, and insist that certain behaviours have always occurred and will continue to do so.[24] Hutter and Williams comment:

> The imposition of moral assumptions and expectations, and their translation into 'natural' laws, is a forceful way of maintaining the female image . . . Deviant behaviour is often regarded as 'unnatural', and 'unnatural' behaviour is usually considered immoral and a freak of nature. The strength and power of the images and stereotypes is reflected in the relative inability of . . . women to negotiate their acceptance or rejection of certain labels and typifications.[25]

The psychological discipline plays a significant role in strengthening the concept of natural laws of behaviour and in encouraging women and men to abide by culturally defined roles. For example, Heather argues that some psychology text-books portray the woman's natural, healthy role as that of loyal wife and devoted mother.[26] Being 'feminine' is also defined as being passive, irrational, dependent and weak, and behaviour which contradicts these traits is regarded as unfeminine.[27] Psychology conducts its 'worship of normality' by portraying any deviance from its definition of women's 'natural' role as pathological or maladjusted.[28]

Certain qualities are linked to masculinity. Masculinity is associated with aggression, rationality, independence, strength and dominance. Failure to conform to these qualities can result in social ostracisation and derision. The man is emasculated – 'he's got no balls'.[29] The internalisation of these attitudes through socialisation (see Chapter 3) is a contributing factor to the high incidence of rape.

The brutality of rape and other forms of violence such as wifebeating distinguishes it from other control mechanisms. Although rape is the primary concern here, the original feminist thesis of rape as an instrument of control must be broadened to include other acts of violence.[30] Violence need not only include the 'legal categories' (rape, murder, assault), but should 'move beyond to include all modes of behaviour that coerce compliance'.[31]

Brownmiller argues that men deliberately and knowingly use rape as a control mechanism. She states that rape is 'a conscious process of intimidation by which *all* men keep *all* women in a state of fear'.[32] Brownmiller's conspiratorial conceptualisation of all men's conscious collusion in rape is difficult to support or even comprehend. However, her contention that rape is an act affecting all women, regardless of whether they are personally raped, makes a major contribution to an understanding of the social implications of rape. It is certainly true that all women, whether raped or not, fear rape and take precautionary measures which limit their freedom.[33]

Hindelang, Gottfredson and Garofalos do not share the opinion that fear of crime inhibits women's behaviour.[34] They believe that women (and men) still do what they want, but change how they do it. For example, they may request a friend to visit them rather than vice versa.

However, Riger and Gordon have found that women's fear of violence sometimes results in their not taking certain jobs,[35] not visiting friends and not venturing out at night for walks or entertainment.[36] Their findings show that twenty-two percent of men and sixty-eight percent of women avoid doing necessary errands (such as shopping) because of the fear of criminal violence. With regard to recreational activities (such as seeing films), twenty-five percent of men and seventy percent of women avoid them because of fear for their safety. Thus the threat of violence lowers the overall quality of women's lives by limiting their range of choices. Hindelang et. al.'s assertion cannot be dismissed entirely, but it should be recognised that even subtle shifts in behaviour due to fear of criminal violence may constitute a significant burden on both women's and men's lives in terms of effort, time and freedom.[37]

Women's caution about leaving the vicinity of their homes and about evincing certain kinds of behaviour is, however, insufficient to protect them from rape. Women are often raped in or near their homes and by men they know.[38] In this study one rapist reported that he found his victim 'in front of her gate and [when the] other lighties came, we . . . raped her in the street'. Behaviour of this sort suggests that rape has achieved a remarkable acceptability in our society. Some rapists seem to regard rape as normal and consequently take no precautions to prevent their own arrest. Others may be aware of the legal consequences of raping but still take few precautions because they believe there is little chance of prosecution.

Sometimes men rape women who appear to defy control of their own lives – women who seem to break the rules. Rape, or other forms of violence, is then inflicted so as to ensure the woman's respect for the man's authority and her renewed or continuing adherence to prevailing notions of feminine behaviour. A more detailed account of aggression and the use of violence in relationships can be found in Chapters 5 and 6. For the purpose of this chapter, statements from two men from the Physically Violent group illustrate how violence is used to ensure control:

> George: We went outside to talk. As we went down the stairs, she said she doesn't want to hear anything, so I smacked her and said 'listen to reason'.

> Ronnie: Girls, you get one who greets you, others who don't. Why? Now the next day you are going to wait for her and give her a smack because she doesn't greet you.
> Vogelman: Have you ever done that?
> Ronnie: I did it once.
> Vogelman: How did you feel afterwards?
> Ronnie: I just felt she won't do it again.

In many societies the marital contract serves to legally secure male control over women. This in turn increases the potential for rape and violence against women. An extreme example occurs among some American Indian buffalo hunters.[39] If a woman commits adultery, her angry husband invites all the unmarried men of his society to rape his wife.

Dobash and Dobash, writing about Western marriages, state that because men have been given the responsibility of controlling women, physical violence becomes a 'legitimate' means to secure such control:

> After marriage, the authority relationships between men and women became more explicit, husbands came to feel that their wives should meet their demands immediately and without question, no matter how reasonable or unreasonable. The major source of contention centered on what might be called 'wifely obligations' and 'husband's authority'.
>
> In our research, it was the real or perceived challenges to his possession, authority and control which most often resulted in the use of violence. A late meal, an unironed shirt, a conversation with any man, no matter how old or young, all served as 'justification' for beatings.[40]

Rape effectively alters women's behaviour within the realm of sexual intimacy.[41] Women are seen as responsible for sexually satisfying men once men are aroused and are expected to accede to sexual intercourse. If a woman chooses not to fulfil this responsibility, the man may force her to have sex through verbal insults, persistent threats or physical violence. Russell says of women's reaction to the 'all or nothing standard of sexuality':

> Rather than experience the unpleasantness, which may include rape, or asserting her unrecognised right not to engage in sexual acts that she doesn't wish, many a woman will accede to this implicit male rule.[42]

The power of rape as a social control mechanism is strengthened markedly by the silence which surrounds it, especially with regard to the non-reporting of rape to the police. The National Institute for Crime and Rehabilitation of Offenders (NICRO) has estimated that only one in twenty rape victims reports her rape.[43] Reasons for not reporting are numerous, ranging from a desire to avoid the trauma of a court trial, to shame.[44] The nature of rape laws means that the victim sometimes has to endure insensitive treatment by the police, suffer humiliation at the hands of the prosecutor and cope with the legal requirements that permit an invasion of her privacy (see Chapter 6).[45]

The victim's feelings of shame are primarily the result of unsympathetic and sexist societal attitudes to raped women (see Chapters 6 and 7). It is therefore understandable that many women do not want to publicly expose what has happened to them. In her marriage, the rape victim may face a similar response. Her husband, even if he is the only person she tells of her rape, may be repulsed and feel she is forever tainted. This could result in separation and the loss of her economic and social support.[46] Women face the possibility of being blamed for the rape by both men and women. The stigma attached to raped women may mean difficulty in finding a sexual partner in the future. Finally, exposure can result in her having to go through the humiliating procedure of police and court investigation. Thus, because women fail to report rape, rape becomes an invisible, privatised problem. Its invisibility means that rapists are often not arrested, rape receives less public attention, its social and political aspects are ignored and it becomes defined (although not always) as a purely personal concern. Solutions are therefore individualised, and rape and its effect as a social control mechanism are not understood and dealt with as social problems. All of this results in a higher incidence of rape and greater restrictions on women's freedom.[47]

Ironically, women are driven to seek the protection of men from rape by men. Thus women relinquish more power to men and collude in their increased control by them.[48] Hanmer explains this:

> The pervasive fear of violence and violence itself, has the effect of driving women to seek protection from men, the very people who commit violence against them. Husbands and boyfriends are seen as protectors of women from the potential violence of unknown men. Women often feel safer in the company of a man in public and the home is portrayed as, and often feels, the safest place of all, even though statistically speaking, women are more likely to be violently assaulted in marriage and by men known to them.[49]

Dependency relationships predicated upon physical protection necessarily restrict freedom and development.[50] If a woman is too afraid to venture out alone at night, for example, she may seek a male partner to accompany her. If she is unable to find a protective partner, she may choose to remain restricted to her home. Her growing dependence on others inhibits her movements and decreases the amount of control she has over her own life and environment.

A deeper understanding of the social control of women in a male-dominated society requires an analytical framework capable of linking patriarchy to the social, economic and political spheres of our society. A feminist theory of society helps to do this. The scope of this work does not permit a detailed explanation of the various strands of feminism. However, since aspects of socialist feminism have been used in this thesis, a brief, simplified account of this theory is provided.

It is necessary from the outset to distinguish radical feminism from socialist feminism. Radical feminists believe that capitalism has little to do with women's oppression, and that women's subjugation is derived rather from the motive force of history, namely men's striving for power and domination over women – the dialectic of sex.[51] Male supremacist attitudes and norms are said to pre-exist and outlast any specific social formation, so that the history of the world is a history of patriarchy. Radical feminists, however, fail to analyse the specificity of the operations of patriarchy through history or of its connection to other forms of domination in the economic and political spheres.[52] A further failing is its conceptualisation of men and women as homogeneous social categories. Radical feminism ignores the fact that in a class and racially stratified society, some men are more dominated than dominating: in South Africa, for example, a black man has less social and political power than a white woman. While it may be true that the majority of people who hold political and economic power are men, not all men have equal control in society.[53]

Socialist feminism moves beyond an exclusive analysis of hierarchical sex structures to include divisions based on class in a more comprehensive enquiry into the workings of society. It does not view the systems of class stratification and patriarchy as either autonomous or identical: rather, they are mutually dependent.[54] In this respect, socialist feminists are unlike traditional Marxists who confine their focus to class divisions, the labour process and the state.[55] For socialist feminists, society is an economic, political and cultural totality in which experience, 'private life' and social existence are crucial factors in the perpetuation of the social system.[56]

Socialist feminists define class divisions as extending beyond income, life style or roles.[57] Classes are defined by ownership and control of the productive resources of a society. To maintain the wealth appropriated from this ownership, capitalists need to extend control beyond the production process. They must rely on advertising to promote sufficient consumption of their products; notions of masculinity to provide a hard-working and competitive labour force; notions of femininity to provide nurturance for the primarily male labour force; the family to instill these notions of masculinity and femininity into children; an education, whether through the family, the schools or the university, which encourages respect for authority and submission to those who wield it; and direct repression through the police, army or male violence to bring into line the rebellious and the non-conforming – including strikers, lesbians and independent women.[58] This is not to suggest that all of these institutions and practices are the manifestion of an all-powerful and coherent capitalist plot. Rather, the interconnections between social relations and political and economic power need to be laid bare if we are to understand the workings of our society.

Socialist feminists argue that although many men may assert that they do not engage in rape or other forms of violence, they nevertheless enjoy privileges, power and control – social, sexual, political and economic – through rape and violence or the threat thereof.[59]

In upholding stereotyped notions of masculinity, men pay a price. They compromise honesty, sensitivity, the capacity to love, the ability to relax in the company of others and sometimes their health.[60] Men are in a position similar to that described by Hegel when he spoke of the dominator himself being narrowed and 'dominated by his compulsion to dominate'.[61]

Dominance and passivity within the sexual arena will constitute a major focus of the next chapter. Both these characteristics contribute to rape. Modes of behaviour, as socialist and liberal feminists have pointed out, have, in part, grown out of sexist socialisation patterns and sexist ideology. The importance of conventional psychological theory as an ideology which reinforces oppressive social relations cannot be underestimated. Many psychological theories of sex differences and rape, as will be shown in Chapter 3, have had the effect of justifying women's oppression. In so doing, they have made it easier for men to rape and have increased the trauma of the rape victim.

NOTES

1 Hanmer, 1981; Hutter and Williams, 1981.
2 Cited in Dahl and Snare, 1978.
3 Cited in Dahl and Snare, 1978, page 42.
4 Smart and Smart, 1978.
5 Barker in Mcintosh, 1978.
6 1981, page 19.
7 Clark and Lewis, 1977.
8 *Sunday Star*, 13 November 1988.
9 Herman, 1979.
10 1982.
11 London Action Rape Group, 1982.
12 London Action Rape Group, 1982.
13 Clark and Lewis, 1977.
14 1973, page 924.
15 Hutter and Williams, 1981; Smart and Smart, 1978.
16 Clark and Lewis, 1977.
17 Spender, 1980.
18 Connell and Wilson, 1974.
19 1977.
20 Hutter and Williams, 1981.
21 Connell and Wilson, 1974; Hutter and Williams, 1981.
22 Chafe, 1977.
23 Chafe, 1977.
24 Heather, 1976.
25 1981, page 23.
26 1976.
27 Lips, 1981.
28 Heather, 1976, pages 49-50.
29 Lips, 1981.
30 Riger and Gordon, 1981.
31 Hanmer, 1981, page 190.
32 1975, page 26.
33 Riger and Gordon, 1981.
34 1978.
35 1981.
36 Gordon, Riger, Le Bailly and Heath, 1980.
37 1978.
38 Bowker, 1978.
39 Hoekel, 1960.
40 1977, page 64.

41 Russell, 1975; Wilson, 1982.
42 1975, page 272.
43 MASA, no date.
44 Herman, 1979; Robin, 1972.
45 Robin, 1977.
46 Herman, 1979.
47 Robin, 1979; Smart and Smart, 1978.
48 Hill, 1982.
49 1981, page 190.
50 Kilpatrick et. al., 1981.
51 Brownmiller, 1975; Firestone, 1979; Koedt, 1972; Millett, 1971.
52 Eisenstein, 1979; Kuhn and Wolpe, 1978.
53 Hodge, 1979.
54 Eisenstein, 1979.
55 Ehrenreich, 1979.
56 Barrett, 1980; Ehrenreich, 1979; Eisenstein, 1979; Hartmann, 1981.
57 Brother, 1979.
58 Brother, 1979; Hartmann, 1981.
59 *Masculinity and Violence*, 1982.
60 Hoch, 1979.
61 Cited in Hoch, 1979, page 18.

Chapter Three

Psychological theories of sex differences and rape

Sexuality has long been the subject of heated debate in the social sciences. Enquiries have ranged from the origins of sex roles to definitions of a feminist sexuality. But there have been few discussions about the close relationship between sex roles and rape. Furthermore, it seems little research has been conducted into psychology's contribution to perpetuating gender stereotypes and rape myths (see Chapter 4).

The intention of this chapter is to focus on the psychology of sexuality – the source of prolific writing – and investigate its contribution to the aetiology of rape. Much of the discussion relies for its framework and many research references on the extensive, insightful and thorough work of Rohrbaugh.[1] Another aim of this section is to pose an alternative paradigm in which to understand sex roles and, more specifically, male development. A different understanding of human sexuality changes conceptions of why men rape.

Herman argues that a society which teaches men to engage in sexual conquest and to be competitive and aggressive, especially in the sphere of sexual relations, must be defined as a rape culture,[2] for it is these characteristics and behaviours that are primary contributors to the incidence of rape.[3]

Herman's argument would not go uncontested by psychological theorists. Many psychologists would disagree with the postulate that the values attached to masculinity and femininity are based on learning instead of instinct and biology. Hutt, for example, in her book *Males and Females*, states:

Too little cognisance is taken of the structure and function of the brain, much less of the constraints set by the nature of its organisation. I make no apology, therefore, for stating the case for the biological bases of psychological sex differences.[4]

Biological theories are reductionist in that they subsume 'complex socially and historically constructed phenomena under the simple category of biological difference'; and they also have serious implications for the possibilities of social transformation.[5] If we are to say that masculinity and femininity are naturally given, then how do we explain historical changes in sex-role behaviour? Would it be possible to establish a more humane way of living? Could the expression of male sexual aggression through rape ever be transcended? These problems and questions make essential an examination of some of the psychobiological theories.

Animal behaviour theories

The most explicit arguments for human nature's constancy and immutability are those based on animal behaviourism. As Morris states:

Behind the facade of modern city life there is the same old naked ape. Only the names have been changed: for 'hunting' read 'working', for 'hunting ground' read 'place of business', for 'home base' read 'house', for 'paid bond' read 'marriage', for 'mate' read 'wife' and so on.[6]

Researchers explain their investigations of animal behaviour, and specifically sex differences, in the quest for (amongst other things) human analogies by arguing that these differences give an indication of biological make-up without contamination by social variables.[7] This premise is faulty, however, because it denies the existence of various systems of social organisation amongst different animal groups. Animals cannot be said to be unsocialised – rather, their socialisation takes a different form.[8]

   The idea that direct extrapolation from animals to humans is valid has serious implications, for it may serve to tacitly condone or at least accept sexual aggression and rape. The following quote from

Gebbard, Gagnon, Pomeroy and Christenseon illustrates the point:

> Any reasonably experienced male has learned to disregard [the] minor protestations of the female . . . a male is supposed to be physically forceful in his sexual behaviour . . . Actually, there is some sound biology behind this supposition. In many mammals, coitus is preceded by a physical struggle . . . The physiological by-products of excitement and exertion − the increased heart rate, increased breathing, muscle tension, the greater supply of blood to the body surfaces, etc. − all of these are also part of a sexual response and it is easy to see how these physiological conditions could facilitate a subsequent sexual response.[9]

Research on animal behaviour, like any other research, may trip up on methodological difficulties. There is the question of experimenter bias − researchers may study particular animal groups whose behaviour supports their central assumptions,[10] and they may be subjective in their interpretations of the animals' behaviour.[11] Examining animals in the artificial setting of a laboratory can also generate artificial behaviour. For example, some research has shown that captivity substantially increases aggression in animals.[12]

Generalisation from animals often rests on the odd assumption that whatever animals do is required, desirable and natural in humans.[13] As Weisstein points out, an extension of such logic is that since animals do not read or receive an academic education, neither should humans − it would be unnatural.[14] The point to be made is that classifying the sexually aggressive behaviour of some animals as desirable (because natural) in part helps to legitimise this kind of sexual behaviour in humans.

French cites some interesting studies of the comparative behaviour of humans and animals. While she does not suggest that comparisons between the two serve any useful function, her summary of animal behaviour points to a significant overlapping in the behaviour of animals and humans.[15] Rohrbaugh reaches a similar conclusion. She too highlights some common characteristics, but says findings yielded by studies are generally disappointing for biologists.[16] Extrapolating from the work of Rosenberg and Weisstein, she comments that a wide variety of social organisation and sex differences pervade the animal species, from the female lion who takes charge of the hunting and the killing and the male marmoset who is responsible for child care, to the male baboon who is responsible for the fighting and the female baboon who does the child care.[17] And even with reference to the latter, male baboons are known to hold and care for their young if their mates die.[18] Among non-humans, therefore, it cannot always be taken as fact that the male plays the aggressor role and the female the nurturant and passive role. Finally, regarding the issue of sexual coercion and aggression amongst animals, French's comments about the rarity of rape amongst animals are worthy of note:

> [An] easy, noncoercive kind of sexuality is true of most animals: aggressive or dominant behaviour interferes with mating, and only when it is eliminated and two sexes enjoy themselves and each other in mutuality can coitus occur. Rape is extremely rare in the animal world. Male monkeys cannot mate unless female monkeys invite them and co-operate; female primates in estrus choose their own partners, and often many partners, one after the other.[19]

Research on human infants

Human newborns, like animals, have often been selected as the subject of research studies by researchers who work within a biological framework because they are believed to be unsocialised.[20] These researchers argue that any sex differences which manifest close to the time of birth can be attributed to biology and so provide an explanation for sex differences in behaviour in adulthood.[21]

Such research makes the claim to have identified sex differences in newborns that continue into adulthood. Male newborns are said to be bigger;[22] have higher sensory thresholds in terms of pain, taste, hearing and smell;[23] have better motor skills and superior energy levels;[24] exhibit more aggression;[25] and to be less amenable to comforting.[26]

In response to this data, Rohrbaugh reports studies that did not discover any sex differences and those which found differences in the opposite direction.[27] She cites Maccoby and Jacklin's exhaustive review of relevant literature which concluded that the reliability of findings was too low to make suppositions about sex differences in newborns.[28] Findings varied from investigation to investigation and for the same infant over a period of time. Some infants were very active as newborns but sluggish as pre-schoolers, for example. Since it is difficult to accurately determine the same infant's behaviour over three or four years, it is even more ambitious to attempt to determine dissimilarities between groups of male and female infants.

It would be both senseless and rigid to deny the possibility of sex differences and their potential effect on behaviour. However, it must equally be acknowledged that behavioural sex differences in infants cannot be attributed solely to biology, as social factors may have a contaminating effect. Parents have different perceptions and responses to male and female infants, and these may cause or exaggerate any differences present at birth.[29]

Sex role stereotyping begins as soon as the infant is defined as male or female.[30] This was borne out in a study where thirty pairs of first time parents, fifteen with newly born daughters and fifteen with sons, were interviewed.[31] Interviews were conducted within a day of the birth. Although medical examination revealed no significant differences between males and females, daughters were said to be finer featured, softer, littler and less attentive than sons.

A crucial determining factor in the establishment of behaviour patterns is the complex interaction of mother and infant, which constitutes a substantial part of the infant's life. Moss has outlined some significant aspects of this interaction.[32] He argues that mothers stimulate their sons to higher activity levels. The significance of this is that heightened physical activity in newborns has been interpreted as increasing the potential for aggression in adulthood.

According to Moss, there is a greater likelihood of mothers responding to tears and fretting in girls. This may be because mothers believe girls to be more vulnerable and in need of greater reassurance.[33] The result may be an increased tendency in females to turn to others for assistance, thus encouraging passive and dependent behaviour.

Rohrbaugh comments:

Not only does the latest research suggest that no discernible sex differences exist at birth, but in addition it points toward a pervasive tendency for parents to perceive infants in terms of gender. If any real biological sex differences do serve as a starting point for the socialisation process, we cannot know what they are as long as sex-role stereotyping is so deeply ingrained that babies are perceived in terms of gender.[34]

The above evidence and the qualities predisposing men to rape (see Chapter 6) suggest that men are not born to dominate or rape. Rather, it is their socialisation, a small part of which is based on their first interaction with their parents, that may lead them to engage in violence and rape.

However, there are still many theorists who disagree with the notion of socialised behaviour and who prefer to postulate that behaviour can be explained in terms of hormonal endowment.[35]

Hormonal theories

Some theorists explain human development and men's apparently superior sex and aggressive drives in terms of hormones. Hormonal theories proved an attractive ally of anti-women's liberation protagonists, particularly in the 1960s, as they provided strong and comprehensible biological arguments about the danger of transforming the 'natural order' of the world.[36]

Hormone studies show that the circulating level of sex hormones – androgen (male) and estrogen (female) – are similarly low in both sexes until the age of ten.[37] Only at the time of puberty is there greater hormonal secretion and the beginning of appreciable differences in hormonal composition in males and females. Females have larger amounts of estrogen, while males have larger amounts of androgen.[38] These hormonal differences are seen as laying the foundation for behavioural sex differences.[39]

Hormones are supposedly linked to behaviour through their role in determining energy flow, which is directed into areas such as sex and aggression. The assumption is that bodily chemistry has a one to one relationship with behavioural patterns and personality. Social factors are considered irrelevant to the relationship between physiological state and behaviour.[40] Rohrbaugh explains how social factors give shape to hormonal response:

> Extensive research has shown that even our private emotions and their interpretation are shaped by the reactions of those around us. While visceral sensations such as heart palpitations, flushing and tremor tell us that we are emotionally

aroused, we have to learn whether that arousal means that we are excited, angry or happy. And we learn to apply these verbal labels by observing others while we are experiencing the physical sensations.[41]

This observation has been supported by experiments conducted by Schachter and Singer and Schachter and Wheeler.[42] Findings suggest that the experience of emotion is reliant on physical arousal and social or external cues, and that physical sensations tend to be labelled according to environmental cues or social surroundings.[43] Thus arousal within the context of a funeral may be translated into sadness, whereas arousal at a rugby match may be translated into excitement. To quote Rohrbaugh again, the conclusion we can draw from this is that:

> A simple one to one relationship does not always exist between body chemicals and their physical effects, on the one hand, and between behaviour and mood on the other. Like all body chemicals, hormones produce a physiological state that must be translated into personality and behaviour through a specific social context. Given the pervasiveness of gender as a filter of perceptions and expectations from birth on, we can reasonably assume that sex roles determine many of these social contexts. Thus, sex roles probably enter into the very way we perceive and interpret our own bodily sensations, including those sensations due to hormones.[44]

Rohrbaugh's assertion that emotions are translated by social cues implies that premature extrapolation from hormonal theories retards the search for an understanding of human conduct[45] and sexually aggressive behaviour.[46]

Hormonal explanations, however, continue to be attractive. According to Archer and Wilson, this is because they provide 'easy and simple solutions', 'pander to our inertia' and become 'a gigantic moral let-out'.[47] Hormonal theories' inability to control for social factors means they must fail to come up with the ultimate explanation for sex differences in sexual and aggressive behaviour.

The big question is whether one of the most influential theories in the world of psychology – psychoanalytic theory – takes sufficient cognisance of social factors and provides a better understanding of sexual aggression.

The work of Freud

The psychoanalytic formulations of Freud have permeated not only the psychological profession, but also many other areas of our society. Within the world of psychology, their influence has extended to research on sex roles and sex differences. Like the other biological theories discussed, Freudian theory assumes a largely predetermined relationship between sex and behaviour.[48] The limited scope of this work makes it impossible to deal with many features of Freudian theory. What follows is a brief description of Freudian arguments and criticisms levelled against them.

Freud's biological bias derives from his concept of psychosexual stages. Freud believed that the development of personality rested on four stages – oral, anal, phallic and genital. In each of these stages, libidinal (sexual) energy is directed towards a particular erogenous zone, for which the stage is named. An erotogenic zone, according to Freud is 'a part of the skin or mucous membrane in which stimuli of a certain sort evoke a feeling of pleasure'.[49]

Sex roles evolve during the oedipal stage (which follows the phallic stage), as boys and girls reach different resolutions of the oedipal conflict. During the oedipal period, the little boy wants to sexually possess his mother and competes with his father for her affection. The boy realises, however, his lack of power and inferiority in relation to his father, and fears that his father, who is the primary disciplinarian in the family, may punish him by castrating him. In the face of this fear and inability to compete, the boy relinquishes his desire for sexual possession of his mother and begins to identify with his father.

Identification with the father results in the boy inculcating his father's attitudes. The boy also incorporates his father's morals and prohibitions, thereby initiating the development of the superego – an internal set of moral standards which act as a conscience and reflect society's and parents' moral standards. It is largely on the basis of these standards that individuals evaluate themselves.[50]

The girl, like the boy, sexually desires her mother. However, as soon as she realises that, unlike her father and brother, she does not possess a penis, she loses her sexual desire for her mother and comes to perceive her mother as responsible for her lack of a penis. The girl turns to her father for fulfilment of this desire for a penis.[51]

Freud believed that the girl's awareness that she lacks a penis means she does not fear castration as retribution for incestuous desires. The result is a diminished sense of justice in women and moral deficiency in adulthood.[52] By not identifying fully with her mother, the girl does not internalise her mother's attributes as successfully as the boy does the father's, and consequently does not develop as strong a superego or sense of self-worth as the boy.[53]

Freud also describes women as being prone to physical vanity, shame, jealousy, passivity, masochism and a lower sexual drive.[54] The last two features have the most important implications for a study of rape.

According to Freud, for females to pass through the psychosexual stages successfully, they must refrain from masturbating with their 'masculine' clitoris (penis substitute) and change to the 'feminine' vagina.[55] This change from active clitoral sexuality to passive vaginal sexuality is generalised to other forms of behaviour. Active or aggressive modes of relating are avoided, and aggression is consequently turned inward, resulting in masochistic behaviour and self-destructive attitudes. In *New Introductory Lectures on Psychoanalysis*, Freud explained this notion:

> The suppression of women's aggressiveness which is prescribed for them constitutionally and imposed on them socially favours the development of powerful masochistic impulses, which succeed, as we know, in binding erotically the destructive trends which have been diverted inwards. Thus masochism, as people say, is truly feminine.[56]

A more specific account of Freud's thoughts on female masochism is found in his paper 'The Economic Problem in Masochism':

> For the real situations are in fact only a kind of make-believe performance of the fantasies – the manifest content is of being pinned, bound, beaten painfully, whipped, in some way mishandled, forced to obey unconditionally, defiled, degraded . . . in them the subject is placed in a situation characteristic of womanhood.[57]

Freud believed men have a greater biological drive for sex. He claimed that men are essentially responsible for reproduction since their biologically determined aggression allows them to coerce women into having sex, whether women wish to have it or not.[58] He wrote:

More constraint has been applied to the libido when it is pressed into the service of the feminine function, and – to speak teleologically – nature takes less careful account of its demands than in the case of masculinity. And the reason for this may lie – thinking once again teleologically – in the fact that the accomplishment of the aim of biology has been entrusted to the aggressiveness of men and has been to some extent independent of women's consent.[59]

Freud's understanding of sex differences in behaviour and attitudes helps augment pessimistic conceptualisations of women and positive assumptions about men. In the context of rape, these perceptions help alter interpretations of the rape act in the rapist's favour. But Freud's ideas have spread their influence further afield. His theories have formed the basis of other psychological theories which have equally negative implications for an analysis of rape. In this regard, it is the work of Deutsch that will be concentrated on. Deutsch was a psychoanalyst – a follower of Freud – and much of her work on sexuality was published in the 1940s.

Post-Freudians

Deutsch was more specific than Freud in her analysis of female masochism and rape.[60] She believed that women unconsciously wish to be raped. Masochism, Deutsch asserted, 'is the most elementary power in a woman's life' and is directly linked to the female's biological predisposition.[61]

The notion of inherent female masochism directs the burden of guilt away from the rapist towards the victim. Another example of this supposition is Abrahamson's conclusions to his study of wives who had been raped by their husbands:

The conclusions reached were that the wives of the sex offenders on the surface behaved toward men in a submissive and masochistic way but latently denied their femininity and showed an aggressive masculine orientation: they unconsciously invited sexual aggression, only to respond to it with coolness and rejection. They stimulated their husbands into attempts to prove themselves, attempts which necessarily ended in frustration and increased their husbands' own doubts about their masculinity. In doing so, the wives unknowingly continued the type of relationship the offender had had with his mother. There can be no doubt that the sexual frustration which the wives caused is one of the factors motivating rape, which might be tentatively described as a displaced attempt to force a seductive but rejecting mother into submission.[62]

A further factor used to devalue women's experience of rape is that women's sexual fantasies are sometimes rape fantasies. Deutsch, for instance, contends that female pubertal fantasies are basically masochistic: 'Girlish fantasies relating to rape often remain unconscious but evince their content in dreams, sometimes in symptoms, and often accompany masturbatory actions.'[63] Deutsch goes still further than this, arguing that young girls' fantasies are not simply generally masochistic, but specifically related to rape:

> In dreams the rape is symbolic: the terrifying male persecutor with knife in hand, the burglar who breaks in at the window, the thief who steals a particularly valuable object, are the most typical and frequently recurring figures in the dreams of young girls.[64]

Deutsch's notion of women's moral deficiency in relation to reports of rape is so detrimental to the rape victim that she again requires quoting:

> Rape fantasies are variants of the seduction fantasies so familiar to us in the lying accounts of hysterical women patients. Both rape and seduction fantasies are deliberately passed on to other persons as true, and they have the typical pseudologic character we found in the more romantic and fantastic lies of puberty. That is, they draw their appearance of truth from the fact that underlying them is a real but repressed experience. It is precisely rape fantasies that often have such irresistible verisimilitude that even the most experienced judges are misled in trials of innocent men accused of rape by hysterical women.[65]

The logic is that some women make false accusations of rape because of their unconscious desire to be raped.

The fact is that false rape accusations do occur and women do have rape fantasies. However, the ordeal to which rape victims are subjected after reporting a rape (see Chapters 6 and 7) makes it unlikely that false accusations would be numerous. Furthermore, there are no indications that false accusations about rape are made more frequently than those about any other kind of crime. It is the responsibility of the legal process, rather than social opinion, to determine the truth in such cases. It must also be noted that indulging in a sexual fantasy – about rape or anything else – is not the same as wanting that fantasy to become real. Finally, with reference to Deutsch, the link between indulging in a fantasy and making a false accusation is hardly a necessary one.

Numerous criticisms have been levelled against Freud by feminists and members of the neo-Freudian school. Mitchell, in *Psychoanalysis and Feminism,* sounds a note of caution. She argues that a rejection of psychoanalysis would be detrimental to feminism.[66] Mitchell understands psychoanalysis as 'not a recommendation *for* a patriarchal society, but an analysis *of* one'.[67] While this is true up to a point, Freud's work, as Mitchell also admits, contains sexist premises and judgements. This study contends, in line with the work of Horney and Thompson of the neo-Freudian school and Mitchell to an extent, that the majority of Freudian concepts should not be discarded, but that the assumptions underlying these concepts should be carefully scrutinised.[68] An unquestioning attitude towards anyone's work, including Freud's, does nothing to advance the discipline of psychology or our understanding of human behaviour.

Criticisms of Freud

Feminists such as De Beauvoir and Millet and neo-Freudians such as Horney and Thompson concur in their rejection of Freud's notion of male as healthy and female as pathological.[67] They are especially critical of his emphasis on biological rather than social factors as the key to human behaviour. Millet articulates this last criticism succinctly. She writes that Freud failed to realise that

women *are* born female in a masculine dominated culture which is bent upon extending its values even to anatomy and is therefore capable of investing biological phenomena with symbolic force.[70]

Neo-Freudians believe that psychoanalytic theory, if it is to more fully comprehend human sexuality, must pay more attention to the role of social and cultural conditioning. They argue that an understanding of sexuality can only be achieved through subjecting biological sex differences to sociological analysis. Thus Thompson, for example, writes that penis envy, which arises from anatomical differences, is not so much a question of anatomy as of politics:

> When such a wish [penis-envy] is expressed the woman is but demanding in this symbolic way some form of equality with men . . . The woman envies the greater freedom of the man, his greater opportunities and his relative lack of conflict about his fundamental drives. The penis as a symbol of aggression stands for the freedom to be, to force one's way, to get what one wants . . . So the attitude called penis envy is similar to the attitude of any underprivileged group towards those in power.[71]

Some psychologists and feminists have gone beyond Horney and Thompson's criticisms to question the very existence of penis envy. Psychologists Conn and Kanner reject the idea of penis envy in women on the basis of empirical and laboratory studies.[72] This has important implications for Freud's theory of female sexuality, since the absence of penis envy would bring into question the female transition from clitoral to vaginal sexuality and the resulting development of masochistic tendencies, including women's unconscious desire to be raped. It also has implications for whether women can gain sexual gratification only through vaginal stimulation.

In writing about penis envy, De Beauvoir comments on the girl's lack of anxiety in recognising male genitals:

> To begin with, there are many little girls who remain ignorant of the male anatomy for some years. Such a child finds it quite natural that there should be men and women, just as there is sun and moon . . . For many others this tiny bit of flesh hanging between boys' legs is insignificant or even laughable; it is a peculiarity that merges with that of clothes or haircut.[73]

De Beauvoir goes on to argue that even if a girl takes an active interest in male genitals, it should not imply that

> she experiences jealousy of it in a really sexual way, still less that she feels deeply affected by the absence of that organ: she wants to get it for herself as she wants to get any and every object, but this desire can remain superficial.[74]

Freud's proposition that vaginal sexuality makes for the passivity so essential to healthy female development is equally (or more) contentious. Cavell points out: 'There are many ways of being active as there are of being human. To pierce and to enter are one kind of activity. To grasp and to hold are another.'[75]

With the emphasis on vaginal sexuality came the judgement that vaginal orgasm is the only healthy and mature orgasm. After extensive research, Masters and Johnson concluded that in fact there is no physiological difference between clitoral and vaginal orgasm.[76] While their findings are not universally accepted, with some such as Hite claiming that differences between vaginal and clitoral orgasms do exist and others like Hoedt arguing that vaginal orgasms are non-existent, there is a strong body of opinion which posits that clitoral and vaginal orgasm are inseparable.[77] Rohrbaugh comments:

> Female anatomy is such that it is physically impossible to have one without the other, for the clitoris is merely the external visible part of an underlying *clitoral system*. These internal organs expand as much or more than the male penis during arousal, and this engorgement is discharged as a unit.[78]

The myths of the 'superior' vaginal orgasm and passive female sexuality raise further questions about Freud's proposal of female masochism and suggestion that women enjoy being raped. As De Beauviour states:

> Pain, in fact, is of masochistic significance only when it is accepted and wanted as proof of servitude. As for the pain of defloration [and rape], it is not closely correlated with pleasure; and as for the sufferings of childbirth, all women fear them and are glad that modern obstetrical methods are doing away with them. Pain has no greater and no less a place in women's sexuality than in man's.

Still it is true that the sexual role of women is largely passive; but the actual performance of that passive part is no
more masochistic than the normal aggressive behaviour of
the male is sadistic.[79]

To conclude, it must again be emphasised that Freud's work should
not be rejected but rather critically analysed. Thus while there is
little disagreement that young children identify with the attributes
of their parents, there is considerable disagreement about just how
that process occurs. While Freud was a rebel in his day, his work
may nevertheless act as a conservative force.[80] Certainly some of
Freud's ideas on female sexuality have helped reinforce, intention-
ally or unintentionally, a number of myths about rape. Freudian
theory overemphasises the biological at the expense of the social,
and therefore remains unable to explain adequately sex differences
in attitudes and behaviour.

One concept which incorporates social theory and makes a significant contribution to an understanding of behavioural sex differences is that of socialisation.

Socialisation

Socialisation can be defined as a process through which people are
acculturated to attitudes and ways of behaving which enable them
to participate in society.[81] The notion that sex role behaviour is
learnt has been verified by numerous studies, ranging from examinations of cross-cultural sex differences[82] to research on
hermaphrodites.[83]

A classic study of differences in cultural socialisation was conducted by Barry and associates.[84] After examining ethnographic
reports of one hundred and ten societies around the world, they
found that socialisation patterns and work roles were responsible,
for example, for pressurising girls into nurturant and submissive
roles and encouraging boys to be more independent and
achievement-orientated. In the societies examined, emphasis on
nurturance as a quality natural to women prepared girls for the
child caring role, while stress on men being independent and active prepared boys for hunting.

Ember's study of the Luo tribe in Kenya highlights the impact
of socialisation on assigned work tasks, as well as its profound ef-

fect on human behavour.[85] The study centred on an examination
of behaviour patterns among Luo girls, Luo boys who had to do
'female work' (because girls in the family were too young to work)
and Luo boys who were not required to do 'female work'. Ember's findings indicate that Luo boys who perform 'female work'
display 'female' character traits such as submissiveness and
dependency.

In South African society, expectations about personality are often
based on occupation. Thus men who do social work or nursing
are often seen as having feminine characteristics, particularly in
terms of their ability to nurture.

Studies of hermaphrodites present one of the most convincing
arguments for the theory that sex role behaviour is largely
learnt.[86] These individuals are often raised such that their sex role
socialisation does not correspond with their sexual anatomy. A boy
with defects in the penile area which conceal his biological sex may
be brought up as a girl. Likewise, a female child may be brought
up as a boy because of enlargement of her clitoris. Research data
reveals that by the age of two, such individuals begin to behave
in a way typical of the sex they were raised as, regardless of their
biological sex.[87] Hampson and Hampson draw out the implications of this:

> In the human psychologic, sexuality is not differentiated when
> the child is born. Rather, psychologic sex becomes differen-
> tiated during the course of the many experiences of growing
> up, including those experiences dictated by his or her own
> bodily equipment. Thus, in the place of the theory of an in-
> nate, constitutional psychologic bisexuality such as that pro-
> posed by Freud . . . we must substitute a concept of psy-
> chologic sexual neutrality in humans at birth. Such psy-
> chosexual neutrality permits the development and perpetua-
> tion of diverse patterns of psychosexual orientation and func-
> tioning in accordance with the life experiences each individual
> may encounter and transact.[88]

Assuming, then, that socialisation does operate in society, the question is how it operates and what its content is. Psychologists[89] and
sociologists[90] tend to stress the positive aspects of the socialisation
process. They argue that children acquire the moral codes, social
skills and sex role behaviours necessary for proper functioning in

our society. While this is valid, it is also true that socialisation is responsible for perpetuating sexist ideas and behaviours which encourage rape and facilitate the social control of women.

In South African and many other societies, socialisation defines as natural that which is social. Naturalism allows for the view that behaviours which have persisted through history must be natural. This suggests that trans-historical behaviours are resilient to change, and, moreover, that attempts to change these behaviours are unnatural and so deviant. The effect is that the social control of women – which has largely survived various upheavals throughout human history – is accepted unquestioningly as the natural order of things.

The truth is, however, that people are never perfectly or identically socialised, so that deviations from – and even transgressions of – sex and other roles always occur. We do not respond to socialisation as computers do to programming. Thus the effects of socialisation are not fixed or even predictable.

Furthermore, if one assumes that history progresses dialectically rather than linearly, and that all things are interconnected and change is continual, then personality features are never permanent and unchangeable. Change is always possible. Change in the form of reducing the incidence of rape requires an understanding of socialisation and commitment to changing modes of relating within social institutions such as the family and the school.

The family

Parents are usually the child's first and most long-lasting human contact. The family is therefore usually the most pivotol institution in shaping the pre-school child's beliefs, values and attitudes. Mead explains the crucial role of parents and other 'meaningful' adults in terms of 'significant others'.[91] For Mead, the first phases of socialisation are characterised by the child adopting the attitudes and roles of its parents. As the child gets older, she or he begins to learn that these parental attitudes and roles are reflected in a much more general reality. For instance, the little boy who plays with dolls soon realises that it is not only his father who finds this unacceptable, but also every 'significant other' with whom he has contact. At this stage the boy begins to relate to both a 'significant other' and a generalised other, which represents society at large. The influential nature of the behaviour of significant others is entrenched by the child's dependence, high degree of curiosity and receptivity to most forms of stimulation.

Bandura's work raises another aspect of learning in the socialisation process. Bandura found that even when they are not actively punished or reinforced, children learn behaviour merely by watching others.[92] He called this process 'modelling'. There are two components to learning through modelling. The first is observational learning – learning new responses from watching the behaviour of another. The second is that a person who has already acquired a particular behaviour may become less or more willing to reproduce it by observing the consequences when another engages in it.[93]

Whether they are conscious of it or not, most parents act as representatives of their society. They help conserve dominant norms and inhibit the development of alternative forms of behaviour. Prevailing sex roles become ingrained through the childhood activities encouraged by parents.

Another major function of the family is its role as a disciplining agent. It is the first place where children learn to accept authority and hierarchy unquestioningly. These relations are expressed in the father's dominant position over the mother, and the child's position in relation to his or her parents. Children are expected to obey their parents even if their commands are unrealistic and their punishments cruel. Over one third of subjects in the study said they had never been (consciously) angry with or questioned their father's or other 'significant adult's' authority, even when severely beaten by them. Two rapists stated:

> He [father] used to hit us hard but I didn't take it hard. I just thought it is my father, I must accept it from him.

> I didn't feel cross. I just thought to myself he [father] is just learning me the right way but I'll see for myself one day when I get bigger. He will have made a man of me or something like that.

Two men from the Physically Violent group commented:

> I wasn't that kind of person that if I get a hiding then I won't like him any more because we were brought up to be kind and courteous.

> They [parents] would scold me or they would give me a big
> hiding and out of that I would know what is wrong and what
> is right.

A man from the Non-Violent group said:

> I knew I was wrong, he never gave me a hiding for nothing.
> Even if I don't like it, I must love him.

Parental behaviour of this sort is not universal. Differences, although not very great ones, occur among and within different classes and race groups.[94] Middle class parents, for example, tend to discipline their children more through withdrawing love than with physical punishment. The kind of discipline used with the subjects of this study occurred in a social context permeated by visible manifestations of violence – wife-beating, gang fights and child abuse. The subjects, probably unlike children from middle class homes, were able to acquiesce more easily to their fathers' violence because they were raised in a subculture of violence. Violence within such a subculture is a legitimate means of resolving conflict. This is one of the familial lessons these children take with them into their school lives and adulthood.

The lessons of violence within the family structure are illustrated in the many reports made by psychologists and social workers dealing with child abuse. Child abuse victims often become child abusers. The explanation for this may be simply that children learn that violence is a means of resolving problems, or alternatively that the abused child identifies with the person in authority – the abuser – because she or he too wants the power of authority. The desire for power may be particularly strong because the abused child feels so powerless. This process has been termed identification with the persecutor. It is also found amongst adults who have experienced extreme trauma and violence. This concept helps explain the phenomenon of the dying concentration camp victims who looked for scraps of SS uniform material to pin on themselves before dying. They felt the uniform material would give them some power and stand in some way between them and death.[95]

After the family, the next most significant institution in a young child's life is the school – assuming, of course, the child has the opportunity to go to school, which is not universally the case.

The school

The school is often narrowly perceived as an institution which provides children with only an academic education. Yet its role extends far beyond this: it also transmits values, attitudes and behaviour. Not all the school's social lessons are entirely new, since they are built on the learning and experiences that have already taken place within the family. Boys and girls are again taught their respective roles and behaviours. Two different forms of control ensure internalisation of desired qualities – external and internal. External controls are penalties used to make the individual toe the line. Penalties may range from corporal punishment to the more subtle teacher disapproval or gossip among school mates. With internal controls, the threat lives in the individual's own consciousness. For internal controls to operate effectively, the family and the school must have successfully inculcated the desired values.[96]

Another crucial role of the school is the stress it places, especially among boys, on individual ambition and competition. The result is that boys begin to rank themselves according to physical strength, sporting prowess and sexual success with girls. When they fail to achieve in an area deemed important, they feel insecure. To overcompensate for their frustrations and insecurities, they may resort to methods of problem-solving instilled by family and school – physical violence and aggression.[97] Such behaviour is made easier by the support and encouragement the boy receives from his peer group and the popular acceptance of violence in the broader culture.

The peer group

Adolescence is a time of biological changes, and one often characterised by conflict, stress and emotional turmoil. The turbulence of adolescence derives primarily from heightened self-consciousness and a desire to make an impression on people; the reorganisation of personality through the discarding of childhood behaviours; a sense of omnipotence; heightened sexuality; changing physical make-up; changing relationship to parents and peers; and increased social expectations placed on adolescents.[98] Adolescence is also a time of role experimentation and this, together with the above factors, makes the adolescent years central in the formation of identity.

Erickson called adolescence a time characterised by 'identity versus role confusion'.[99] Commenting on adolescents' preoccupation with social expectations and their attempts to develop an identity, Erickson wrote:

> They are sometimes morbidly, often curiously, preoccupied with what they appear to be in the eyes of others as compared with what they are and with the question of how to connect the earlier cultivated roles and skills with the ideal prototypes of the day.[100]

The mental anguish and quest for independence from parents induce the adolescent to find a group of friends who can provide support and affirmation. But acceptance by any group requires conformity to the norms and standards of that group. This might mean modifying or changing behaviour and developing an interpersonal identification with the group's aims and activities. Thus in Riverlea, a male wanting to become part of a wider circle of friends may have to evince more aggression, increase his physical strength and show more sexual assertiveness in order to participate in group activities such as fighting and womanising. The peer group has the awesome power to pressurise individuals to conform and to ostracise deviants, making it an effective instrument in eliciting stereotypical sex role behaviour.

All these social institutions, supplemented by others too numerous to detail, help to mould experiences, attitudes and behaviour. The greatest significance of this lies in the fact that behaviour is demonstrably the result of social, rather than biological, factors. In the words of Oakley, 'to be masculine and feminine is as much a function of dress, gesture, occupation, social network and personality, as it is of possessing a particular set of genitals'.[101]

This chapter has attempted to illustrate that moralities, ideas, beliefs and academic enquiry play a role in developing and reinforcing stereotypical notions of sex role behaviour. These in turn contribute to the incidence of rape, as the next few chapters will attempt to illustrate. A closer examination will be made of those activities of boyhood and manhood that help develop men's perception of women as sexual objects – a perception which is a necessary precondition for rape.

Notes

1 1981.
2 1979.
3 Herman, 1979; Russell, 1975; Wilson, 1983.
4 1972, page 17.
5 Barrett, 1980, page 12.
6 1967, page 43.
7 Rohrbaugh, 1981.
8 Rohrbaugh, 1981.
9 1965, pages 177-8.
10 Rosenberg, 1973; cited in Rohrbaugh, 1981. A good illustration of this is that
    many studies choose to focus on the rhesus monkey species. In this species,
    females fulfil the task of nurturing the young and are passive and submissive,
    while the males are domineering and aggressive. Yet the rhesus monkey is fur-
    ther removed from humans on the evolutionary scale than is the gibbon, whose
    males and females demonstrate few differences in physical appearance or be-
    haviour (Rosenberg, 1973; cited in Rohrbaugh, 1981).
11 Rosenberg, 1973; Rosenthal, 1966; cited in Rohrbaugh, 1981.
12 Wilson, 1983.
13 Weisstein, 1971; Wilson, 1983.
14 1971; cited in Rohrbaugh, 1981.
15 1986.
16 1981.
17 1973; 1971.
18 Morgan, 1972; cited in French, 1986.
19 1986, page 10.
20 Hutt, 1972; Rosenberg and Sutton-Smith, 1972.
21 Rohrbaugh, 1981.
22 Rosenberg and Sutton-Smith, 1972; cited in Rohrbaugh, 1981.
23 Garai and Scheinfeld, 1968.
24 Garai and Scheinfeld, 1968; Rosenberg and Sutton-Smith, 1972.
25 Maccoby and Jacklin, 1974.
26 Rosenberg and Sutton-Smith, 1972.
27 1981.
28 1974.
29 Rogers, 1976; Rubin, Provenzano and Luria, 1974.
30 Rubin, Provenzano and Luria, 1974.
31 Rohrbaugh, 1981.
32 1967; cited in Rohrbaugh, 1981.
33 1967.
34 1981, page 25.
35 Bardwick, 1971; Dawson, 1979; Money and Erhardt, 1972.
36 Crook, 1970.
37 Lunde and Hamburg, 1972.
38 Archer, 1976; Rohrbaugh, 1981.
39 Rohrbaugh, 1981.
40 Rogers, 1976; Rohrbaugh, 1981.
41 1981, page 31.
42 1962; 1962; cited in Rohrbaugh, 1981.
43 Rohrbaugh, 1981; Schneider, 1976.
44 1981, page 32.
45 1976, page 176.
46 Rada, 1983.

47 Archer, 1976; Wilson, 1983.
48 Ullian, 1976.
49 1925, page 99.
50 Freud, 1897; 1905; 1924.
51 Freud, 1905; 1924; 1925.
52 In 1925, Freud wrote that: 'Women show less sense of justice, are less willing to submit to the great necessities of life, and are more often influenced in their judgements by feelings of affection and hostility' (page 190). In 1933, he wrote: 'The fact that women must be regarded as having little sense of justice is no doubt related to the predominance of envy in their mental life; for the demand for justice is a modification of envy and lays down the condition subject to which one can put envy aside' (page 134).
53 Freud, 1924; 1925 (1933).
54 1924; 1925; 1933.
55 1924; 1925.
56 1933, page 116; cited in Rohrbaugh, 1981.
57 1924, page 258.
58 Rohrbaugh, 1981.
59 1933, pages 131-2.
60 1944.
61 1944; cited in Edwards, 1981.
62 1960, page 165; cited in Edwards, 1981.
63 1944, page 255; cited in Edwards, 1981.
64 1944, page 255.
65 1944, page 256.
66 1974.
67 Mitchell, 1974, page XV.
68 Horney, 1967; Thompson, 1943.
69 De Beauvoir, 1972; Millet, 1970; Horney, 1967; Thompson, 1943.
70 1970, page 100.
71 1943, page 124.
72 Conn and Kanner, 1947; Katcher, 1955. Conn and Kanner and Katcher, as cited by Rohrbaugh, attempted to assess children's knowledge of genital sex differences in the oedipal stage. They did this through experiments involving doll playing, interviews and identification of persons in pictures. Both studies found that approximately fifty percent of the children were unaware of genital sex differences. Conn and Kanner's findings also suggested that children who were aware that girls did not have penises were not traumatised by their knowledge. However, because psychoanalysis is concerned with the operations of the unconscious, the validity of empirical studies is open to question.
73 1972, page 300.
74 1972, page 300.
75 1974, page 164; cited in Rohrbaugh, 1981.
76 1966.
77 Hite, 1976; Koedt, 1974.
78 1981, page 275.
79 1972, page 419.
80 French, 1986.
81 Berger and Berger, 1976; Pikunas, 1976.
82 Barry, Bacon and Child, 1957; Embers, 1973.
83 Hampson and Hampson, 1961; cited in Rohrbaugh, 1981.
84 1957.
85 1973.
86 Hampson and Hampson, 1961; cited in Rohrbaugh, 1981.

87 Rohrbaugh, 1981.
88 1961, page 1 406.
89 Pikunas, 1976; Schneider, 1976.
90 Berger and Berger, 1976.
91 1934.
92 1965; 1971.
93 Schneider, 1976.
94 Kerckhoff, 1972.
95 West, 1985.
96 Berger and Berger, 1976.
97 Tolson, 1977.
98 Hjelle and Ziegler, 1981; Jersild and Alpern, 1974; Pikunus, 1976.
99 1963.
100 1963, page 261.
101 1972, page 158.

Chapter Four

Rape-promoting factors: Sexuality and rape

This chapter focuses on those rape-promoting factors which have a strong sexual orientation. While it is difficult to divorce other rape-promoting conditions such as work alienation, racial oppression and economic exploitation (see Chapter 5) from their association with sexuality, there are factors which are more sexualised than others. This differentiation has thus been imposed in order to gain greater clarity about sexuality and rape. The distinction also emphasises that rape is neither an act of violence nor an act of sexual passion — it is a crime of *sexual violence*.

This chapter has been divided into three sub-sections: rape myths; rape-encouraging institutions, behaviours and ideologies; and the sexual conquest. It will be demonstrated throughout that rape exists because, at least in part, of the ideologies and institutions which dehumanise women and are essential to the social construction of masculinity.

Rape myths

Rape myths do not approximate reality. Their widespread internalisation decreases social censure for rape. The myths need to be examined in order to achieve greater understanding of rape and more widespread condemnation of it. In propogating a false account of what rape is, rape myths give men tacit permission to rape and help them rationalise and evade responsibility for their sexually violent behaviour.

A widely accepted view of rape is that it is a sexual act perpetrated for sexual gratification by men who, in the face of women's sexual provocation, have lost their normal self-control. Men's sexual appetites are seen as so powerful and volatile that they may be uncontrollably aroused by a woman's dress, presence or movements. Women are expected to be conscious of this, especially if they choose to be sexually intimate with men they might not wish to have sexual intercourse with. It is their responsibility to impose appropriate limits so as to curb the male's powerful sexual drives. Medea and Thompson discuss adolescents' perception of this responsibility:

> Opinions varied from one social group to another as to just what a boy could stand before he lost control. In one group, it was his hand on her breast, under her blouse, but not under her bra. That was very conservative. In another, he could maintain control of himself if he touched a girl above the waist only, provided he used just his hands . . . Young boys had a remarkable variation in breaking points.[1]

They go on to say:

> We would prefer to establish that, if women flirt they are not inviting rape. If they kiss a man good night, they are not inviting rape. Even, and this should raise a few hackles, even if they should be guilty of 'teasing' a man, they are not inviting rape.[2]

These extracts serve to question the notion that men's sexual cravings are uncontrollable. This myth, like many of the others dealt with in this chapter, is part of the fiction surrounding rape, a fiction which naturalises male violence against women. Rape myths in no way explain the reasons for rape. Their popularity, however, necessitates a thoroughgoing enquiry into their content and effects.

The ideology of men's intemperate sexuality and women's sexual provocation has its roots in the concepts of male sexual aggression, female sexual passivity and the sexual objectification of women. This ideology has penetrated the minds of rapists and the general public. Witness the comments made by men from the three groups, beginning with a rapist:

> If I go to a girl and ask her [to have sex], and she says no, obviously I can't control myself . . . I must have that sex with her.

A man from the Physically Violent group said:

> There is a thing as rape. I mean look, you get guys that get tempted, something runs away with their mind . . . They see a girl walking with a mini and he goes and rapes her. You find with guys, it's in them. It's like a sport, they feel like forcing a lady instead of asking her nicely.

A subject in the Non-Violent group believed:

> The sex wants of men are greater than that of women. Women maybe are to blame [for rape] to a certain extent in the way they dress.

In addition to assuming women's responsibility for preventing rape, these statements reflect the belief that rape is a sexually spontaneous act inflicted upon an unknown victim. Findings from studies indicate otherwise.[3] At least fifty percent of rape attacks in first world countries involve men known to the victim and take place in the victim's own home. Only fifteen percent of rapes are said to occur in the rapist's home and approximately twenty-nine percent in other places.[4] Of rapes occurring in familiar situations – in the victim's own home and by an acquaintance or friend – a great number are planned. Amir's study finds that of reported rapes, seventy-one percent are premeditated, eleven percent are partially planned and only eighteen percent are not premeditated.[5] My own study revealed similar results. Fifty-five percent of the rapes occurred in the victim's home, sixty-six percent were premeditated, twenty-two percent were partially planned, and eleven percent were impulsive.

The myth that rape is a spontaneous act relates to the assumption that men are sometimes so overwhelmingly attracted to women's physical beauty that, helpless in the grip of their uncontrollable sex drives, they have no choice but to rape. According to two men from the Physically Violent group, men rape

> because of a woman's body. They see it and they think I am going to get that woman or I am going to rape her.

because he wants to get his sexual satisfaction and he would like to have a beautiful woman.

Rapists, however, did not mention the victim's physical attractiveness as a motivating factor for the rape. Thus while some men are attracted to women purely on the basis of their looks, this form of sexual attraction is not sufficient to provoke rape.

The need to conquer and control is the primary ingredient of any rape. It may also be argued that conquest of a stereotypically attractive woman may provide the rapist with a greater sense of self. Even in normal day to day heterosexual relationships, men may feel more self-confident after sleeping with a woman valued by other men for her physical beauty. The crucial difference, of course, in the two situations is that in the latter case the physically attractive woman freely chooses her sexual partner, but in the first has no such choice.

The question, then, is are conventionally physically attractive women more vulnerable to rape? At present there is no empirical data to support this. However, what is clear is that even if conventionally physically beautiful women are more vulnerable, other women who do not fall into this category are not invulnerable. Researchers[6] and the daily newspapers report that rapes are frequently perpetrated on conventionally unattractive females, such as young girls and very old women.

Central to the sexual rape myths discussed has been the notion that men rape for sexual gratification. As some rapists put it, men rape because of 'lust and lack of sex'. Although this sentiment is at odds with reality, it does have some measure of truth. Sex is something that men seek to gain when raping a woman, and those rapists more concerned with sexual gratification may use less physical violence than others. This type of rapist may not despise women to the same extent as his more violent counterparts. He overpowers, threatens and manipulates, but he does not physically brutalise the woman. Yet even in these cases, sex is entangled with so many other factors that isolating it as the sole cause of rape would be a mistake. Male socialisation and society's emphasis on sexual activity have made sex the most visible reason for raping. However, as will be illustrated, rapists use sex to fulfil non-sexual needs: the need for power, to dominate and to prove their masculinity.

In the light of this, structural theories focusing on the sexual nature of rape should be viewed with caution. For example, a study by Svalastoga attributes a high incidence of rape to an excess of males in the sex ratio. A surplus of men makes the hunt for sexual partners more tense, he writes.[7]

Theories of sexual access seem to rest largely on the concept of frustration, relative deprivation and deviance. It is postulated that when men are unable to attain what they desire (in this case, sex with women), they become frustrated and their potential for aggression is increased (see Chapter 5). This aggressive potential is intensified if other men have sexual partners, as those without feel relatively deprived. Relative deprivation is often related to an increase in aggression. Rape then becomes a means of coercion to correct perceived deprivation and to take forcibly what is not available through legitimate avenues.[8]

Lester's study brings into question the validity of the sexual access theories.[9] He found no relationship at all between sex ratio and the incidence of rape. There are further studies which show that the vast majority of rapists have been involved in a consenting sexual relationship at the time of their raping.[10] These findings are partially substantiated by the present study, where six of the nine rapists had sexual relations with a partner at the time of their rape. Research on the criminal careers of rapists also suggests that rapists are not obsessed with sexual gratification. Rabkin found, after reviewing much of the research on criminal histories, that compared with other sex offenders, rapists have longer criminal records including crimes not sexually related.[11] Due to problems in gaining information about the criminal activities of other sex offenders, this aspect was not investigated in the present study.

Linked to the perception of rape as a sexual crime is the belief that women derive sexual enjoyment from being raped. This is a view held by many rapists,[12] and is also supported by some orthodox psychoanalytic doctrine (see Chapter 3). The reality of women's experience is very different.[13] Women report feeling depressed, upset, hurt, humiliated, angry and physically sick.[14] Women's physical reaction during rape is another indicator of their sexual response. Physical responses typically include involuntary tightening of the vaginal muscles, making sexual intercourse very painful for the woman and causing bruising and tearing of her muscles.[15] One would also expect that if women found rape sexually pleasing, their sexual activities after being raped would not be negatively affected. Feldman-Summors, Gordon and Meagher found

that rape victims, prior to being raped, and non-raped women engaged in similar amounts of sexual activity and experienced similar levels of satisfaction. One week after the rape, however, victims' responses on sixteen of the twenty-three items tested showed
decreased sexual fulfilment. The only behaviours not rated as less
gratifying after the rape were those 'involving masturbation and
primarily affectional behaviours such as holding hands, hugging,
and talking with or being held by one's partner'.[17] Although satisfaction increased slightly two months after the rape for some subjects, it did not reach the degree of satisfaction experienced before
the rape.

How can the rapist's false assumptions be explained? A rapist's
claim that 'I pulled off her trousers and gave her a smack and after that she was pleased with me', and his later comment about
the same victim – 'I knew when I am finished [with the rape], it
will all be okay between me and she' – illustrate how influential
traditional concepts of male sexual dominance and female sexual
passivity are in reinforcing beliefs about women enjoying rape. Says
Herman:

> Many rapists believe that women enjoy sado-masochistic
> sex . . . In one instance where a 63-year-old woman was
> robbed and raped at gunpoint by a 24-year-old man, her as-
> sailant threw her a kiss and said before running away, 'I bet
> I made your day'. Some offenders have been incredulous
> when arrested, complaining that they may have been a little
> rough, but the woman enjoyed their advances. The rapist's
> attraction to dominance and violence stems from his view of
> sexuality which he interprets to mean 'man ravishes, wom-
> an submits'.[18]

It is to be expected that if rapists believe that women enjoy rape,
they will also believe that women 'look for' rape. Three rapists
made the following statements:

> Women look for it . . . look how they dress.

> Some women look for it. Those who go to night clubs without
> hardly any clothes on and getting drunk, that is looking for it.

> Now and then you get girls that want it. They go after it.

They are walking around at night looking for men . . . and then when the boys come they want to chicken out . . . Then the guys just take them into the school yard.

The injurious effects of this myth have also been discussed by Russell.[19] She writes of a woman who was hospitalised for a few days after being raped by an 'apparent good Samaritan'. At the hospital, she was interviewed by a male psychiatrist who asked questions such as 'Haven't you really been rushing towards this very thing all your life?'. When she returned home she was met by the wrath of her husband, who said, 'If that's what you wanted, why didn't you come to me?'. The idea that women who are raped 'look for it' was so real for her husband that he proceeded to rape her himself.

Amir discusses the idea that women 'look for' rape in terms of his 'victim precipitation' theory.[20] Victim precipitation refers to 'an assumption or definition by the male that the female consented or implied that she was consenting to sexual relations with him, although her consent was withdrawn prior to the act'.[21] This notion can be extended to imply that a woman choosing to enter certain 'vulnerable' situations must assume a level of risk. Thus taking a lift with a stranger may be regarded as behaviour 'precipitative' of rape, possibly resulting in the court discounting the victim's testimony. So-called 'precipitative' behaviour may also provide the rapist with an excuse which relieves him of responsibility for the act. As the Dublin Rape Crisis Centre report states:

The popularity of the belief that a woman seduces a man into rape by incautious behaviour, is part of the smokescreen that men throw up to obscure their actions.[22]

Women who wear sexually revealing clothes or behave in a sexually flirtatious manner are not seeking rape. They may be looking for sexual attention, or enjoy the excitement and adventure of flirtation, but this is worlds apart from wanting the coercion, terror and violence of rape. This issue is brilliantly dealt with in the film 'The Accused', recently screened in South Africa. This film, based on a real incident, tells the story of a young woman who is gang-raped in a bar in the United States to the cheers of numerous onlookers. While the victim flirts with two of the offenders before the rape, clearly enjoying the sexual attention she receives, the rape is brutal and pitiless, with each moment torture to the victim.

Of Wolfe and Baker's sample of eighty-six convicted rapists, virtually all insisted, despite considerable evidence to the contrary, that their behaviour could not be referred to as rape or that it was justified by the particular circumstances.[23] A similar finding is reported by Sailly and Marolla in their study of convicted rapists.[24] Empirical[25] and clinical[26] evidence indicates that rape myths are more likely to be held by rapists than by males in the general population; and that these fictional sentiments may help to provoke the prepetration of their crime and define their perception of themselves as lovers.[27] Rape myths provide one of the best means for the rapist to rationalise his sexually violent conduct.

Rape-encouraging institutions, behaviours and ideologies

Contrary to popular belief, rape is not something which women can lie back and enjoy when they realise escape is impossible. For the victim, sex during rape is humiliating and dehumanising.[28]

For male rapists, however, their perception of women as sex objects and their belief that women are not worthy of respect may make sex in rape pleasurable. For men in general, consensual sex with women in everyday life may become laden with similar – although not the same – values. Sex may fail to be an expression of love or a means to provide both partners with sexual pleasure, and become an act of conquest, designed to make men feel the way that 'real men' should – powerful and virile.[29]

Contempt for women underlies most acts of rape. This contempt is bred and nurtured by sexist ideology which casts women as inferior to men. It is also linked to the sharp distinction society draws between acceptable male and female behaviour. The emphasis on difference helps intensify men's negative attitudes towards women. Russell has commented on this issue:

> The remarkable thing is not that rape occurs, but that we have managed for so long to see it as a rare and deviant act, when it is, in fact, so embedded in our cultural norms, as a result of the clash between the feminine and masculine mystiques.[30]

Sexist ideas, undue emphasis on the differentness of the sexes and dislike of a fellow human being are usually not sufficient to provoke rape. Dehumanisation of the individual is also necessary. Before understanding what dehumanisation means, one must understand what it means to see another as human. To be seen as human, an individual must be accorded identity and community. Kelman speaks of this process in the following way:

> To accord a person identity is to perceive him as an individual, independent and distinguishable from others, capable of making choices, and entitled to live his own life on the basis of his own goals and others'. To accord a person community is to perceive him – along with one's self – as part of an interconnected network of individuals who care for each other, who recognise each other's individuality and who respect each other's rights.[31]

Based on such a formulation, dehumanisation of people is widespread in terms of the perceptions individuals have of other racial groups, classes and the other sex. With reference to the dehumanisation of women, Litewka argues:

> To hate someone, you must first dehumanise them, make them sub-human . . . When men objectify women, they take the female's humanness away, making her less than human, non-specific, sub-human. This allows men to carry out their role with women, exert their power over them. But if a man has a bit of decency lurking in his brain (and I like to think most do), he hates himself for having been evil enough to destroy the female: that is, evil enough to have taken a whole breathing thinking feeling human being and to have made something less than human of it.[32]

Dehumanisation probably occurs in its most extreme form in war. It is a necessary prerequisite for any army to believe that the enemy is less than human. This makes the enemy easier to kill. The implications for 'enemy women' are extremely serious. Brownmiller documents a report made by an American Marine forward observer during the Vietnam war:

> The main thing was that if an operation was covered by the press there were certain things we weren't supposed to do, but if there was no press there, it was okay. I saw one case where a woman was shot by a sniper, one of our snipers.

When we got up to her she was asking for water. And the lieutenant said to kill her. So he ripped off her clothes, they stabbed her in both breasts, then spread her eagle and shoved an 'E tool' up her vagina, an entrenching tool, and she was still asking for water. And then they took that out and they used a tree limb and then she was shot.[33]

Such extreme brutality points to the violence which men probably regarded as good citizens are able to perpetrate against (enemy) women. Their actions must obviously be understood within the extreme context in which they were executed – within a group, and in an atmosphere of intense hatred, anger, fear and violence. However, that context alone cannot explain such sadism. The dehumanisation of the woman was a further necessary factor in reducing the moral restraint against extreme violence towards her.[34]

In everyday life, the dehumanisation and rape of women does not occur within the same extreme context. This may in part explain why rapists seldom engage in the level of brutality described above. Much of the root of the rapist's dehumanisation of women lies in a culture made up of patriarchal institutions, particular socialisation patterns and sexist activities in adulthood. The effect of these institutions and behaviours can be seen in the adolescent male's early sexual experience, which is usually masturbatory.

Masturbation

Before the heightened sexuality that marks adolescent heterosexual relationships begins, the boy experiences his sexuality in a genital and privatised way through masturbation.[35] By the end of adolescence, most boys have experienced orgasm from masturbation.[36] Yet despite this common experience and the present era of sexual liberation, masturbation, or 'shovelling' or 'skommeling' as it is called in Riverlea, still evokes feelings of guilt among a cross-section of men. Below are the respective comments about masturbation from men from the Rape, the Physically Violent and the Non-Violent groups.

I felt guilty because I knew I was doing something wrong.

I used to always feel guilty that something might happen.

I think it was good at first and then afterwards it was like a bring down, like a drug . . . it's sort of a guilty feeling you have afterwards.

A major source of male guilt lies in the perception that masturbation is an inappropriate, anti-social behaviour. This leads to feelings of demasculinisation.[37] A rapist from the study explains the implication of this association between masturbation and demasculinisation for women's sexual role:

I mean, what's the use of going to masturbate? Why sit in a toilet and jerk yourself off? For what reason, when there is girls to do it?

Another rapist commented:

The guys used to say if your come is like white then you are mature, and my come was like not so white, so I didn't feel so hot.[38]

This points to another reason for the guilt and uncertainty which surround masturbation: lack of adequate sex education. The social expectation that adolescent boys (and men) be confident and knowledgeable about sex inhibits their expression of doubts and uncertainties. Consequently, they sometimes accept incorrect information without question or learn about sex and sexuality by chance.[39] Misinformation can result in the internalisation of myths about male and female sexual responses – such as the notion that women get sexually aroused by physical force. In this way, sexual ignorance can and does play a contributing role in rape. The question that arises from this postulation is, does the reality of the victim's experience not contradict the rapist's expectations? One would expect the rapist to see that his victim is not enjoying the rape. Yet this is not the case, and even when the rapist is doubtful, he is able to employ various rationalisations to make his behaviour seem acceptable. The rapist's attempts to make his sexual aggression benign are discussed in Chapter 7.

The feelings of guilt stemming from masturbation devalue it as a source of sexual pleasure. Masturbation nevertheless does help release sexual tension and reinforce feelings of masculinity in the male masturbator. The latter occurs primarily through fantasies and achieving orgasm. In the male's masturbatory fantasies, he is often the dominator and controller while the woman is the passive sexual object. This is reflected in rapists' descriptions of their masturbatory fantasies:

> You just scheme of all the positions you know . . . like a cherry is hanging on, it's like a stage show and they are doing just what they want to with her.

> I felt like a man . . . I had sex with some beautiful sex symbol.

Masturbatory fantasies in which women are abused are not unusual or deviant; they are partly by-products of popular media images and the desire to exert control and power over women. While indulging in a rape fantasy does not mean the man in reality will or wants to rape (any more than the woman who fantasises about rape wants to be raped), masturbation in a society in which women are not always accorded full human status may mark the beginning for many men of the association between sexual activity and objectification of women. The association becomes further entrenched in the male psyche with his experience of dating relationships.

Dating relationships

A boy's first sexual encounter with a girl usually takes place within a dating relationship. While the dating relationship can and does provide an avenue through which to experience joy and affection and does help to facilitate the intensity of adolescent love, it may also have harmful effects on heterosexual relating because it reinforces sex-role stereotypes and provides many boys with the first personal experience of sexual aggression. This pattern of behaviour may be carried into adult life and be reflected in its most extreme form as rape.[40]

Male initiative is the major theme in dating relationships, whether in adolescence or adulthood. The male asks the girl or woman out, plans their activities and, if more affluent, provides transportation and pays their way. The male assumes his role as initiator as a result of unconscious or conscious compliance to the peer culture norm, sex role training which emphasises assertiveness and the desire to have sex with women. The last sometimes leads men to search for women in order to have sex. Two rapists commented:

> We used to meet with the ouens and go and ride around the night clubs and get the cherries in the shebeens.

> I mean, that's all a man looks for [sex] in a woman. I mean, at our age that's all guys go to discos for – one night stands; in fact last night I had one.

Physical or verbal sexual harrassment is also part of a man's sexual initiative. As told by a member of the Physically Violent group and a rapist respectively:

> After that we walked home, on the way we saw a chick on the other side of the road and Jimmy went for her. We said 'hey leave her, she has never done anything', but he went and grabbed her bag and he kissed her.

> Well I've been involved in a lot [of fights] through my mouth, through my funny remarks . . . I remarked to this white lady 'you've got a lovely pair of tits', so she reckons 'don't get personal, what have you?'. So I reckon 'okay sorry'.

Millet writes that the ascendancy of the concept of male superiority derives from the teachings of the family.[41] She argues that romantic love in no way deadens this notion or enhances the status of women. In fact, the ideology of romantic love conceals women's sexual oppression and their economic dependence on men. According to Millet, love nourishes women's acceptance of inferiority, household drudgery, passivity, dependence and male sexual aggression.

While it is true that romantic love may not enhance the status of women, Millet is mistaken in holding the ideology of love responsible for perpetuating women's inferiority and submissiveness. Rather, what is to blame is the ideology of loyalty and monogamy. Women's socialised notion of loyalty in heterosexual relationships tells them that they should preserve marriage, no matter what the cost to themselves. The ideology of loyalty is strengthened by women's fear of independence and social ostracism. Whatever the content of women's relationships and marriages, it is likely that when in love, they do feel more content, confident and perhaps even superior to other women who are not married or involved in an exclusive heterosexual relationship.

In the dating situation, where two people are acquaintances, the woman may expect the man to take responsibility for their welfare. Ironically, this attitude makes the woman particularly vulnerable to potential sexual aggression. Medea and Thompson cite an example of a female university student who, because she was locked out of her residence and did not have any money, accepted her date's offer of a motel room where he proceeded to rape her.[42] Of her behaviour, Medea and Thompson say:

> No sensible woman, if she ever thought about it, would allow the roof over her head to be dependent on a man with whom she has only had a short acquaintance, a man she has no reason to trust. And no adult should need someone else to arrange where she is going to lay her head. But in the present dating system, women commonly expect men to take care of them, and therefore situations develop in which a woman can't take care of herself.[43]

A study by Kanin and Parsell of college women in the United States seems to confirm the widespread occurrence of sexual aggression in dating behaviour.[44] About fifty-six percent of the two hundred and ninety-one female respondents reported experiences of physically offensive behaviour at some level of sexual intimacy during the academic year. The study suggests that men often perceive women in the dating situation as suitable sexual targets. The study also scotches the myth that sexually offensive behaviour is a rarity among academics or intellectuals. Reported rapes on university campuses in South Africa, while not numerous, nevertheless appear to have become part of the annual university calender.

In the context of dating and sexual intimacy, men often tend to quantify the success of their sexual encounters. They measure them on a physical intimacy scale, with sexual intercourse rated the ultimate achievement. This may mean that if a particular point in erotic intimacy is reached on one occasion, the man expects to reach even greater heights on the next. However, for some men there is no need for a 'next time'. They believe that a woman who agrees to a date or engages in petting has in reality consented to sexual intercourse. It is particularly in these situations, when physical coercion follows sexual intimacy, that the courts find difficulty in defining rape. As has been argued above, when intercourse occurs against the woman's wishes, irrespective of the level of sexual intimacy reached, this is an act of rape.

In the present study, the replies to the question 'What would you do if a girl refused your sexual approach?' illustrate the tactics used in date rape, the most common being physical force and verbal persuasion.[45] Two rapists replied:

I would keep on until she accepted me as a friend or boyfriend. I'd keep on harrassing her to have sex with me. I will try and force her.

Well, a little force, threats and speak nicely a little.

The attitude of men from the Physically Violent group was not very different, but it never resulted in them raping:

I would feel very bad [if a girl said no]. I would run up a temper and would like to smack her to get the frustration out, but something like that never happened to me. I would say it's up to you, I wouldn't force her.

I would feel a little 'nie gelukkig'. The next day I won't leave it, I want her to give in.
Vogelman: What would happen if she didn't?
Eric: I would like to get violent.
Vogelman: Have you ever done that?
Eric: No.

A similar attitude was expressed by men from the Non-Violent group. Higher frustration tolerance levels and fear of legal and police action seem to have prevented their anger from being expressed in rape.

I get a little cross and just leave her . . . I could easily get into trouble if I force her; then she can make a case against me.

If she don't want to give me I can't force her, because I'm going to get into trouble doing that. By hitting other people's children, forcing sex out of them, that goes to court.

I will just leave her, she will just bring you into trouble.

The idea that 'I would rape if there were no legal consequences' has been investigated by Malamuth and his co-researchers. In one of their studies, male subjects were of the opinion that half the male population would rape if there were no legal threats.[46] Importantly, over half the non-rapist male subjects in this study and sixty-nine percent in another stated that they would rape if there were no danger of prosecution.[47] These shocking figures may be the result of the common perception that rape is really perfectly ordinary.[48] Malamuth gives as an example of such an attitude actor James Caan, who, many years ago, after viewing the abominable conditions of an Ohio prison, stated: 'I'm not going to do anything wrong anymore, except maybe for an occasional rape.'[49]

What emerges from this discussion is that the power relationships of the dating situation and the widespread belief in the normality of sexual aggression provide a negative model for male-female sexual interaction. The impersonalisation of sexual relations, which usually begins in dates, is one more factor in the aetiology of rape.

Sex talk

Discussions of sex among men – a popular male pastime – often reflect a callous attitude towards women. One might expect that men would want to speak about their sexual fantasies and experiences since sex is a pleasurable area of life which evokes strong emotions – contentment, satisfaction, anxiety and anger. In fact, if men did not discuss sex, this would be an unhealthy sign suggestive of sexual repression. However, some of the discussions held in the company of men are by no means healthy. Rather than revolving around pleasurable fantasies, mutual gratification, doubts, reassurances or ideas for improving relationships, talk often centres on the level of physical intimacy attained or boasts about sexual prowess. Such boasts are often tinged with aggression, as reflected in a statement I recently overheard at a bar in the centre of Johannesburg: 'I fucked her so good it hurt her.'

In these discussions, the promiscuous woman is verbally defiled and dehumanised. This contrasts with the sympathy and respect sometimes accorded the monogamous woman. The comments below are from members of the Physically Violent and Rape group respectively:

> I never talk about the chick I'm going out with. I never talk about my steady girlfriend, I would feel guilty about it. But if it's a chick I meet and have sex with her, okay, then we will talk about it because she means nothing to me.

> You see if it's a girl I'm not serious about, I will think about telling them . . . because you can see when a girl is like a whore. She comes to you, she asks you to have sex with her. Girls like that I don't respect; then I tell my friends hey this chick came to me and hey I did this and I did that. But when I'm serious about a girl, I won't do that.

There were a few men who refused, for various reasons, to engage in these discussions. One rapist said:

> I was always very specific about my own cherry because she was exception. That's how all of us operate in the company I know – the special girl gets special treatment, the others they are nothing. But as I grew up, I learnt that it wasn't nice to discuss a girl afterwards, after she had pleased you.

A man from the Non-Violent group commented:

> If I am telling you I made so and so with a girl, that guy is not going to keep it for himself, maybe he is going to see that girl and tell her 'oh, you are a whore'. That's why I don't trust anybody, I keep it for myself rather.

One reason some men don't speak about their sexual partners is that they fear the woman will be called a 'whore'. A man from the Non-Violent group asked: 'If you talk about your girlfriend, what is he going to think about your girlfriend?.' Thomas believes that men's dread of female promiscuity and their

> insistence on female chastity cannot be explained by reference to the fact of childbirth and elaboration thereon, the solution is more likely to be found in the desire of men for absolute property in women.[50]

A number of critical conceptualisations flow from this. Firstly, women who are not the property of one man (those not in an exclusive sexual relationship) are perceived as the property of all men. In essence they lose their physical and sexual autonomy. Secondly, women become the victims of sexual double standards – concupiscence in women is seen as a show of unfeminine and pathological behaviour, whilst in men it is an illustration of masculinity. For women in exclusive sexual relationships, 'unfaithful' behaviour can lead to more injurious accusations because such actions are seen as a betrayal of lover or husband and of home and family.[51] As Engels, generations ago, remarked:

> What for women is a crime entailing due legal and social consequences, is regarded in the case of a man as being honourable or, at most, as a slight moral stain that one bears with pleasure.[52]

Women encounter sexual double standards in many spheres of life. In the area of prostitution, the female prostitute suffers more legal and personal retribution than does her male client (see section on prostitution). In the workplace, women often face harsher penalties for sexual indiscretion than do men.[53] In rape cases, rape victims can endure as much social ostracism as rapists. The victim is often distrusted because of her perceived complicity in the act, or is thought foolish for permitting the rape to happen. The rapist, on the other hand, although possibly criticised for such sexual behaviour, may at the same time be regarded as sexually daring or as 'sewing his wild oats'.[54]

A prime illustration of the distinction which the male-oriented systems in Western countries make between 'good' and 'bad' women is an incident which occurred during the famous Peter Sutcliffe trial in England in the early 1980s. Sutcliffe was responsible for murdering numerous women, among whom were prostitutes. The Attorney General, commenting on Sutcliffe's victims, stated: 'Some were prostitutes, but perhaps the saddest aspect of this case is that some were not.'[55] Implicit in this statement is the notion that prostitutes, because of their sexual licentiousness and 'sinful' behaviour, forfeit their right to legal protection and social sympathy. As Eardley writes in his article 'Masculinity Acquitted':

> What we are invited to be really angry about is that, unlike

that other folk-hero the original Jack, Sutcliffe broke the rules
and killed 'respectable' women – our wives, mothers and
daughters.[56]

Women often behave in ways which do not comply with social and
sexual norms. They may walk unaccompanied in the streets at
night, have lesbian relationships or demonstrate independence by
living alone. Any of these activities may be considered provocative because the woman is not abiding by socially defined norms.
Women who break the rules which bind them are seen as renounc-
ing the rules which protect them. Hill describes this state of affairs in the following way:

> She was hitch-hiking (she asked for it). She was wearing a
> low-cut dress (she asked for it). She left her door open (she
> asked for it). She seemed friendly in the pub. She came up
> for coffee. I only wanted to talk to her and she told me to
> fuck off. *She's* a lesbian. She's a prostitute. She's had two
> abortions. She had to be punished. Feminists: bitter, frigid,
> man haters: what you need is a good fuck.[57]

A discussion of sexual promiscuity would be incomplete without
mentioning the pressure on men to be sexually active. This is well
described by a rapist interviewed by Levine and Koenig:

> The guys who do have sex, it's just a big laugh, and they're
> supposed to be normal. And anybody who hasn't had sex,
> who waits around until maybe they care about somebody to
> have it with, they're right out of the picture. They aren't even
> looked at as normal.[58]

The social pressure to be normal and the fear of being seen as unmasculine play a part in encouraging men to engage in impersona-
lised sex. One of the ways men are easily able to attain impersona-
lised sex is by frequenting prostitutes.

Prostitution

Like pornography and rape, prostitution helps contribute to a perception of women as objects to be degraded and abused[59] and, as

in rape, it generally involves a relationship between two people (rapist and victim, client and prostitute) of which the essence is male domination. Thus amongst the numerous reasons for men frequenting prostitutes (marital dissatisfaction, sex, social needs), the need to express power remains strong: the nature of the trans-action is fundamentally that of client purchasing power over a prostitute. In Rosenblum's study, a prostitute says of her clients:

> What they're buying, in a way, is power. You're supposed to please them, follow orders. Even in the case of masochists, who like to follow orders themselves, you're still following his order to give him orders.[60]

In order to make the association between rape and prostitution clearer, let us look briefly at prostitution and its relationship to women's social position. The role of the prostitute has been likened to that of the wife.[61] As early as 1892, some South African wom-en wrote of this similarity. Emily Conybeare, in her article 'Wom-anly Women and Social Purity', wrote of women who marry for status and the security of a good home.[62] She believed these mar-riages lacked affection, and quoted a female colleague who described them as 'a desecration of holy things and as much prosti-tution as the girl who sells herself on the street'. An analagous opin-ion is expressed by Marro in 'La Puberte': 'The only difference between women who sell themselves in prostitution and those who sell themselves in marriage is the price and the length of time the contract runs.'[63]

Some prostitutes make the same point. They see no difference between their role and that of women in general. Said Michelle, about her life as a prostitute in Johannesburg:

> I'm not ashamed of what I do or did. It's my job – so what? Most women are prostitutes in some way or other, it's just that some of us do it right out and are honest about it and others do it in a roundabout manner.[64]

A subject from the Physically Violent group feels the same way:

> Well maybe every women is a prostitute, because even a de-cent girl or your girlfriend, if you don't provide her with nice big lunches or a dop afterwards, all out of your own pocket, then you are still going to slip up. You are not going to come

right. So they might not be walking the streets but in a way what is the difference?

A rapist said:

> I think you don't have to go to one [prostitute] . . . You know there's lots of cherries that wants it, but as the society laid the laws that it's the men's work to talk for it, then I believe it's unnecessary to go and buy it if you can talk it through.

The parallels between prostitutes and 'normal' married women have been drawn to include rights of sexual access. In marriage, for example, sex is believed to be the man's right and the woman's duty. She is expected to be sexually accessible at all times. If she is not, the husband can in South Africa, with the support of the law, refuse to take 'no' for an answer. A husband cannot rape his wife. At most, rape can be viewed as an 'aggravating circumstance' when a husband is convicted of assaulting his wife. This law makes marriage a contract of property, with the husband as owner.

While some female sexual and social stereotypes may entail a degree of prostitution, to postulate that all women, and particularly those married, are prostitutes is absurd. Firstly and most importantly, such a statement ignores the many women who are not subservient, in marriage or outside of it, and who take control of all aspects of their lives, including their sexuality. Secondly, the non-prostitute woman is not necessarily subject to the same degradation that prostitutes experience as a result of their actions.

Prostitutes are distinguished from other women through their particular vulnerability to male violence.[65] Their clients' need to express power often manifests itself in physical force and rape. When this occurs, the contract between client and prostitute becomes null and void. In everyday life, women who are prostitutes are denied autonomy of choice. The notion is that 'if she has sex with other men, she has no right to refuse me'. A member of the Rape group said:

> If I know she is a prostitute, I would never take 'no' for an answer. You just take it for granted that if she is sleeping with other men, why not with you? I scheme people that pay

for sex is stupid. There's something with people who can't
approach a cherry with words or force, maybe they have a
lot of money to waste − R30 to R40 for a few minutes, it's
unnecessary.

Prostitutes are further distinguished from other women in that they
command less social status and respect. The prostitute, De Beauvoir writes, is 'denied the rights of a person, she sums up all the
forms of feminine slavery at once'.[66] Furthermore, although some
prostitutes claim to be satisfied with their jobs, the expressed desire
of many prostitutes to leave prostitution because of its oppressive
nature implies that the parallels between women in general and
prostitutes are exaggerated.

The distinction between prostitutes and rape victims, however,
is not always clear. This is particularly apparent in times of war
when women are often forced to become 'prostitutes' to service
the occupying army.[67] Brownmiller cites an example of an S.S.
policeman who threatened a Jewish girl with rape, saying he would
'get her next time and pay her five Zlotys'. Brownmiller interprets
that he was trying 'to turn an act of rape into an act of whoring
in which the victim shared responsibility'.[68]

The thin line between prostitution and rape is recognised by some
men. Said a subject from the Non-Violent group:

Some people say why don't you do it through a shebeen, and
buy somebody some liquor and then ask her for something
instead of raping her, so you can't say what's the difference
between rape and this prostitution business.

However, for some men who do accept the contractual agreement
in prostitution and the obligations that go with it, frequenting a
prostitute is not the same as raping a woman or winning her over.
Having sex with a prostitute does not fulfil their power needs. Said
two rapists:

I don't think she [a prostitute] would have satisfied me. I
wouldn't have had to fight for it, that night it was worth fighting for.

Those who just lie down and open their legs, it's not real
fun . . . [it's] like shooting buck with a big telescope −
there's no hunting, there's no real fun, no excitement.

The earlier postulation that prostitution and rape encapsulate the male assertion of power through sex does not mean, as the rapist would clearly agree, that raping and visiting a prostitute are equivalents. They are different in three primary respects. Firstly, in rape aggressive and coercive behaviour are fundamental to the act. This is usually not the case with prostitution. Secondly, the rape victim generally exercises no control over the sexual interaction whereas the prostitute usually does. For example, the prostitute will generally only agree to perform certain sexual acts if she feels comfortable doing so and if payment is appropriate. Furthermore, unlike the rape victim, some prostitutes have control over the nature of their sexual conduct – they will make their own decisions about when and how to have sex. Thirdly, power, as the rapists' comments above indicate, is a stronger motive in rape because rape always entails complete control of the woman without her consent. To this extent, clients of prostitutes in Johannesburg whom I interviewed in a previous study defined themselves as completely different from rapists, whom they saw as 'mad'.

An idea prevalent in our society is that rape and prostitution are both phenomena that will always be present. In my study of clients of prostitutes, interviewees commented:

There will always be people [rapists] who are mad.

Rapists have something wrong with them. They were born that way and will always be that way and nothing can be done about it.

It [prostitution] will never be stopped. It's the oldest profession in the world.

It [prostitution] already is legalised. The police don't ever bother them and magistrates realise that men and women will always make love and therefore there is nothing they can do.[69]

The argument that rape and prostitution are timeless, immutable facts of life has strong naturalistic connotations. Naturalism declares what *is* to be natural, and does not see that present realities may be changeable in the future. In so doing, naturalism stifles exploration of human potential. It denies human agency and depoliticises human society. Naturalism has served as a rationalisation for those who have called for the legalisation of prostitution. They further justify their call by arguing that people have a right to pursue whatever profession they wish, and that prostitution will reduce the incidence of venereal disease (through institutionalised medical examinations), crime and rape.

Brownmiller is convinced that legalising prostitution would aggravate women's oppression:

> My horror at the idea of legalised prostitution is not that it doesn't work as a rape deterrent, but that it institutionalises the concept that it is a man's monetary right, if not his divine right, to gain access to the female body, and that sex is a female service that should not be denied the civilised male . . . Indeed, until the day is reached when prostitution is totally eliminated, the false perception of sexual access as an adjunct of male power and privilege will continue.[70]

The greater prevalence of female prostitution compared to male prostitution appears to support the idea that men have a stronger sexual drive than women. Women's sexual needs are not seen as sufficiently strong to demand their satisfaction in the market place, while men's sexual urges are such that men are prepared to pay for sex. In this way prostitution, like pornography and rape, contributes to the image of women as docile objects of sexual desire and men as sex-hungry, domineering subjects. It is in this context that prostitution helps to promote rape. When 'young men learn that females may be bought for a price, and that acts of sex command set prices, then how should they not also conclude that, that which may be bought may also be taken without the civility of monetary exchange'.[71] This view was expressed clearly by the rapist who said he would not pay or accept a 'no' from a prostitute because she had had sex with many other men.

Legalisation of prostitution and pornography could help institutionalise the notion that women's sexual role is to satisfy men's 'uncontrollable' sex drive. The liberal supposition that legalisation of these institutions is an extension of men and women's civil rights, while not without validity, can therefore not be accepted on face value. It is not at all clear that legalisation of prostitution and pornography grants freedom of choice when it contributes to the incidence of violence against women.[72] Thus while prostitute and client and the reader of pornography may have freedom of choice, the rapist's victim certainly does not. It is for these reasons that the fight against prostitution – and pornography – contribute to the fight against rape.

Pornography

Pornography has been defined as the 'explicit description or exhibition of sexual activity in literature [or] films [which are] intended to stimulate erotic rather than aesthetic feelings'.[73] It has also been described as 'erotica in which the theme is sexual degradation of another person'.[74] Since rape too is an act of defilement, and since sexual aggression is a primary component of much (although certainly not all) pornography, the connection between rape and pornography merits serious investigation.

Before beginning this examination, one must ask about pornography the same question we asked about rape: why, if some pornography degrades women, is it tacitly accepted and so widely disseminated in many Western countries? One answer, quite simply, is that people in these countries have become so desensitised to the humiliation suffered by women through male violence that censorship of offensive pornography is not considered important.[75] In South Africa the situation is different. Pornography is prohibited in terms of the Publication and Entertainments Act of 1963 and the Publications Act of 1974.[76] The motivation behind the South African Government's censorship of pornography appears to be conservative – to conserve the family and Christian values. It is on the continuum of conservative attitudes to a broad range of issues: sex education, abortion, homosexuality, lesbianism and day care and rape crisis centres. What is more disturbing about the milieu in South Africa is that although possession of pornographic material carries daunting penalties, the demand is such that it is widely available. This suggests that laws are not always sufficient to transform attitudes and behaviour. Education and different socialisation patterns are also required.

Research has indicated that between eighty[77] and ninety-two percent[78] of men in Western countries have voluntarily obtained pornographic material. In the present study, fifty percent admitted to reading or seeing pornography during their school years.[79] Besides providing sexual arousal, pornography assisted in the construction of fantasies during masturbation.

Men's enjoyment of pornography gives a clue to the kinds of images of women and sex in which they take pleasure. The underlying message of much pornography is that women's bodies are available for men's use and enjoyment.[80] This is true whether the pornography is subtle or explicit. In 'soft' pornography, which is often found in advertisements, the static images of women, clothed, semi-clothed or naked, hint at the innumerable possibilities they promise for male pleasure. 'Hard core' pornography details these possibilities and helps to define and reinforce men's sexual self-image of their own power and control.[81] Coward discusses the effect of such images in encouraging rape:

> In porn, women are represented as voracious, eager and available for whatever men want . . . porn puts into circulation images of sexuality that have definite meanings connected with them; sexual pleasure for men is initiation and dominance, and for women submission to men's depersonalised needs . . . It reinforces ideologies of masculinity and femininity. Men are seen as initiators, the source of active desire. Women are seen as . . . responsive to men (to their actions or looking), not as responsible in their own right. This is one reason for the commonness of rape and the leniency of punishment; there is a thin dividing line between initiation (normal sex) and force (criminal sex).[82]

Pornography, however, is not limited to depictions of male initiation and domination. It can include sexual scenes involving lesbians, children, old women and depictions of torture and brutal violence.

Lesbians have often been the target of men's sexual aggression, partly because they devalue men's sexual potency. Lesbians' sexual preference means they don't need men, and this may make men feel inadequate.[83] Pornography helps 'reassure men and allay fears of impotence'[84] through scenes such as a man interrupting a lesbian love act 'wielding what he would like to think they really need – his "angry" prick'.[85]

In her article 'On the Other Side of the Billboard . . .', Faraday describes some of the forbidden frontiers which have been touched by pornography:

> Porn magazines . . . constantly encourage readers to over-

come their repugnance at new methods of 'getting it off'. Once desensitised, they are then ready to encounter the 'harder' stuff both in thought and practice. A recent copy of Forum contained an article on 'Passionate Grandmothers', and the avid enthusiast can find specialist magazines with pictures of older women in shiny boots and black knickers. There is still a big market for photographs of women in gym slips but how long before the thrill gives way to the 'need' for already available photographs of eight or nine year old children poised in the act of fucking, whilst grinning at the cameraman for approval? Screw, a widely available magazine in the United States of America, carried a photograph of a mastectomy patient in one of its S/M features, suggesting breast mutilation as a form of 'sexual excitement'. And, of course, at the most extreme, there are the 'snuff' movies emerging from South America, in which women are sexually assaulted, mutilated and finally butchered.[86]

These examples demonstrate another major preoccupation of some pornography: the expression of male power, psychologically and physically, through the humiliation, intimidation and violation of women. Pornography depicting this reflects and promotes the notion that female submission and male dominance, both in rape and everyday sexual behaviour, are not only natural, but erotic and desirable.[87] Feminists such as Brownmiller and Lips contend that the defilement of women, which marks the division between erotica and pornography, strengthens the male fantasy that 'every women wants to be raped, or at least possessed and dominated sexually, and that no real woman cares if she gets kicked around a bit in the process'.[88]

The idea that pornography contributes to rape has not been accepted by all writers. Some maintain pornography has little or no relationship to sexual violence. Their argument is based on the theory that arousal does not necessarily result in imitative behaviour.[89] This is in turn based on the fact that while some rapists claim that pornographic material provoked them to rape, there are a great deal more men who are able to control any aggressive impulse prompted by pornographic material.

The argument that men who watch or read pornography which incorporates rape do not necessarily model themselves on the male protagonists, is probably valid. Just as a woman's rape fantasy will not lead her to try get raped, a man's rape fantasy based on porno-graphic images does not mean he will rape. There is no one to one, causal relationship between pornography and rape. Trying to prove such a relationship would raise some hair-raising methodological problems because of the difficulty in controlling for the many ex-traneous variables that lead to sexual violence. However, in general, feminists have never posited a direct causal link between pornog-raphy and rape; rather, they have seen pornography as a contribut-ing factor. Research into whether rape is modeled would have to contend with the possibility that imitation of pornographic por-trayals of violence need not be immediate. There is a likelihood that emulation would take place in times of heightened emotional-ity and uncertainty, both of which often occur in situations of sex-ual interplay.

Another argument cited against the role of pornography in rape is that many rapists and sex offenders are indifferent to pornogra-phy. According to Gerbhard:

> About all that can be said is that strong response to pornog-raphy is associated with imaginativeness, ability to project, and sensitivity, all of which generally increase as education increases, and with youthfulness, and that these qualities ac-count for the differences we have found between sex offenders in general, and non-sex offenders. Since the majority of sex offenders are not well educated nor particularly youthful, their responsiveness to pornography is correspondingly less. Comparison of the response to pornography and the response to the sight or thought of females reveals that the latter is a more effective stimulus.[90]

Gerbhard is mistaken in presuming that sex offenders are not too well educated or youthful. In this study, the mean age of rapists was 24,5. Most research shows that only eight percent of rapists are forty years or older, while fifty to sixty percent are between fifteen and twenty-five years old[91] and are distributed right across class lines and educational standards.[92] An example of the latter is a rape case in which five Soweto teachers were accused of plying a young girl with drinks and then gang raping her.[93] A further flaw in Gerbhard's argument is that he does not consider that men's thoughts about women may also result from their exposure to pornography.

There is, however, a growing body of research which points to pornography's influence on rape, aggression and violence against women.[94] The findings of Donnerstein's study indicate an association between the subjects' observation of 'aggressive erotica' and increased aggression, measured, in this case, by the subjects' preparedness to utilise a shock machine to shock others.[95]

A study designed to measure the effect of pornography on sexual arousal was conducted by Malamuth and Check.[96] In this study, male undergraduate students were requested to listen to one of three stories: a 'rape abhorrence' story where the victim dislikes the experience throughout; a 'rape arousal' story where the victim becomes involuntarily sexually excited; and a story of 'mutually desired' sexual intercourse. All subjects were then told a story of a male student raping a petrified female student in an alley. The results of the study were that subjects exposed to the rape arousal and mutually desired sex stories became more sexually aroused (as measured by tumescence of the penis) by the depiction of a rape in an alley than were subjects exposed to the rape abhorrence story. The conclusions drawn are that portrayals of the victim enjoying her rape experience stimulate sexual arousal, while images of a victim's negative experience tend to lower arousal during the reading of a rape story. Thus positive images of rape make rape seem attractive to men.

In the realm of self-generated fantasy, Malamuth found that subjects who had watched rape slides and then listened to a verbal account of rape invented more sexually violent fantasies than did subjects exposed to slides of mutually desired sex and a verbal depiction of rape.[97]

While bearing in mind the difficulty of positing a one to one, causal relationship between pornography and rape, Court's examination of the link between pornography and rape in South Africa is suggestive.[98] He gives figures to show that in England, America, Australia, New Zealand, Denmark and Sweden, where more liberal approaches to pornography were adopted, there was a greater increase in rape from 1960 to 1977 than in South Africa where legal prohibitions reduce the availability of pornography. This led Court to conclude that:

(a) The incidence of rape has increased where liberalisation of pornography legislation has taken place;

(b) These increases have occurred concurrently with legislative changes;

(c) Limited availability of pornography results in less rape.

Before Court's argument can be accepted, further investigation into other possible reasons for the increasing incidence of rape in the countries (outside of South Africa) he examines is necessary. It is possible, for example that more progressive attitudes towards rape victims between 1960 and 1977 encouraged more reporting of rape. Also, while the increasing incidence of rape in those countries where liberalisation of pornography occurred does point to a relationship between pornography and rape, that does not explain why the incidence of rape in South Africa per capita is higher than in some countries where pornography is freely available.

Whatever the arguments about the extent of pornography's influence on violence and rape, it is certainly true that pornography is not as harmless as some suggest. The greater proportion of pornography perpetuates images of women as 'anonymous, panting playthings, adult toys, dehumanised objects to be used, abused, broken and discarded'.[99] Pornography can have a powerful impact on adolescent boys and adult men. It promotes sexual stereotypes and depicts male domination and rape as sexually desirable. Its continuing existence must therefore be regarded with the utmost pessimism.

Language

Language has played a significant role in promoting the sexist attitudes described in this chapter. While language is commonly understood as a neutral facilitator of communication, in reality it mirrors the prevailing culture while also teaching and entrenching the attitudes which helped to create it.[100] Language in a sexist society therefore contains many words which are sexist. The prevalence of words such as 'chairman', 'spokesman' or 'sportsman' assume that a person is male unless proved otherwise. This contributes to upholding a male-centered culture. While proposals that words like 'chairman' be changed to 'chair' or 'chairperson' are often met with cynicism and accusations of pettiness, changes to language are important because they acknowledge women's participation in society in the very language with which we express our social being.

An excellent illustration of how language can reflect the reification of women is contained in a rapist's description of his participation in a gang rape with thirteen other men in which a woman was severely assaulted and raped for two hours:

> You can't get your satisfaction out of this woman lying there like a piece of pole in front of you. A woman you rape will never give her best.

He and his mates had not assaulted, raped, defiled and humiliated a human being: they had used a 'piece of pole'.

Contemporary sexual vocabulary has no term for normal, healthy sexuality in women.[101] For men, however, the terms 'virile' and 'potent' describe healthy male sexuality. Thus language gives to men and withholds from women healthy sexual power. In language, as in life, men dominate the sexual arena. Without a name, healthy female sexuality is at best hazily and insubstantially conceived, at worst denied.[102]

Associated with the need many men have to be sexually dominant is their fear of being impotent or sexually inadequate. Hoch explains how language has reflected both male sexual prowess and male anxiety about impotence:

> There are numerous celebrations for the man of super bedroom potency. He is called stud, stallion, bull, beef, cock, sword, blade, stickman, a walking phallus . . . On the other hand, there is not even a word available in our language to describe an impotent man – the whole subject is so feared that a noun which might acknowledge the malfactor is literally repressed.[103]

The statements below made by a rapist and a physically violent man respectively reflect this fear:

> I've been always worrying about my penis, man. How the girls will feel if I've got a small penis. You see it will worry me to think, what will this chickie think to say this oke is still a kid.

> When I hear [other men's] stories, I think maybe I didn't come right with a chick. I tend to lie and say, 'What you mean I didn't come right?'. But then if they want to know about my experience, then I just say 'I don't want to talk about it because there is nothing to talk about' – just lying not to feel bad in front of them. You know how it's like if you don't come right, they think you are a moffie.

To avoid being thought effeminate or 'not man enough', some men display their masculinity at every available opportunity – be it through sex, violence or rape.

Language is also a mechanism for the social control of women. Women who show a sexual appetite or have healthy sex lives are often labelled 'whore' or 'slut'. These terms rob the sexually active woman of social status and human dignity. Women may feel compelled to avoid behaviours which may invite these labels. The sexual double standard operates linguistically here too. There are no derogatory words to describe the male equivalent of the sexually promiscuous woman.[104]

Colloquialisms for sexual intercourse further entrench male domination and female passivity. Says Greer:

> All the vulgar linguistic emphasis is placed upon the poking element, fucking, screwing, rooting, shagging are all acts performed upon the passive female.[105]

Comments from subjects in the present study verify Greer's analysis:

> I pomped her about three times.

> You just put your cock up a cunt.

Brownmiller comments on the terminology used for sexual intercourse:

> The sex act . . . has its 'modus operandi' in something men call penetration. Penetration, however, describes what the man does. The feminist Barbara Mehrhof has suggested that if women were in charge of sex and the language, the same act could well be called enclosure.[106]

A consequence of the male-centredness of language is that there are few words which adequately describe women's sexual experience and, in particular, rape.[107] Schulz argues that considering the extreme nature of the violence and degradation involved in the act of rape, the term 'rape' is innocuous:

> The organs and processes of sex and elimination provide us

with a set of terms in English, which we designate 'dirty words' . . . it is ironic that the most vicious sexual act of all is not among them. We have no four letter word for the act of taking women sexually by force.[108]

There is only one word designated to describe the diverse experiences of the rapist and his victim. The neutrality of the word 'rape' is therefore said to be an inaccurate description of the pain, fear and trauma experienced by the victim and the culpability of the offender. Spender remarks:

Because there is no name which represents the trauma of being taken by force, the horror of the rape victim can be compounded. When an act cannot be accurately named, it cannot be readily verified, to oneself, or to others. A woman who has been attacked in this way has no other name except rape to describe the event, but with the inbuilt neutrality of meaning, rape is precisely what she does not mean . . . Women need a word which renames male violence and misogyny and which asserts their blameless nature, a word which places the responsibility for rape where it belongs – in the dominant group.[109]

Language and other socialising systems and institutions are formative in defining women and men. They are responsible, as stated above, for the social construction of masculinity. An important part of masculinity is sexual conquest, in turn an essential feature of rape.

The conquest

Sexual conquest is a central characteristic of heterosexual relations and rape. The primary features of sexual conquest are the desire for sexual gratification, and a sense of triumph following gratification, both of these feelings unaccompanied by consideration of the woman's needs and feelings. Litewka gives an account of what conquest means to men:

Conquest logically follows objectification and fixation. I mean, after all, what the hell's the sense of objectifying and fixating if you're not going to get off your ass and do a little conquering? And when we do conquer, what is the trophy? In the old days it might have been a lock of hair or a garter strap. A ring can also announce your achievement. But always, your own knowledge of what transpired is your reward – being pleased with yourself and being able to say to yourself 'I am a man'. And if others have knowledge of your conquest, your knowing that they know is as great an award as any.[110]

The desire of many men to win and to dominate is not confined to sex, but manifests in all spheres of life, including sport, business, academia and interpersonal relationships. Because sex is so intimately related to desire, fear and love, it can be a very naked, primal, revealing expression of self. And it is within this primal area that men's need to conquer is often intensely acted out. The importance of the sexual conquest is reflected in the widespread belief that sexual intercourse with a woman marks the graduation from adolescence to manhood. Attaining the treasured trophy of a woman's body gives the adolescent a new-found sense of confidence and superiority. A rapist and a man from the Physically Violent group stated respectively:

It [having sex] was in fact the greatest thing that happened, because all the guys that was at the party with me, that came with me in fact, they knew it's the first time that I'm now like going out with a cherry. They know me, you check, and they all anxious to hear what happened. Then I told them, like how it was like this, and how it was like that . . . I felt like I had just proved my manhood.

The first time I had it was with a married woman. She showed me how to go about it. That was my first teenage love affair. I felt like any guy, I felt proud. And I felt I was a step ahead of those other buddies of mine.

A man's early sexual experiences may nourish particular notions of sexual behaviour. The first experience does not necessarily provide a model for all future sexual behaviour, but if it is repeated the male may begin to feel more comfortable with it and will, unless challenged, repeat it many times.[111] Casual sex is common to the initiation of many individuals into the world of sexual intercourse. One rapist, for example, described his initial sexual experience as follows:

> I just had it, no one taught me. It just happened. I met her at the disco and we went off and had sex . . . We just went to any place. I liked it . . . It was just a one night stand.

The first sexual experience of another rapist was of gang rape. At the time he was twelve years old and in the company of a few older friends. On the way home from a social event, they picked up a young woman hitchhiking, plied her with alcohol and raped her for a 'whole night'. He discovered where to insert his penis because:

> It was the big ous first . . . Seeing them telling her, 'okay, lay still, open up'. We were all standing around her. Okay one ou is finished and the next one comes, then I come, you know what I mean . . . That is how I started with sex.

This first sexual experience, devoid of tenderness and based on coercion and debasement of the woman, was repeated in adulthood by his again raping. It is difficult to ascertain what influence this initial experience had on his later raping behaviour. However, since he was never charged for his initial offence and participated with a group of men who were all supportive of raping the victim, it is likely that his impression that rape is socially acceptable was either created or augmented. The experience of the rapist described above contradicts the findings of Groth and Birnbaum who state, 'in no case have we ever found that rape was the first sex experience [of rapists]'.[112] While the case mentioned in this research may be unusual, it does suggest that more attention should be paid to the adolescent sexual experiences of rapists.

Sexual conquest is also a feature of men's intrapsychic life. Men tend to introject, at a young age, all the feelings that come with sexual conquest. These feelings are 'taken into the self and become part of his [their] inner life'.[113] Thus the male self is filled with the spirit of virility and dominance, and the lurking threat of 'femininity' is further repressed or destroyed. It is the wish to satisfy the virility mystique and to stamp out any unmasculine behaviour that strengthens a man's desire to rape. Russell's description of a victim's experience of an attempted rape explains this point:

Her would-be rapist felt very embarrassed when he could not get an erection. 'Play with me,' he commanded, to which she contemptuously replied, 'Who's raping who here? That's ridiculous, man!' According to the informant he then felt very foolish and ashamed. 'I had the upper hand from then on . . . I gave him a hell of a time. He drove me to town. He was very frightened that I would phone the police, and I told him I sure would, and that if he ever did it again, I'd find out.' Since he had the physical strength to pin her down and remove her pants, he could also have made her 'play' with him. But it seems that she was able instead to play on his feelings of being unmanly for not being able to rape her without assistance. It is a sad consequence of subscribing to the virility mystique that a man feels bad about not being brutal enough to rape a woman.[114]

The pressure to conform and comply with the virility mystique is more intense in militarised societies or war situations, such as exist in South Africa. The reason for this is that the very real dangers of combat augment not only a general level of anxiety, but also insecurity about control and power – and so about masculinity. As outlined above, the insecurity of some men is such that they may conform to a group will to rape 'enemy' women. Komisar gives an example:

In 1966, an American patrol held a nineteen year-old Vietnamese girl captive for several days, taking turns raping her and finally murdering her. The sergeant planned the crime in advance, telling the soldiers during the mission's briefing that the girl would improve their 'morale'. When one soldier refused to take part in the rape, the sergeant called him 'queer' and 'chicken', another testified later that he joined in the assault to avoid such insults.[115]

In everyday heterosexual behaviour, sexual and masculine insecurity may be intensified by the fear of sexual rejection. The failure to conquer a woman sexually means that a man's individual prowess is questioned both by himself and by others. Some men defend against the possibility of failure to conquer by not initiating sexual relations. Others do it through lying or boasting about their sexual exploits, or, as in the case of some rapists, by being overly aggressive. One rapist described his sexual initiative in the following way:

> I had to scrape up all the courage I had and I told her exactly what I wanted. I told her listen I'm going to take you and I'm going to have you.

Results of this study show that among rapists, the most frequently used means of coping with sexual rejection or the inability to conquer is either by simply not accepting a woman's refusal, or by interpreting the woman's unwillingness as 'playing hard to get'. According to Chappell, Geis, Schafer and Siegel, the rapist's anxieties about sexual rejection and his subsequent rape behaviour are related to the sexual permissiveness of the particular society:

> A rejected male in a non-permissive setting is more able to sustain his self-image by alleging that it is the setting itself that is responsible for any sexual setback he suffers . . . In the permissive setting, the rejected male becomes more hard-pressed to interpret his rejection . . . forcible rape represents a response arising out of the chaos of a beleaguered self image.[116]

The findings of Geis and Geis's study[117] contradict Chappell et. al.'s hypothesis.[118] Geis and Geis found no significant relationship between sexual permissiveness in society and rape. While a sexually permissive society cannot, by itself, account for rape, Chappell et. al.'s conclusions are worth further investigation in the light of the sexual objectification of women, the conquest mystique and other rape-encouraging variables so dominant in, for example, South African society.

One of the negative consequences for men of the need to conquer is that they spend so much time strategising, that they often forget about the pleasure of physical intimacy. Wives and girl-friends, who have already been conquered and are willing and available to have sex, may be considered less desirable than other women who have not been won over. Of course, another reason wives and girlfriends may be considered less sexually attractive is because of sexual boredom. Sexual boredom is not exclusive to men, and probably occurs at some point in most marriages or long-term heterosexual relationships. Sexual boredom and the male desire to conquer may result in affairs or 'one night stands'. While an occasional 'one night stand' may be physically enjoyable for both the man and the woman, some men find them sexually and emotionally unfulfilling, although they admit to having them continually. There may be a variety of reasons for single men being sexually promiscuous without finding it pleasurable. One may be that by involving themselves in superficial relationships, they avoid intimacy. Another reason is that 'sleeping around' provides a feeling of accomplishment. The preoccupation with virility may override feelings of emotional alienation. This emphasis on virility is illustrated in its most extreme form by a rapist's account of a gang rape:

> She was wet already, and it just wasn't right to me. I just
> felt I'm another one. I'm just the last one. Most of the times
> when I have sex with a cherry, then I want to lay next to
> her and talk about it . . . in that specific situation there was
> no time for that, so I just got up and washed myself and that
> was the end of it . . . The thing was just to prove myself,
> because that was the very first time I actually did it with
> friends around.

In order for men to cope with some of the alienation that comes with sexual conquest, they may need to separate their sexual behaviour from their emotions. Hoch explains:

> The split that Christian and Platonic philosophy makes between man's 'higher' spiritual and 'lower' carnal functions, between mind and body, is thus reproduced in a further split between the higher and lower parts of the body, between the psyche and the penis. The psyche just thinks, the penis acts.[119]

This split is also seen in the words men use to describe their genitals. Their penis becomes 'it' or 'John' – something distinct from their personality and the rest of their body. The fact that 'John' has sexual intercourse, rather than the man himself, helps the individual detach from the act.

The crude quantification of physical intimacy and the generalised objectification of women account in part for some men's lack of concern about the quality of their relationships with women. Gross insensitivity towards women's sexual desires is not uncommon. On the issue of sexual insensitivity, Seaman writes:

The women in my survey have struggled, often valiantly, to establish their own sexual identities, to discover what it is they really like and want.

And then they learned that most of the men don't want to hear. For as various as these women were in their tastes and proclivities, their complaints about men were depressingly repetitive. Men make love as if they are following a program . . . They are humourless . . . They are too fast . . . They are cruel to women who require finger stimulation, making them feel that this is a loathsome aberration . . . They are interested in 'target' organs only, and they fail to appreciate the total body sensuality of women . . . And above all, they ignore the woman's statements about what she likes.[120]

Some men go further: they ignore any pain the woman may experience. A member of the Non-Violent group said of his experience with a virgin:

> I was feeling lekker. You know it was exciting. The first time she cried, it was hurting and all that, and all I was thinking is that it's good and real nice.

An additional feature of many men's approach to sex, especially with sexually promiscuous women, is their lack of concern about the possible consequences of their actions. Very few of the rapists or the men from the non-raping groups contemplate the possibility of the woman falling pregnant. Nor is their concern aroused if pregnancy does result. Considering some rapists' general attitudes towards pregnant women with whom they have been involved, this is not surprising. A pregnant woman is a burden not worth having around. Said one rapist:

> I have had plenty of chicks. I mean I have experienced many, I have got five kids already from screwing around. Okay, like with these chicks my intention was to get married to them, but once a chick is maybe pregnant from you, they change so much. I mean they are nice to you before, but once they get pregnant, she thinks she has got some sort of bond between you, that is going to keep you. And she changes, you know she is not the kind of person you thought she was and that is what puts me off.

Thus while pregnant married women are generally nurtured,[121] the responses of many men to pregnancy in single women are callous. De Beauvoir has commented on these attitudes:

> They [men] have easily resigned themselves to woman's tribulations . . . The painful burden of pregnancy – that heavy payment exacted from woman in exchange for a brief and uncertain pleasure – has even been the subject of much facetiousness. 'Five minutes pleasure: nine months pain', and 'it goes in easier than it comes out' – an amusing contrast. But there is sadism in this philosophy. Many men enjoy feminine misery and repudiate the idea that it is desirable to ameliorate it.[122]

The reader may question the emphasis on sexuality and conquest in a work on male violence. The reason for such an emphasis is that life in the bedroom is closely entwined with the assertion of power, the most vital constituent of rape. It is also necessary to excise the myth that sexual inequality disappears during lovemaking. Sex cannot be divorced from everyday behaviour. The outside world and social attitudes do not suddenly all disappear when the man takes off his clothes. Sexist attitudes and behaviours are likely to be taken into the lovemaking situation, making this 'moment of apparent equality' into a moment which 'harshly exposes the inequality between men and women, and economic and social power become crucial elements in our lovemaking'.[123] Thus the status of women as possessions of men frequently manifests itself in heterosexual relationships. As one rapist explained:

> The type of cherry that I like is like the one I have now. Not because of her looks, but because of her manners, her way of thinking and doing things . . . And if I want to have sex, she's my woman, I'm entitled, I mean not legally – we are not married.

Conquest always involves assertion and domination. This is as true for the arena of sexual interaction as for any other. To account for the widespread desire for and execution of sexual conquest, however, it may be necessary to look not only at male domination, but female acquiescence, which itself similarly reflects sexist socialisation. In her article 'Female Sexual Alienation', Phelps quotes a woman as saying:

In each of our lives, there was a first man for whom we were prepared like lambs for the slaughter. My fantasy of him was a composite of Prince Valiant, Gary Cooper and my father. Trained in submission, in silence, I awaited him through a series of adolescent boyfriends who were not masterful enough to fit the dream . . . because I would not really graduate to the estate of womanhood until I had been taken by a strong man.[124]

The incorporation of female passivity and male domination into sexual responses perpetuates prevailing heterosocial and heterosexual behaviour. But abiding by behavioural norms is far more difficult for women because they are subject to contradictory social expectations. Although women are defined primarily as sex objects, only tacit recognition is given to their sexual needs. The consequence, says Millet, is that: 'There isn't a woman alive who is not obsessed with her sexual desirability. Not her sexual desire, her sexual desirability.'[125] The actions of many men intensify the notion both men and women have of sex – as something that is done to women. Says a rapist of his sexual behaviour:

This one cherry, I've been using her for a long time just sexually. And a lot of guys have been using her for that because she was built lekker.

Women are unlikely to obtain sexual satisfaction from interaction of this sort. Nonetheless, numerous women continue to engage in unsatisfying sexual intercourse because they believe it is important to men and see it as a means of becoming close to them.[126] This may help to account in part for research data which indicates that only twenty to thirty[127] percent of women regularly experience orgasm during sexual intercourse, and that thirty-four percent of women fake orgasm repeatedly.[128]

Paradoxically, men's desire for control also impedes their own sexual and emotional gratification and exploration:

The most unfortunate misconception our culture has assigned to sexual functioning is the assumption, by both men and women, that men, by divine guidance and infallible instinct, are able to discern exactly what a woman wants sexually and when she wants it. Probably this fallacy has interfered with natural sexual interaction as much as any other single factor.[129]

Sawyer puts this more strongly:

It is not really possible for two persons to have a free relationship when one holds the balance of power over the other . . . Persons bent on dominance are inhibited from developing themselves.[130]

Sexual control also finds expression in violent behaviour. There is a tendency in our society to conflate aggression, violence and sexuality.[131] This is depicted in the popular media. Now a cliche in movies is the scene where after an argument between a man and a woman who apparently do not like each other, the man forces himself on the woman through an aggressive kiss, the woman initially resists and then herself becomes overwhelmingly passionate. The picture of 'normal' heterosexual relations as consisting of an aggressive male forcing himself on a woman who seems to fear sex with him, but who unconsciously wants to be overpowered, makes the line between rape and 'normal' heterosexuality thin indeed.[132]

For some feminists, rape and everyday sexual behaviour are one and the same thing. According to Medea and Thompson:

Rape is not a special isolated act. It is not an aberration, a deviation from the norms of sexual and social behaviour . . . Rape is simply at the end of the continuum of male-aggressive, female-passive patterns, and an arbitrary line has been drawn to mark it off from the rest of such relationships. That the line is superficially imposed accounts for the tremendous confusion that arises when we try to talk about rape. It accounts for the difficulty that the laws and courts have in prosecuting a rapist. It accounts for the fact that the average person will condemn rape as a crime equivalent to murder but will have little sympathy for the actual victim of a rape . . . We muddle around trying to draw artificial lines in the actual behaviour of real persons and we find it cannot be done. If it happens in an alley, it's rape; if it happens in bed, it's love; if the man is a stranger, it's rape; if he's your date, it's love. If he hits you full in the face, it's rape; if he merely overpowers you, it's love.[133]

A paper by the London Action Rape Group put it in another way:

> He asks her to sleep with him . . . she refuses. He tries to persuade her. He tells her he loves her . . . He calls her a prude, immature, frigid. He says he 'needs' sex, so if she doesn't come across, he'll have to find a girl who will. Each time they meet he carries on a bit further, a bit further ('Why not go all the way'). Each time she finally tells him to stop and breaks away, he gets angry, he rages, he sulks; he tells her how bad it is for me to be left 'excited'. He works towards his goal, which is her vagina. He means to have, to possess this woman.
>
> This is not rape, this is normal everyday stuff. The magazines call it young love.[134]

The convergence of heterosexual behaviour and rape means women who have been violated don't always see themselves as victims. Instead of demanding a change in the aggressive behaviour of men, these women respond by blaming themselves for not taking proper precautions.[135] Other women may also believe the rape victim is responsible for her rape. Victim-blaming often helps other women feel more secure and safe about themselves. By blaming rape victims for not taking sufficient precautions, women make themselves feel safe from the danger of rape. They believe that because they take what they perceive to be appropriate precautions, they will escape being raped.

The offender frequently does not consider himself a rapist (see Chapters 5 and 6). He considers himself a lover and his victim a sexual partner, because, in his own terms, he behaved like a lover should – aggressive, domineering and forceful. One rapist said of rape victims:

> You get some who fall in love with their rapists . . . To be raped is nothing, it's just like having sex with your husband.

While there may be similarities between heterosexual behaviour and rape, they are not the same. Heterosexual sex, unlike rape, can involve feelings of tenderness and affection. Furthermore, male domination in sexual behaviour is not directly comparable to the aggressive and violent acts characteristic of rape.

But the very uncertainty about similarities and dissimilarities is an effect of the sexist behaviours and perceptions outlined in this chapter, and the uncertainty can be relieved not by definitive answers, of which there are none, but by a transformation of male-female relationships in society. Russell suggests that in a society which considers it masculine to be loving and concerned, to be attentive to the wishes of others, to detest domination, oppression, exploitation and violence, to see women as human beings, to value personality and character more than physical attributes, to cherish long-term relationships rather than 'one night stands' – in such a society men would not rape.[136]

South African society is, however, not like this. For the majority of men and women, the experience of apartheid South African society is of degradation and humiliation. They live with work alienation, racial discrimination, political oppression and poor living conditions. This, as will be argued in the next chapter, creates in men a sense of powerlessness and low self worth. They can, because of women's objectification and inferior position in society, use women to boost their self image. Sometimes this may mean raping them.

Notes

1   1972, page 44.
2   Page 44.
3   Amir, 1971; Bell, 1981; MASA, no date.
4   Amir, 1971.
5   1971.
6   Clark and Lewis, 1977; MASA, no date.
7   1962.
8   Chappell, Geis, Schafer and Siegel, 1977.
9   1974.
10 Deming and Eppy, 1981; MASA, no date; Medea and Thompson, 1972.
11 1979.
12 Sailly and Marolla, 1984.
13 Finkelhor and Yllo, 1982; Levine and Koenig, 1983.
14 Dublin Rape Crisis Centre, 1981; Frank, Turner and Duffy, 1979.
15 Dublin Rape Crisis Centre, 1981.
16 1979.
17 Kilpatrick, Resiek and Veronen, 1981, page 109.
18 1979, page 47.
19 1975, page 258.
20 1971.
21 McNickle Rosel, 1977, page 78.
22 Dublin Rape Crisis Centre Report, 1981, page 207.
23 1980.

24 1984.
25 Field, 1978.
26 Clark and Lewis, 1977; Gage and Schurr, 1976.
27 Burt, 1978, 1980.
28 Brownmiller, 1975; Wilson, 1983.
29 Hoch, 1979.
30 1975, page 274.
31 1973, pages 48-49.
32 1977, page 240.
33 Cited in Peske, 1982, page 113.
34 Kelman, 1973.
35 Pikunas, 1976; Sorenson, 1973.
36 Simon and Gagnon, 1977.
37 Simon and Gagnon, 1977; Sorenson, 1973.
38 'Come' is a colloquialism for both orgasm and semen.
39 Cohn, 1974.
40 Weis and Borges, 1977.
41 Millett, 1970.
42 Medea and Thompson, 1972.
43 1972, page 41.
44 1977.
45 Other tactics include drugging and intoxication.
46 Malamuth, Haber and Feschback, 1972.
47 Malamuth and Check, 1979.
48 Malamuth, 1981.
49 *Newsweek*, 1975, page 48.
50 1959, page 216.
51 McIntosh, 1978; Smart and Smart, 1978; Vogelman, 1982.
52 1972, pages 82-83.
53 Williams, 1977.
54 Lips, 1981.
55 Eardley, 1982, page 5.
56 1982, page 5.
57 1982, page 41.
58 Levine and Koenig, 1983, page 40.
59 Brownmiller, 1976; McIntosh, 1978; Millett 1970.
60 1975, page 178.
61 De Beauvoir, 1972.
62 1892, page 6.
63 Cited in De Beauvoir, 1972, page 569.
64. *Sunday Express*, 1981, page 10.
65 Eardley, 1982.
66 De Beauvoir, 1972, page 569.
67 Brownmiller, 1974; Dublin Rape Crisis Centre, 1981; Sanday, 1981.
68 1974, page 76.
69 Vogelman, 1982, page 79; page 73.
70 1975, page 392.
71 Brownmiller, 1975, page 391.
72 Brownmiller, 1975; Kristol, 1977.
73 *Oxford Concise Dictionary*, 1976, page 860.
74 Lips, 1981, page 120.
75 Dworkin, 1981; Kristol, 1977.
76 Court, 1974.
77 Wallace and Wehmer, 1977.

78 Althanasiou, Shaver and Tavis, 1970.
79 Cody Wilson (1977) provides empirical data on age of first experience, and of the characteristics of patrons of pornographic bookstores and movies.
80 Faust, 1980.
81 Coward, 1982; Faust, 1980.
82 1982, pages 52-53.
83 Litewka, 1977.
84 Wilson, 1983, page 166.
85 Faraday, 1982, page 31.
86 1982, pages 31-32.
87 Faraday, 1982; Lips, 1982; Wilson, 1983.
88 Lips, 1982, page 120.
89 Faust, 1980; *The Report of the Commission on Obscenity and Pornography*, 1970.
90 1965, page 673.
91 MacDonald, 1971; *Uniform Crime Reports*, 1981.
92 MASA, no date.
93 Sowetan, 1983.
94 Brownmiller, 1975; Donnerstein, 1980; Malamuth, 1979; Malamuth and Check, 1979.
95 1980.
96 1979.
97 Malamuth, 1979.
98 1979.
99 Brownmiller, 1975, page 394.
100 Schulz, 1975.
101 Hage, 1972.
102 Spender, 1980
103 Hoch, 1979.
104 Lips, 1981.
105 1971, page 41.
106 1975, page 334.
107 Spender, 1980.
108 Schulz, 1975 (b), page 67.
109 Spender, 1980, page 180.
110 1977, page 232.
111 It is suggested that the comfortable feeling that rapists experience in repeating the behaviour patterns of their initial heterosexual encounter does not necessarily indicate satisfaction with this mode of behaviour. It may merely reflect a rigidity in their sexual behaviour. The findings of Groth (1979) and the present study reveal that approximately one third of the rapists had experienced sexual trauma. The trauma may be the product of witnessing an ugly sexual encounter, or due to problems in early heterosexual contact. According to Glueck (1952-5), only ten percent of all rapists derived pleasure from their first ejaculation, forty-three percent felt mildly anxious or disgusted and thirty-one percent felt severe anxiety or disgust. Seventy-three percent still experienced moderate to severe anxiety after sexual intercourse in adulthood.
112 1980; cited in Paske, 1982.
113 Klein, 1957, page 5.
114 1975, page 263.
115 Date unkown, page 153.
116 1977, page 231.
117 1979.
118 Chappell et. al., 1977.
119 1979, page 152.

120 1972, page 101.
121 Lips, 1981.
122 1972, page 455.
123 Eardley, 1982, page 5.
124 1979, page 21.
125 1970, page 40.
126 Bardwick, 1971.
127 Fisher, 1973.
128 Hite, 1976.
129 Masters and Johnson, 1970, page 87.
130 1974, page 171.
131 Herman, 1979.
132 Connell and Wilson, 1974; Herman, 1979
133 1972, pages 11-12.
134 1982, page 42.
135 Herman, 1979; Russell, 1975.
136 1975.

Chapter Five

Rape-promoting factors in the economic, social and political spheres

Although rape-promoting factors in the economic, social and political spheres are closely linked to sexuality and masculinity, they have been separated so as to enhance clarity. Since an essential ingredient of rape is a man's need to gain power and build up his depleted self-concept, it is necessary to investigate both those non-sexual areas of men's daily life which cause or exacerbate a sense of powerlessness and demasculinisation, and those that allow for an expression of potency. The first area includes work alienation, racial oppression and community life, while the second includes the culture of violence, masculinity and power.

Work alienation

In Riverlea, as elsewhere in South African society, a person's status is linked to the amount of money earned from a 'respectable' job. A railway technician in Riverlea, for example, may earn the same amount of money as a middle class social worker, but will not have the equivalent social standing in broader society. Since broader society is generally dominated by the middle and wealthier classes, the attitudes, conduct and occupational positions of these classes are likely to be attributed greater value than those of the poverty-stricken working class communities. Within the dominant middle class perceptual framework, all the men in the present study would probably have been accorded low social status because they were unemployed or occupied low status, low paying jobs. In Riverlea itself, however, because only some two percent of the working population could be classified as managers and administrative workers, blue collar work does not imply low status for the worker. This is particularly the case below the railway line, where few occupy white collar jobs.

Ideally, work should provide a number of psychological benefits. It should satisfy needs for stimulation and a sense of belonging, structure a person's time and provide social relationships with others.[1] Over and above this, because definitions of work are intimately related to definitions of masculinity, men achieve a sense of personal worth from their jobs.

A subject's statement that the ideal man 'should be strong . . . and should be able to do a man's job' points to a perception that the characteristics of a successful worker are bound up with those of a successful man. Says Tolson:

> As individuals, men are brought up to value work as an end in itself, and to fix their personal identities around particular occupations. The roots of gender identity are interfused with expectations of achievement – 'become someone' through working, 'make something of yourself'. It is this personal identity that insists on the 'right to work', to be a breadwinner for the family, and which is threatened by lay-off or redundancy. There is in our society a collective masculine culture of work that makes firm distinctions between 'work' and 'non-work', 'work' and 'leisure', or 'career' and 'family' . . . As he moves between the demarcated spheres of his existence, a man must negotiate barriers of definition and find ways of coping with the shifting of his identity.[2]

Two important factors emerge from Tolson's statement. The first is that unemployment, a condition with which many men in Riverlea are familiar, is often perceived as a personal failing rather than as a fault of the economic system. Two social work students who were completing their practical work course in Riverlea, and who had come across numerous families whose members were unable to find work, commented in an interview that unemployment is considered a personal failing not only by the unemployed individual, but also often by his family.

The second factor mentioned by Tolson is the behavioural consequences of unemployment and dissatisfaction with work. With reference to unemployment, Eisenfeld and Lazarsfeld, in their article 'The Psychological Effects of Unemployment', conclude:

> We find that all writers who have described the course of unemployment seem to agree on the following points: first there is shock, which is followed by an active hunt for a job, during which the individual is still optimistic and unresigned; he still maintains an unbroken attitude.
> Second, when all efforts fail, the individual becomes pessimistic, anxious and suffers active distress: this is the most crucial state of all. And third, the individual becomes fatalistic and adapts himself to his new state but with a narrower scope. He now has a broken attitude.[3]

Yankelovich's study of American male workers found that eighty percent were dissatisfied with their jobs.[4] In the South African context, where coloured workers suffer less favourable working conditions, lower wages, poorer safety measures and more exploitative relationships with their employers – dissatisfaction with work is likely to be even greater.

In South Africa, as in most countries, blue collar production is often characterised by a division of labour in which work is broken down into repetitive and simple actions. The work becomes monotonous and the worker bored, and he fails to identify with the completed product.[5] Bell asserts:

> Many jobs force the person to pretend to be something he is not. As a result the person may feel alienated from what he does. Often the alienation the worker feels is due to a feeling of powerlessness, of having no control over what he does.[6]

Passivity and powerlessness run counter to the 'appropriate' masculine feelings. Thus a man who expects his work to make him feel masculine and in control, and who finds it doesn't, is likely to experience frustration. The degree of frustration is based on two factors: the strength of the person's desire to achieve the frustrated goal – for example, work satisfaction, and the degree to which the goal is interfered with – boring work, a racist supervisor.[7] According to Miller's 'frustration – aggression hypothesis', frustration often leads to aggression, but the aggression is not necessarily directed against the immediate source of frustration.[8] This may, be due to the source's superior power and the great risks involved. For instance, a male worker's fear of losing his job might prevent him from directing his aggression at the immediate source of his hardship – the machine or his boss – to another less dangerous source. Dollard and his associates have called this 'displacement'.[9] Two interrelated questions arise: The first is, if men do not always aggress against the source of frustration because of fear, against whom do they aggress? And the second, why do rapists express their aggression sexually?

The answer to the first question is dependent on a number of factors: Is the target readily available? Will the individual gain power by expressing his aggression against the particular target? Will his aggression compensate sufficiently for the areas of his life with which he feels dissatisfied? Does the assault conform with his ideas and morals? And what are the likely consequences?

Regarding the second question, the perfect victim for the rapist is a woman. She is visible and easily accessible. Compared to other men, the rapist has a more extreme perception of women as passive sexual objects who should always guarantee a man's requests. He believes he can overpower and control her without too many negative economic or social consequences. The rapist, like most criminals, assumes he will not be apprehended for his offence. And considering the amount of unreported rapes, the probability of apprehension and legal prosecution is not high. For the rapist, a woman can occasionally threaten his masculinity, but she is rarely any match for his physical strength. In addition, she can restore his eroded sense of male power. The mechanism best able to fulfil these requisites quickly is rape. It provides short-term relief to frustration, alters his self-concept immediately and can be justified by social norms.

Are all rapists working class men?

Since the sample of men interviewed in this study was drawn from a largely working class community, the link between working class men and rape needs to be considered. Alienation and lack of power in the workplace affects the majority of working class men. This does not mean, however, that because rape helps to compensate for feelings of powerlessness, all working class men will rape.

Accepting that not all working class men rape, would it be more accurate to suggest that because working class men experience heightened frustration in their workplace and in their community, they are more likely to rape than men from other more privileged social and economic strata?

The answer to this question is 'no'. Work dissatisfaction is not unique to the working class. It occurs across all classes and occupations. Furthermore, occupational frustration and dissatisfaction are related not only to objective work conditions, but also to individual expectations. Often individuals from the wealthier classes have higher hopes than those who have always experienced extreme deprivation. Unmet expectations can spark frustration and anger. Berkowitz gives the example of unemployed men who, after a long period of unemployment, become apathetic and resigned rather than violent.[10]

Work dissatisfaction in isolation does not cause rape, but it can act as a contributing factor. When it is combined with numerous other factors, such as sexual inadequacy, dehumanising attitudes towards women, sexist beliefs and expectations and unmet power needs, all of which are not exclusive to the working class, rape can result. This helps explain why some members of the working class rape and others do not.

It is a commonly held stereotype that all rapists are working class and middle class men do not rape. In the past, much of American and Canadian research tacitly supported this supposition.[11] In his study of rape, McCaldon stated that 'rapists are mainly from the lower socio-economic groups'.[12] According to Mohr, seventy-five percent of rapists are from low socio-economic backgrounds.[13]

While not wanting to rule out the possibility that the majority of rapists are from working class and poverty-stricken backgrounds, such conclusions should be approached with caution. According to Davis, the police and courts perceive men from working class backgrounds as more likely rapists than men from the middle class.[14] In a similar vein, Clark and Lewis posit that the judicial process appears to find it difficult to believe that a man who belongs to a more affluent class than his victim would want to rape her.[15] Middle class men may escape suspicion or arrest for rape because the rape cases in which they are involved are not reported. This is partly due to the fact that in affluent areas, people live further apart from each other and have more privacy, making it easier to keep rape a secret.[16] The victims of middle class rapists are sometimes in vulnerable economic and social positions and may be unwilling to bring the rape to the attention of the police. Says David on this issue:

> It seems, in fact, that men of the capitalist class and their middle class partners are immune to prosecution because they commit their sexual assaults with the same unchallenged authority that legitimises their daily assaults on the labour and dignity of working people.[17]

While accepting the argument that middle class men probably manage to escape prosecution for sexual offences more easily than do working class men, it is incorrect to assert, as David does, that they are immune from arrest and legal penalties.[18]

Although working class men may not be more likely to rape than other men, it remains important to focus on those conditions of working class life which may promote rape. The working class men interviewed experienced a number of life factors which may have heightened frustration and therefore the potential for aggression. They were all unemployed or experienced alienation in their work place. Like many others in Riverlea, their housing was inadequate, with up to twelve people sharing a small, two-bedroomed house. Again like many other Riverlea residents, they had more or less permanent financial problems. Besides struggling to provide financial support to their families of origin or their own nuclear families, they also owed regular hire purchase payments on household items such as furniture and hi-fis. Experiences of a subculture of violence were common among all the subjects. Riverlea is the site of many home-based gangs. Social workers with a knowledge of Riverlea report that one of the community's primary problems is wife-beating and child abuse. All the subjects, excluding those from the Non-Violent group, were active within this culture of abuse.

Race

Riverlea is designated a coloured residential area and the subject population of the present study is comprised exclusively of this racial group. The majority of coloured men in South Africa suffer racial discrimination, are economically and politically powerless and have a reputation, like other black men, of being rapists.

Hypotheses that 'blacks are more likely to fight than whites' and that 'the majority of rapists are black' appear in a great deal of the research on rape.[19] Firestone's *The Dialectic of Sex: The Case for Feminist Revolution* was one of the first feminist works to deal with this question.[20] For Firestone, racism is an extension of sexism.[21] Using the conceptualisation that 'races are no more than the various parents and siblings of the Family of Man', she posits, within the framework of American society, the father as the white man, the mother as the white woman and the children as the black people.[22] Basing her formulation on Freud's oedipal theory, she goes on to argue that because of the desire of the son to kill the father and sleep with the mother, black men have an insatiable hunger to sleep with white women. And, to 'be a man', the black man must

> untie himself from his bond with the white female, relating to her if at all only in a degrading way. In addition, due to his virulent hatred and jealousy of her Possessor, the white man, he may lust after her as a thing to be conquered in order to revenge himself on the white man.[23]

According to Amir, eighty-two percent of rapists are black.[24] MacDonald asserts that black rapists were 'over fives times the expected number of Negroes among the two hundred and fifty-three offenders who raped women', and MacKellar states that ninety percent of all reported rapes are perpetrated by black men.[25] The reason given is that:

> Blacks raised in the hard life of the ghetto learn that they can get what they want only by seizing it. Violence is the rule in the game for survival. Women are fair prey: to obtain a woman one subdues her.[26]

Feminists such as Brownmiller have also adopted the view that black men are more likely to rape than white men.[27] She believes that racial oppression has denied black men fulfilment of their need – as men – to dominate. They must therefore resort to rape. She says of black men and 'ghetto inhabitants':

> Corporate executive dining rooms and climbs up Mount Everest are not usually accessible to those who form the sub-

culture of violence. Access to a female body – through force – is within their ken.[28]

On the issue of black men raping white women, Russell comments:

If some black men see rape of white women as an act of revenge or as a justifiable expression of hostility towards whites, I think it is equally realistic for white women to be less trusting of black men than many of them are.[29]

A closer reading of Amir and some other studies will hopefully restore some semblance of reality to white men and women's perception of the 'black threat'.[30] Amir reports that ninety-three percent of reported rapes are intra-racial – the rapist and the victim belonging to the same race group – while in South Africa, the estimate is between ninety-five and ninety-eight percent.[31] Findings from the present study yield similar results – none of the rapists raped anyone outside of their racial group. Furthermore, none of them admitted to physically assaulting white or African women, and only one verbally assaulted a white woman.

The reasons for intra-racial rape are complex and at this stage very little research has been conducted. There are, however, three suggested reasons for its predominance over inter-racial rape in this particular study. The first is that coloured women are more accessible to coloured men than are women from other racial categories. The second is that rapists may prefer to rape in their own community because they are more familiar with the setting and possible dangers. Since the Group Areas Act legislates that coloureds have to live within the same residential area, this would help to ensure that the victims of coloured rapists tend to be coloured women who reside in their community. The third is that raping a coloured woman is easier than raping a white woman because of her more vulnerable social and economic position, and a perception that there would be less stringent legal consequences. This perception is based on the view that courts in South Africa tend to give less harsh sentences to black men whose victims are black women than to those who raped white women.

Many white men believe that black men are imbued with uncontainable sexual desire and that black women are able to tolerate sexual excesses. Davis says of the consequences of this perception:

Once the notion is accepted that black men harbour irresist-
ible, animal-like sexual urges, the entire race is invested with
bestiality. If black men are ravishers of white women, black
women must welcome the sexual attentions of white men.
'Loose' women and whores, their claims of rape will always
lack legitimacy.[32]

In spite of this, the incidence of white men raping black women
is low in South Africa.[33] No figures are available to assess whether
this has increased or decreased in recent years. What does seem
to have increased in 1988 are public reports of white men raping
their black domestic workers. Without ascertaining figures from
previous years, it is difficult to assess whether this is in fact a new
rape trend.

What is clear, though, is that these cases tend to be characterised
by lengthy and extreme abuse. In one case, two black teenage
domestic workers reported that they were kept 'as sex slaves for
over four months'.[34] A report in the *Star* newspaper described
another such incident, this time involving a twenty-four year old
black woman:

> The woman, a newly employed domestic worker, was held
> as a sex slave for five days at a Forest Hill, Johannesburg
> home and raped five times by her employer . . . [At his
> home] she was ordered to clean up his bedroom. After she
> had done so, her employer entered the room and demanded
> she remove her underwear. When she refused, she was as-
> saulted until she removed her clothing. She was then raped
> and held until Sunday. During this period, she was raped
> a further four times.[35]

Despite these reports, it still seems that the phenomenon of white
men raping black women is not very common. This may be the
result of white men's perception of black women as inferior, even
less than human. For white men, sex with black women, whether
coerced or not, may be perceived as socially embarrassing. Conviction would intensify such embarrassment. Ironically, it is white
men's relative respect for white women which makes white wom-
en more susceptible to rape by this group of men. Rape by white
men indicates that factors which encourage rape also exist within
white communities.

Nevertheless, the myth of the black rapist is perpetuated by researchers who analyse rape purely on the basis of cases reported. Black men, because they are discriminated against and lack power in society, are easier to arrest and convict. This has meant that they have had to take a disproportionate amount of blame for the incidence of rape, thus confirming the myth.[36] The truth, however, remains – as one South African health guidance booklet put it: 'Rape is common among all race groups.'[37] Racial genetics cannot account for rape. They do not explain why some black men rape and others do not. For one coloured man to rape and another not to, feelings of powerlessness, exploitation and racial subjection must act in concert with other sexual, psychological and 'masculine' variables.

The culture of violence

Violence has always been part of human behaviour. It was once requisite for physical survival in a dangerous environment. But in present times, when human survival depends less on anatomical strength, violence continues to increase. By 1981, it was estimated that there had been four million homicides in the twentieth century. Figures for rape and assault exceed this number many times over. While no accurate figures are available of people killed through war, the number is thought to run into hundreds of millions.[38] To understand its prevalence, we must therefore return to two key components in any study of human social phenomena: the social milieu and social learning.

Violence is an integral part of South African culture. It was an important component of white colonial settlement and has continued to feature prominently in political control. It is also used to deal with conflict in social groupings such as the family, the school, the community and peer groups. Crime in South Africa has reached epidemic proportions. According to official figures, approximately thirty murders are committed each day in South Africa. The actual incidence is probably higher.

Riverlea belongs to the geographical region known as the Witwatersrand. It is estimated that on average nearly ten people are murdered every day on the Witwatersrand.[39] This is 'roughly equivalent to the murder rate of New York, Los Angeles and Chicago combined'.[40] The pervasiveness of violence in South Africa can be attributed to numerous factors, including unemployment, poor wages, alcohol and drug abuse, racial and class conflict, and a social acceptance of violence as an appropriate means to attain personal and societal goals. Within such a setting, Shapiro's comments with reference to the United States would hold true for South Africa. She writes that 'attacks on women are as certain . . as death and taxes – more certain than taxes, since some manage not to pay'.[41]

Rape can be linked to a prevailing culture, rather than merely a subculture, of violence. This argument extends Amir's postulate regarding working class violence.[42] Amir maintains that the excessive emphasis on violent and 'machisimo' behaviour in working class and black communities is a principal cause of rape, and that rape is merely a reflection of the subcultures of these groups. Amir's theory, however, does not explain the occurrence of rape in the dominant culture of white, middle class society.

The subcultures of violence that exist within communities should not be studied in a social vacuum. Wilson points out:

> Rape represents an act of machismo and sadistic domination, not only in the ghetto but also outside of it. It is not the subculture alone that is violent; our whole culture is suffused with beliefs in male supremacy, dominance and aggression.[43]

Some investigation has been conducted above into the wide spectrum of cultural and subcultural trends which elicit rapists' violence. Three of the most important factors will be discussed below. Although this analysis is specifically aimed at understanding the development of violent behaviour in rapists, it also provides some understanding of the violent behaviour of subjects in the Physically Violent group.

The family

The family commonly evokes stress and violence.[44] Families can be a source of nurturance and support. At the same time, members are stressed by constant and intimate interaction with one another and need to be able to solve problems harmoniously. In working class homes, crowded living conditions tend to aggravate this stress. In this study, for example, most subjects reported living in a two bedroomed house which accommodated six or seven people. In most families, power and authority are vested in the male head of the house, who is usually the father. Consequently, resolution of differences is not only dealt with amicably through discussion and inamicably through forced removal from the house, separation or divorce, but also through male authority and violence. Such violence is a frequent and sanctioned activity because of the norms of male dominance and family privacy which operate in society.[45]

Using Bandura's theory of modelling, it is likely that the violent behaviour of fathers is frequently modelled by their sons.[46] This is especially significant in the sons' relations with women, since the violence which they witness is usually directed at their mothers. Unlike subjects in the Non-Violent group, the majority of subjects in the Rape and Physically Violent groups had observed their fathers assaulting their mothers:

He used to hit her with fists and on two nights he stabbed her.

He would hit her a lot with a belt.

He beat her, even once with an axe.

He used to punch her and hit her until she bleeds.

Their mothers' responses were often traditionally feminine – passive and accepting. Said one rapist: 'She just used to take it all the years. It's like this and I must accept it.' The nature of parental conflict and the effects of sex role socialisation are reproduced in rape behaviour. As Melani and Fodaski explain:

We find, in the early lives of many convicted rapists, an indication of great parental friction, with a violent father abusing an ineffectual mother. The culturally established images of male aggressiveness and female weakness, learned from the parents and approved by society in general, are thus duplicated symbolically and physically in the explosive act of rape.[47]

Observation, however, is not the only means of learning about violence. Some children learn about it through their own victimisation. Violence against children occurs more often in working class families where physical punishment is used by parents to ensure obedience. In middle class families, while violence does occur, psychological pressure is the predominant method of eliciting the child's co-operation.[48] It must be stressed that physical punishment is not common to all working class children and that the level of physical coercion is not the same in all families. For example, most of the subjects in the Non-Violent group were never beaten, and at most received a slap across the face. In contrast, as children, rapists and physically violent men had more brutal and more frequent violent encounters with their fathers. Two rapists reported:

> He would hit with his fist and with his belt until we had blue marks.

> He used to donder me . . . say about twice a week . . . with his belt. He used to work at the leather works and he had a special belt. I still got the marks on my backside through him.

Two physically violent men said:

> I got a fair amount of hidings, maybe ten a week with a flat hand across my backside. Then later on he started with a fan belt tied to a piece of wood.

> He beat us with a sjambok. He would undress us and hit us . . . nearly every day.

Removing a child from a violent environment does not necessarily prevent violent behaviour in adulthood. Some researchers, such as Renvoize and Gelles, believe no experience of violence can ever be eradicated from the mind.[49] If a boy is raised in a violent family, socialised in a culture in which masculinity and aggression are intimately linked, is punished through violence and receives insufficient love, it is to be anticipated that he will at some point in his life resort to violence. The boy learns that violence is normal, is a simple means to get what he wants and to control the behaviour of others. This learning manifests itself when, as an adult, he decides which woman he wants and forces her into submission through rape.

Renvoize quotes a doctor who gave evidence to the Select Committee on Violence in Marriage in Great Britain as giving the following answer to questions about whether violent children have a low frustration tolerance and the likelihood of detecting low tolerance levels at an early age:

> We do not need a special test for this. All one needs is to observe these children and one can see a pattern developing. By the time they are about seven, they are having temper tantrums, they are losing their temper, attacking adults, even in play, quite viciously. They have been brought up in an environment of violence and they have seen their father battering their mother. By the time they are fourteen, male children can really let rip with violence and if something does upset them, they have learned that violence does pay. One must realise that if there is a background of family violence, the children are at risk and unless something is done for these children, they will become the battering husbands [or rapists] of the next generation.[50]

Similarly, Pizzey writes:

> It is hardly surprising that this child grows into the man who explodes when he is frustrated. At an age when small children are learning about society and how they are expected to respond to the demands made on them by the world they live in, they have a learned pattern of response from their fathers who solve all problems with their fists. If something annoys and upsets them, their response is to annihilate it.[51]

There is much evidence which supports this point of view. Guttmacher's study of homicidal offenders in America concludes that most of the offenders had experienced a violent upbringing and identified themselves with their aggressors, believing that aggression was a cure for frustration.[52] Tanay found that sixty-seven percent of murderers in his sample had been exposed to violence in childhood.[53] Similarly, Walters' work with a group of twenty men sentenced to death by American courts revealed that most of them had been brutally punished as children.[54]

Results from this study did not show a significant difference between rapists and physically violent men: seventy-eight percent of the rapists and eighty-nine percent of the physically violent men had experienced physical and psychological abuse as children.

The question, once again, is why does the inculcation and socialisation of violence not always lead to rape?

While learning by example is instrumental to the child's behaviour, the process for the rapist may be an ambivalent one. Tolson illuminates the male child's ambiguous feelings towards his father:

A boy's gender identification is disturbed by his alienation from his father and by his perception of father's absence from the home. Father appears alien, not only because he legislates and punishes, but also more significantly, because his 'masculine presence' can only be construed in physical absence – his distance from family affairs. Father is an outsider because he goes 'out to work'. The brutality of his presence lies not so much in acts of domestic violence (though these cannot be minimised), as in general masculine estrangement conditioned by the reality of work.[55]

Hartley takes Tolson's point one step further:

Fathers are not at home nearly as much as mothers are. This means that the major psychodynamic process by which sex roles are learned – the process of identification – is available only minimally to boys since their natural identification objects, their fathers, are simply not around much of the time to serve as models. The absence of fathers means, again, that much of male behaviour has to be learned by trial and error and indirection.[56]

While Tolson and Hartley give valuable insights into the young boy's ambivalence towards his father, father's absence does not lessen his importance as a role model. What power the father loses as a model through his absence, he makes up through his status. In addition to the boy's perception of his father's greater physical strength and his frequent, unchallenged aggression towards other family members, the boy also experiences the other authority in the family – his mother – deferring to father.

Tolson and Hartley tend to ignore other factors which might remove the father from the household. Some of the boy's ambivalence about his father's lack of commitment and haphazard relationship with him may be the result of separation, divorce, drinking binges and affairs with other women. From an analysis of the interviews, unfaithful fathers were twice as common for subjects in the rape sample as for subjects in the physically violent and nonviolent samples.

As Tolson and Hartley point out, the father's absence produces insecurity in the son, since the boy attempts to identify with someone who is often absent. 'I felt sorry inside' was how one rapist described his feelings about his father's absence. Stemming from feelings of uncertainty is a need for recognition and a desire to compete and aggress in order to conceal the inner vulnerability. Boys hide their insecurity by using the patterns of relating learned at home: violence, aggression and control, particularly in relation to women. Behaving in this manner conceals the vulnerability that might be derided as a sign of weakness.

The work of Bradbury and Pleck suggests that the boy's relationship with his mother may be a factor in promoting violence and rape.[57] The son's relationship with his mother changes from one of absolute dependence and intimacy at the time of birth, to one in which he sees his mother as servant and nurse – a somewhat inferior person. The boy learns that he is in a position to both dominate and be dominated. Sons dominate because they have been given some special status. They are taught that it is natural to make more demands of their mothers than of their fathers. In later life, this demand pattern becomes manifest in relation to other women – their girlfriends, lovers and wives. Ironically, it is this experience of female physical and psychological support in adult life that may be threatening to the man, as it reminds him he can be weak – he requires others, needs care, has feelings and is not as independent as he believed himself to be. Sometimes responsibility for his weakness may be projected on to the woman. If she does not demonstrate sufficient affection, he may blame her for not confirming his image of manhood. This can lead to rape and violence as the man tries to reassert his masculinity.[58]

Another area of possible conflict with the mother is that of discipline. The enforcement of extreme discipline is generally the domain of the father, while the mother usually takes responsibility for day to day discipline and control. It is possible that some mothers, partly because they have limited opportunity to express their power both outside the home and inside it when their husbands are present, may punish their children excessively as a means of relieving themselves of their frustration and gaining a sense of control and power.[59] The boy's responses to his father's and mother's disciplinary measures are very different. As we have seen (in Chapter 3), the boy's socialised acceptance of male authority and status allows him to respect his father, even when severely beaten by him. In contrast, the mother's less tyrannical disciplinary techniques of shouting or hitting can provoke resentment, since such behaviour conflicts with the boy's expectations of her as nurturer. Sometimes his resentment takes the form of violence: he hits, or pushes her away or fantasises about hurting her. As the years proceed, his aggression may become more subtle and be enacted through silence, tone of voice or look.[60] This mode of conduct is echoed in adulthood in his heterosocial and heterosexual relationships. Increasing alienation and heightened insecurities about masculinity can mean that the aggressive behaviour of the younger years increases when the male reaches adulthood. He must show angry feelings towards women in a more direct fashion, and one mechanism that provides gratification is rape.

The boy's conceptualisation of his mother as 'other' and inferior results in his rejection of any of the qualities associated with her. To be 'like a woman' is a disgrace. This he learns not only through experience, but also through the direct messages conveyed by both his mother and father, as well as the popular media. He obliterates the feminine in himself by controlling and dominating those who are female. Says Tweedie:

A boy, reared by a woman, perceives that he is not as she is, that he must reject his beloved to gain himself, that paradise must be lost to achieve manhood. Whatever the beloved is, he must not be. Is she emotional? Then he must be unfeeling. Is she gentle? Then he must be aggressive. Is she kind? Then he must be unkind. His earliest model, from whence his earliest comfort came, must be obliterated. Many men manage this difficult transition and confine its injuries to themselves. Others, rapists among them, do not. The necessary split is too painful, the motion too grievous. And who do they blame for the murder of their souls, unconsciously? Women.[61]

Some researchers argue that the behaviour of many rapists towards their wives is a reproduction of their experiences of their rejecting mothers. A good example of one such piece of work is that of Abrahamsen. After conducting research tests on the wives of convicted rapists, he concluded that:

> The wives of the sex offenders . . . stimulated their husbands into attempts to prove themselves, attempts which necessarily ended in frustration and increased their husbands' own doubts about their masculinity. In doing so, the wives unknowingly continued the type of relationship the offender had had with his mother. There can be no doubt that the sexual frustration which the wives caused is one of the factors motivating rape, which might be tentatively described as a displaced attempt to force a seductive but rejecting mother into submission.[62]

Abrahamsen's findings should be read with caution, since they contain a hint that responsibility for rape lies with the offender's wife and mother. Whatever the root causes of rape, offenders must take responsibility before the law for their own actions. This does not mean, however, that the rapist's behaviour should not be understood within the framework of his history. Rape is a gruesome crime and the responses to it are understandably emotional, but if we are to forget the tragic social and psychological background of many offenders and its contributing role in rape, we will not get closer to a comprehensive understanding or solution to the crime.[64] As Tweedie puts it, rape is in part an act fuelled by rage, vindictiveness and revenge – 'repayment in kind for childhood injuries received'.[64]

The community as a source of violence

Amir's theory of subcultural violence is borne out by the social relations and conditions within working class communities in South Africa and within the community from which the subjects of this study were drawn.[65] Racial oppression and exploitation are aggravated by squalid living conditions such as those found in Riverlea. As far as health care goes, for example, there are two small outpatient clinics, there are few doctors, the hospital is some distance away and transport expenses are high for families faced with unemployment and poor wages. Housing is inadequate, and welfare practitioners in the community report that educational and recreational facilities are insufficient. These conditions are likely to result in feelings of anger, powerlessness and frustration within the community. Violence functions as a means of control of one's environment and provides an outlet for aggression. Gang fights, assaults and rapes are common features of Riverlea life. As one subject from the Non-Violent group commented:

> In Riverlea, there is too much gangster fights, and on the weekends it's murders, rapes and assaults, but it's a lekker place.

This statement indicates an acceptance of violence which would probably not be found in a more affluent community where extreme and overt public violence is seldom experienced. Acceptance becomes tacit encouragement of this violence. Paradoxically, violence as a symbol of strength and power in the machismo ethos can be seen as a means of regaining human dignity, esteem and respect. The statement made by a rapist illustrates this:

> I felt proud of myself. You see we have a small township and if that thing [massive fist fight] happens in our township then I feel a bit like a hero because I started the whole thing. It was a good feeling.

Most of the subjects in the present study had been involved in brutal aggressive behaviour. The following account by a rapist represents the level of brutality engaged in by many of the subjects:

> We were at a braai and . . . I was drunk and this ou was drunk. I went inside and fetched a bush knife, so I stabbed this ou on his hand and he collapsed, and they took him to hospital. When he came out, he got all his friends together, and when I went out of the house, they all attacked me with bush knives. They stabbed me in the back . . . I went to hospital.
>
> The second time I was in a fight . . . I was fighting with this chap and I also chopped his hand with a butcher knife. I chopped his hand paralysed. Then his friends came and they threw me with a brick and broke my jaw and then I was rushed to hospital.

This raises the question, how often do rapists engage in other kinds of violent acts? Many researchers, particularly those dealing with rapists from low socio-economic areas, report that rapists often have a record of other violent offences.[66] In this study, eighty-eight percent of the rapists had committed other violent crimes in addition to rape. To make a more definitive statement about rape as part of the subculture of violence, it would be worthwhile exploring the incidence of other violent acts amongst middle class rapists.

A feature of a subculture of violence is the 'shared commitment to violence and a shared concept of aggressive masculinity'.[67] In Riverlea and other communities, this is expressed in its most intense form in gang fights and gang rapes. In the present study, almost forty-five percent of rapists participated in gang rapes. Although there are no figures for the proportion of gang rapes among other rapes committed in South Africa, a superficial study of local newspaper reports on rape suggests a similar tendency to that in the United States, where one in four rapes is a gang rape.

In a community with a high level of alienation and conflict, gang rape provides a rationale for solidarity and interaction based on male bonding and masculine validation.[68] Since gang rape necessarily involves group interaction, there is a strong pressure to conform to the violent behaviour and contemptuous attitude towards women displayed by the group. Conformity to the group norm provides those in the group with a sense of acceptance and power. This is particularly important considering that many of those who participate in gang rape often feel powerless in their social and working lives.

Physical violence as a means of validating masculinity

The responses of some of the subjects in this study indicate that there is often no apparent reason for their violent behaviour. This account was given by a rapist:

I had newspaper money that I used to buy the newspaper with every afternoon for the people at home. I forgot about the newspaper money and we went down to my friend's house. On the way we found this guy, the newspaper vendor. Then I just kicked him . . . Then my friends just kicked him . . . I don't know why. Even in court before the magistrate I didn't know why.

A subject in the Physically Violent group said:

> I was sitting with a friend of mine and I asked this guy for a light. I said something, I don't know what, and I think he took it hard. He got up and said that's not the way I should talk. I said I just asked for a light, and he said okay he would meet me outside and okay we started to fight.

It is suggested that a significant motivating factor for this apparently irrational violence is men's need to validate their masculinity. The form of violence which this validation takes will differ according to the individual's perceptions, feelings and life conditions. A man who continually assaults others, but never rapes, probably has different perceptions of women from those of a rapist. He is likely to feel less aggressive towards women, objectify them less and place less emphasis on sexual conquest.

The rapist's behaviour during rape is similarly influenced by his attitude to his victim. This is an important point, since it suggests that the rapist does not view all women in the same light. Although no woman could ever measure up to his standards, he does objectify some women less than others. For instance, he may have different perceptions of his lover and a female acquaintance. With regard to a wife or a lover, the rapist may see her as more human because of the greater intimacy he has with her.

This does not mean that rapists do not demonstrate high levels of violence towards their wives or lovers to whom they generally grant some human status. It does, however, imply that they can be expected to behave in a more brutal fashion towards women who do not have the benefit of this status. Thus in situations where the rapist feels aggressive, insecure or disenchanted with a woman's behaviour, the female acquaintance has more to fear than does the wife or lover.

The rapist's perception of people does not only influence the nature of his masculinity-validating behaviour, it also affects how he feels afterwards. This is evidenced in a rapist's greater remorse after beating up a man than after sexually violating a woman (see Chapter 7). The reason for this was that he saw the man he victimised as having feelings and being able to experience pain. The victimised woman on, the other hand, was nothing more than a 'nice pussy' who enjoyed a bit of sexual coercion. These different views of men and women may also stem from the rapist's ability to identify more with a man's hurt because of his own previous experiences of pain. The level of empathy and concern about the anguish and pain of others is often based on the similarity that exists between the sympathiser and the victim. Thus men often find it easier to identify with the worries and hurt of other men than of women.

The validation of masculinity is indeed the 'fix' many men require to survive and to secure pleasure. One of the major ingredients of this 'fix' is man's competitive spirit and his desire to conquer and win. The fulfillment of this ambition is sometimes dependent on his victim being an able competitor. If his victim consents without a fight, the excitement of the conquest is undermined. On the issue of male victims' resistance to assault, some of the comments from the Rapist and Physically Violent groups respectively, were:

> I won't hit him, I won't get my satisfaction. I won't be able to hit a guy if he doesn't hit me back. That's bad because I like to get my satisfaction.

> It would be better if he would have been more stronger . . . What is the use of hitting a guy who is holding his head and looking scared?

Feelings about female victims' resistance are in many ways similar. Although the majority of rapists preferred that their victims did not resist continually, they admitted to being 'turned on' by at least some resistance.

Conquest of the victim is not as gratifying if it is accomplished through mechanisms not associated with masculinity. Thus while patience and tactics may finally result in triumph, the use of brute force provides a quicker victory and a loftier glorification of manhood because of its identification with the desired masculine traits of potency and strength. Two men from the Physically Violent group described the feelings engendered by a fight in this way:

> By having a fight, you can prove your strength. Every guy likes to do that.

I felt good. I felt I am strong and tough.

However, because of the convergence of sex and male domination, acts of force within the sexual arena are often not perceived as aggression. Medea and Thompson assert that

> killing and hitting are seen as real acts of aggression by one person against another, regardless of whether they are taken to court; they are acts which may provoke revenge. Strangely, however, in the case of rape that connection – that it is an act of aggression regardless of whether or not it is prosecutable – is not made. Sometimes it is not made in the mind of the victim. It is seldom made in the minds of the people the victim will have to deal with after the attack.[69]

Clearly, if the rapist shares this perception, then coercion may not be sufficient to validate his masculinity. He therefore engages in extreme physical brutality: he puts sharp objects up his victim's vagina, cuts her breasts, urinates on her, and hits, punches and kicks her. Often it is only when this happens that the rapist, the public and sometimes even the victim will classify rape as an aggressive act.

For the rapist, women are 'legitimate' victims and violence is an acceptable form of male behaviour. Violence restores his power and is the easiest and most recognisable assertion of everything defined as masculine. The behaviour described below is an example of the type of explosive responses rapists often resort to when they believe they are not receiving the treatment they deserve:

> I was coming in my people's house, coming from work. I came in the house and I see these two guys sitting there and I see my sussie passing in the lobby. My cousin is also coming in and suddenly I get jealous because I only have coffee in a saucer and they are eating here. I get funny thoughts that they are boyfriends and they are coming to have a nice time in my people's house, so I smacked the one boy . . . And then the other one opened the door and I grabbed hold of him and gave him a few shots. Then my sister came and she shouts at me and so I just turned around and gave her a smack too. And my cousin she also wants to talk and I smacked her too.

This rapist appeared to be conveying the message to his sister and cousin that he would not tolerate a questioning of his authority. Under no circumstances would he lose the power granted to him as a son, brother and a male.

Rape and destruction of property

Although multiple causation is a feature of every rape, recent studies and most feminist writers stress that a cardinal feature of rape is the rapist's desire to express his power and superiority over his victim.[70] Most writers point, as this study has done, to the rapist's admission that he does not always find rape sexually pleasurable. The predominance of power needs is further evidenced by the overwhelming amount of rapists' statements about feeling strong, powerful and in control during the rape.

These feelings suggest that rape not only ensures the victim's obedience, but also alters the rapist's self-perception and his perception of his victim. Kipnis's work on power, although not dealing specifically with rapists, seems applicable to them.[71] Kipnis found that men who had power devalued the virtues of the less powerful and saw them as objects to be manipulated. This finding suggests why rapists use increasingly degrading violence as the rape proceeds; for if the rapist achieves more power as the rape goes on, and so further devalues and objectifies his victim, then acts of brutality become easier to perform. Thus in the rapist's perception, the more vulnerable his victim becomes during the rape, through, for example, begging or crying, the more it confirms in his eyes that she is not worthy of respect. This in turn justifies and elicits further violence.

Throughout this investigation, power has been described as an essential component of the motivation to rape and the rape behaviour itself (see Chapter 6). What remains to be dealt with in this subsection is the relationship between power and the desire to destroy another man's property.

Once rapists have introjected the socialised masculine norms of competitiveness, conquest, aggression, power and force, they often attempt to transform the masculine ethos into actuality by raping another man's sexual partner. This would be an illustration of greater power relative to another man, who is proved incapable of safeguarding and controlling 'his' woman. This type of rape serves to affirm the rapist's masculinity while destroying that of another man.[72] And in this process, women are clearly cast as the property of men. A few comments by rapists demonstrate this:

> I knew a girl, they took her from another guy . . . She was with this guy at the club. Those guys took her from that guy. They told that guy either we going to screw you or we are going to screw her, so he left her. There were about thirty guys . . . They took her to Soweto and raped her.

> When I feel I want a cherry, especially at night, say at a disco or a party . . then I would wait for her and whoever she is with, we would take her from him and put her in the car and take out a knife depending on who the cherry is.

The second rapist, in qualifying the type of man he would take a 'cherry' from, clearly sees women as the property of men. Women are there to serve 'the boys' and provide them with sexual pleasure. The rapist's statement below also implies that solidarity among men inhibits competitiveness:

> If I am with a ou I know, I wouldn't take a cherry from him. If the ou is not part of the gang, together we would take her as a cut for the boys.

A particularly gruesome gang rape which demonstrated the extremity which men will go to humiliate other men and their partners occurred on the Witwatersrand in April 1989. Of interest is that the rapists, who were black, did not differentiate on the basis of race in choosing their victims. *Business Day* reported the rape in the following manner:

> A man was forced to rape a woman at gunpoint by four men who had raped her minutes earlier on Friday night.
> The incident, which occurred near the isolated Nasrec centre in south Johannesburg, began at about 10.30pm when a white couple in a parked car were held up by four black men.
> The gang, armed with guns, forced the couple out of the

car and each raped the woman while her companion was held at gunpoint.

A short while later, a black couple who were driving past were forcibly stopped by the gang. The black woman was raped by one of the gang members.

The gang then forced the black man to rape the white woman. Afterwards the gang chased the black couple away. The white couple were then locked in the boot of their car and the four men drove off in another car.

They were released after police were alerted shortly afterwards by the black couple.[73]

The rapists in this case clearly had little regard for their rape victims – black or white. The humiliation of the men was compounded by their helplessness to prevent the violence perpetrated against their loved ones. Furthermore, the men were forced to participate in the rape. The black man, probably through physical threats to both himself or his partner, was made to rape. And both men became party to the crime by having to observe the offence without being able to stop it.

Wartime and political rapes are the classic confirmation that rape is an act in which the offender exhibits his power to other men. Previous mention was made of the Vietnam war. Two other infamous war cases are worthy of mention. The first is the 'Rape of Nanking', where the invading Japanese troops in 1947 perpetrated twenty thousand rapes in the first month of their occupation of that city.[74] The second example is that of the 1971 Bangladesh war. The West Pakastani army, who had minimal financial resources to conduct a war, had to find a cheap method of destroying their (male) enemy's will to resist. The method they devised was the raping of enemy women. As a matter of military strategy, two to four hundred thousand Bengali women were purposefully raped. These rapes were considered, carefully decided upon and efficiently carried out. According to war correspondents, pornographic movies were shown to the West Pakistani soldiers in order to sexually excite them, after which they were sent out to rape the imprisoned Bengali women.[75]

The honest writing of Elridge Cleaver sheds light on the use and sexual abuse of women in political struggle.[76] Cleaver, an American black consciousness activist in the 1960s, confessed that he blazoned his hostility towards the white man by raping white women:

I became a rapist. To refine my technique and modus oper-
andi, I started out by practising on black girls in ghet-
tos . . . and when I considered myself smooth enough, I
crossed the tracks and sought out white prey.

Rape was an insurrectionary act. It delighted me that I was
defying and trampling upon the white man's law, upon his
system of values, and that I was defiling his women – and
this point, I believe, was the most satisfying to me because
I was very resentful over the historical fact of how the white
man had used the black woman. I felt I was getting
revenge.[77]

Raping white women was Cleaver's way of showing his equality
with or supremacy over the white man. If there were another simple method of exacting his revenge, Cleaver may have resorted to
it, but women's inferior status in society made them easy targets.
One other salient point that can be drawn from Cleaver's statement is that by admitting to raping black girls for practice, he highlights the fact that irrespective of race, women are regarded as non-
feeling sexual objects. Medea and Thompson ask: 'Where was his
black consciousness when he raped black sisters for practice?' They
answer their own question: 'It was there, but it was a man's black
consciousness.'[78]

Horos cites the response of a husband to his wife's rape: 'I wanted
to kill that bastard, I wanted to destroy him for what he'd done
to me.'[79] This suggests, again, that for some men, women do not
exist in their own right (see Chapter 2). Rape is seen by men as
an offensive act because it damages men's property, and the offense
is sexual because the property vandalised is sexual. In Horos's example, the man's first reaction was to want 'to kill' the rapist not
for what he did to his wife, but for humiliating him. When this
attitude is combined with the 'she must have wanted it' myth, it
is no wonder that married women are very reluctant to report rapes;
and if they do they can often expect no real support from their
husbands. Says Wilson:

Our responses give considerable support to the view that
many women perceived their husbands as relating to them
in a landlord-property type situation. In effect, the husband
will consider his property as being damaged and assume as
well that his property contributed towards the violation.[80]

Levett also explains why some rape victims do not receive appropriate support from their husbands or boyfriends:

> It is likely that the man will have a sense of having been wronged by another in that, feeling proprietary towards his wife or girlfriend, he has been forced to share her with someone else. This results in indignation and even, in the extreme, . . . a wish to kill the assailant and he may storm out in search of him, leaving the woman unsupported and feeling her needs unmet and misunderstood.[81]

Some victims report that the inability of their husbands to adjust to the fact that they had been raped eventually made divorce the only viable solution.[82] Many of the problems rape victims encounter with their husbands or boyfriends seem, in part, due to these men believing common rape myths.[84] The men regard the women as tainted and blame them for their victimisation.[83]

As long as men are fixated on aggression and domination, rape and insensitive male responses to it will continue. The success of rape prevention is partly dependent on men ceasing to see women as 'trophies' for which they compete. Only when making love to a woman is not a conquest, will the power struggle between men not end in the violent assertion of power over women.

Alcohol

It is necessary to explore whether alcohol has an exacerbating effect on rape-promoting factors which are not explicitly sexual. This is especially required because of the widespread use of alcohol in Riverlea. While alcohol appears to be consumed by the majority of men, the level of consumption seems to differ according to the man's family history of alcoholism, life dissatisfaction and the desire to escape from society's pressures and expectations.

The issue of whether alcohol increases male sexual arousal has been the subject of debate. In general, research indicates that large amounts of alcohol inhibit sexual responsiveness.[85] However, low levels of alcohol intake are said to 'promote sexual activity by lowering inhibitions, causing euphoria and greasing the wheels of social interactions'.[86] Some researchers have posited a physiological relationship between sexual arousal and alcohol, while others have argued that alcohol is the only socially acceptable excuse for relating in ways ordinarily unacceptable in more sober social surroundings.[87] Without wishing to delve into the pros and cons of the debate, it appears that whatever the cause, alcohol does heighten sexual responsiveness.

Aggression has also been related to alcohol intake.[88] As with the debate about alcohol and sexual arousal, there has been wide discussion about whether alcohol's effect on aggression is actually physiological or the consequence of societal beliefs and expectations.[89] Again, a similar conclusion is reached – for whatever reason, alcohol can evoke aggression.

Male socialisation has meant that aggression is often translated into violence. Alcohol, by acting as a disinhibitor, accelerates this process. Thus when people are under the influence of alcohol, events like the ones described by two rapists are not uncommon:

> I start fighting when I am drunk . . . I was at a party, and when I ran out, there was this other guy. Then he shook me and I don't take any shit when I am drunk. I grabbed him and I hit him and when I turned my back he stabbed me in the back . . . I don't feel good fighting, it's just alcohol that makes me do it.

> When I'm drunk I can't control myself . . . One other night . . . when we were sitting and drinking at another friend's place, then that story [about who owned the Valium] came up again. I got aggressive. I just started hitting, then he pushed me and I fell with my back on the railing there . . . and I fell next to a bottle, and that was the first time I stabbed someone.

In her study *Web of Violence*, Renvoize provides data on alcohol's effect on physical violence.[90] She cites the Addiction Research Unit of the Institute of Psychiatry in England, who found that fifty percent of a sample of one hundred alcoholics had beaten their wives. Giving evidence to Britain's Select Committee on Violence, the Tyneside Marriage Guidance Council stated that:

> Drinking is almost invariably associated with violent behaviour on the part of the husband. Newcastle Brown Ale seems to make husbands very aggressive and lowers their

'frustration tolerance level' so that what would, in other circumstances, invoke a harsh word, now invokes a blow.[91]

Low frustration tolerance is related to another feature of drinking, which some men from the present study admitted to – losing control and memory loss. Two members of the Physically Violent group commented:

You just lose your mind.

Drinking . . . blackens your whole mind.

A member of the Rape group stated:

> That's why I don't like to drink . . . when I'm drunk I can't control myself. Like one occasion with my friend, I was sitting in Newclare in his car, I just decided I must walk home. And I can't remember that.

What then is the scenario when a woman rejects the sexual advances of an intoxicated man who has a low frustration tolerance and has the potential to lose control and think irrationally? Taking into account that rejection sometimes means devaluation of masculinity, it is possible that, 'unable to retaliate with lucid verbalisation, the intoxicated participant may resort to some other techniques of establishing his identity and saving face'.[92] One of these techniques is rape.

A rapist's statement that 'I feel strong but I am not that kind of person when I am sober . . . When I am drunk I feel big', highlights two important implications that alcohol has for identity change. The first is that in his intoxicated state, the man loses touch with his previous moral and social codes and thus behaves in a manner inconsistent with these codes. The second, related implication is that a man who feels inadequate might want to demonstrate the new-found strength alcohol has provided him with through rape.

Considering Goode's findings – that in forty percent of cases involving male sexual aggression, the offender was classified drunk;[93] and the fact that alcohol tends to magnify some of the attitudes and behaviours contributing to rape; alcohol can be said to have a strong association with rape.

Thus far this study has placed alcohol and other rape-promoting factors within the context of the social control of women, sexist ideology and men's life experiences of sexual insecurity, alienation and powerlessness. Rape, it has been argued, helps transform some of the negative feelings that result from these life experiences. In order to study this proposal in finer detail, this study now moves from an examination of the causes of rape to focus on the rapist's experience during and after the rape.

Notes

1 Bell, 1981.
2 1977, page 13.
3 1938, page 378; cited in Kelvin and Jarrett, 1985.
4 1974.
5 Turner, 1972.
6 1981, page 111.
7 Miller, 1941.
8 1941.
9 1939.
10 1972.
11 Eisenhower, 1969; Katzenbach, 1967.
12 1967, page 193.
13 1965.
14 1979.
15 1975.
16 Marsden, 1978; MASA, no date.
17 1979, page 148.
18 1979.
19 Erlanger, 1974, page 285.
20 1971.
21 Cited in Davis, 1982.
22 Page 181.
23 Page 181.
24 1971.
25 McDonald, 1971, page 51; MacKeller, 1975.
26 1975, page 72.
27 1975.
28 1975, page 194.
29 1974, page 163.
30 Amir, 1971; Herman, 1979; Schiff, 1969; Shapiro and Shapiro, 1979.
31 MASA, no date.
32 1979, page 147.
33 MASA, no date.
34 *The Star*, 22 October 1988.
35 22 October 1988.
36 Davis, 1979.
37 MASA, no date, page 5.
38 Bell, 1981.
39 *Weekly Guardian*, 27 November 1988.

40 *Weekly Guardian*, 27 November 1988.
41 1979, page 469.
42 1971.
43 1983, page 67.
44 Gelles, 1974.
45 Marsden, 1978. Marsden believes that the likelihood of violence within the family is so high that one can identify the times of day and the places in the home where the violence will probably occur: 'the kitchen at teatime where the couple meet, ostensibly for a companionable meal but in fact to discharge the accumulated aggression of the day; the bedroom late in the evening, where the man returns after drinking; but not the bathroom where, despite the adverts, individuals tend to spend time alone' (page 112).
46 1971.
47 1974, page 85.
48 Berger and Berger, 1976.
49 Gelles, 1974; Renvoize, 1979.
50 1979, page 74.
51 1974, page 79.
52 1960.
53 Tanay, 1969.
54 Walters, 1975.
55 1977, page 24.
56 1974, page 25.
57 Bradbury, 1982; Pleck, 1979.
58 Bradbury, 1982.
59 Pleck, 1979.
60 Bradbury, 1982.
61 Tweedie in Levine and Koenig, 1983, page VI.
62 1960, page 165.
63 Paske, 1982.
64 Tweedie in Levine and Koenig, 1983, page VII.
65 1971.
66 Amir, 1971; Groth, 1979; Rabkin, 1979.
67 Deming and Eppy, 1981, page 364.
68 Brownmiller, 1975.
69 1974, page 12.
70 Bell, 1981; Brownmiller, 1975; Field, 1978; Herman, 1979; Mayne and Levett, 1977; Wilson, 1983.
71 Kipnis, 1972.
72 Griffin, 1971.
73 *Business Day*, 17 April 1989.
74 Paske, 1986.
75 Medea and Thompson, 1972.
76 1968.
77 1968, page 72. Cited in Medea and Thompson, 1972.
78 Medea and Thompson, 1972, page 33.
79 1974, page 96.
80 1978, page 61.
81 1981, pages 60-61.
82 Weis and Borges, 1973.
83 Levett, 1981.
84 Levett, 1981; Wilson, 1978.
85 Briddel and Wilson, 1976; Farkas and Rosen, 1976.
86 Gebhard, 1965, page 485.

87 Krech, Crutchfield and Livson, 1974.
88 Gelles, 1972.
89 Davidson and Neale, 1978.
90 Renvoize, 1979.
91 Cited in Renvoize, 1979, page 40.
92 Hepburn, 1973, page 425.
93 Goode, 1978.

Chapter Six

The rape

To date, academic and feminist research has tended to ignore the rapist's experience of rape. A far greater emphasis has been placed on the victim's experience of rape. Descriptions of her feelings and responses during and after the rape have been detailed in many works.[1] Such literature has advanced our understanding of rape and the struggle to eradicate it from the repertoire of human violence. It has also reduced the alienation experienced by many victims after being raped. For many of them, learning about other victims' experiences has reduced the social stigma of being raped and has helped them regain confidence and establish bonds of friendship and support with other women.[2]

But minimal research has been conducted into the rapist's behaviour and feelings during the rape; his response to his victim's possible resistance; his actions and feelings after the rape; and his treatment by the police and courts. In investigating these areas, the rapist's experiences will be detailed and analysed so that he – and his crime – can be better understood.

Events preceding rape

Rapists tend to exploit situations in which women are vulnerable to attack. This may mean raping women who are psychologically and economically powerless, physically disabled, mentally retarded, sleeping, very young or very old.[3] Rapists in this study took the opportunity of raping adult women who were hiking, standing alone, intoxicated, being sexually intimate or in need of an escort home. The common threads running through the rape situations described in this study are that the victims were alone, and that they were not in a position to easily defend themselves.

According to the rapists, many of the rapes were preceded by the woman being in a sexually intimate situation with another man or the offender himself. An example of the former is the rapist who waited for a friend to finish having sex with a girl and then proceeded to rape her with the assistance of another friend:

> There was a girl, we were in the same standard. I also heard she was a girl who mucks around. We went to another friend's flat. He was busy with her and I watched through the louvre doors – and I see the guy busy and then he's finished. Then one of my classmates came with me . . . and held her legs . . . and I had sex with her.

A superficial sexual encounter with a woman was the precursor to another rape:

> There was this girl, Rosemary. We were in the park and were kissing, kissing, kissing. Then I wanted to pull her panties down – she said 'no'. Then I said, ek sal jou slaan. She sort of gave in and then we had sex.

The behaviour of Rosemary's rapist again exposes the destructive effects of 'all or nothing' sexual standards. Many men expect to have sexual intercourse if the woman expresses sexual affection. Women's refusal to go 'all the way' is therefore frequently a forerunner to men's use of force and coercion.

Location

The majority of rapes are perpetrated in relatively safe environments where the victim is alone and the rapist will not be seen or interrupted. In this study, the most common location for rape was the victim's or rapist's home. Approximately fifty-five percent of rapes were committed in one of these locations.[4] The second most common place was large open spaces. Just over forty-four percent of rapes were committed in the veld or parks distant from highly populated areas.

These findings closely approximate those of other research. Figures from various studies of rapes occurring within all types of homes (rapist's, victim's and other homes) are as follows: Amir – sixty-seven percent; MacDonald – fifty-eight percent; Medea and Thompson – fifty-seven percent; and Peters, Meyer and Carroll – fifty-two percent.[5] This study encountered no reports of rapes in cars. Research into car rapes has yielded widely differing results: Amir – fifteen percent; MacDonald – twenty-six percent; Peters, Meyer and Carroll – eight and a half percent; and Svalasgota – four percent.[6] According to Medea and Thompson, eighteen percent of all unreported rape cases take place in a car, and twenty percent of such rapes occur in parks and alleys.[7]

The conclusion drawn from these statistics is that both public and domestic locations may be perilous. The myth that women can avoid rape by avoiding dark alleys should be laid to rest.

The location of rapes indicates that a sizeable proportion of rapes are planned. In the example described below, the rapist's immense desire for 'sexual gratification' did not make him rape the 'girl' on the dancefloor. He managed to control his sexual urges and at the same time think about finding a private place:

> We went to the disco and I left my girlfriend at home. I danced with this one girl and without me trying anything, she was keeping me warm and I thought this is my chance. The first thing in my mind is sex. I danced a few numbers and took her out. Then I remembered a nice place, no one is there, it's not in town, it's past Eldorado Park. We went outside under a tree, there was no one around. I then took her, she had no chance.

In the above case, the woman appears to have been sexually assertive. But 'liberation' from feminine passivity is an ambiguous advantage for women. For while women now supposedly have the right to choose whom they want to have sex with and when, they are still trapped by society's double standards of respectability. When women walk late at night, hitchhike or go to discos or shebeens by themselves, they may be called 'loose' and regarded as easy, even 'fair', targets. These were the insinuations the victim, in the case cited above, had to endure. Medea and Thompson write:

> A woman can say 'no' all day, but if she has gotten herself

into what, by Victorian standards, is a compromising situation, she will not be believed. At the present time, the rapist
has the best of both worlds – women who are taking more
risks, and a society which says that if they take those risks
they deserve whatever they get.[8]

Timing

This study does not include data on the frequency of rape during
various seasons, days of the week or times of the day. Katz and
Mazur have assessed much of the literature dealing with this issue.[9] They conclude that there is a higher incidence of rape in the
evenings, on weekends and during the summer months. If we accept the rationale that 'summer allows greater opportunity for rape,
because more social intercourse occurs', then we must also accept
the implication that rape often entails social contact between rapist
and victim prior to the rape.[10] This serves to undermine the myth
that rape is a spontaneous act committed mainly by strangers.

The rapist's experience

In the interests of clarity, the rapist's experience has been broken
up into component parts, although these are clearly interconnected. They include the rapist's pattern of interaction, which tends
to involve the threat of force, actual force and various other
manipulatory techniques; the rapist's responses to his victim's behaviour; the language which the rapist uses; his sexual behaviour
during the rape; the length of the rape; and the rapist's feelings
during the rape.

Patterns of interaction

When men have power over women, the possibility of rape exists.
During rape, power may be expressed in different ways. Tedeschi,
Schlenker and Bonoma describe two different patterns of interaction used to gain power in a two-person encounter.[11] Both of these
patterns were employed by rapists in this study. The first is an
open method of coercion whereby the assertion of power is not con-

cealed. The second mode of interaction involves manipulation. With this method, the power-seeker's intent is disguised. Rapists in this study tended to favour the open method of coercion, using either the threat of force or force itself. At times, however, this mode of interaction was interspersed with manipulatory techniques.

Threat of force

Instilling fear is an effective means of ensuring compliance. Rapists instil fear by making a variety of threats which focus on the victim's social and physical vulnerability. The threat of physical assault is the most recurrent. Four rapists in the present study commented:

> I will say 'ek sal jou slaan', then she sort of gives in . . . With Charmaine, Abigail, Rose, I've done it, say, about three or four times.

> I threatened to beat her and she must have got scared.

> I didn't klap her. I only threatened her. I didn't even have to say any onbeskofde words.

> I never slap for sex. I sometimes say, I am going to slap you.

To give more weight to their threats of physical injury, some rapists display their weapons and what their weapons are capable of to their victims:

> No weapons were used on her. We would take out a knife and show her but not do anything with it.

The same rapist said of his experience in another rape:

> When we got to the veld, I took out my gun and fired a shot into the air to frighten her. She was frightened because she could see that it wasn't a toy.

The exhibition and use of violent weapons serve another purpose – that of validating masculinity and power. By demonstrating to his victim his ability to handle aggressive armoury, the rapist en-

gages in traditional machismo behaviour and at the same time illustrates his domination over the woman. In this case, firing into
the air displayed a lack of concern about the gun's noise. This
would have increased the victim's fear and feelings of helplessness,
for the rapist's confidence that he would not be heard meant he
believed her screams for assistance would be futile, and it certainly meant they would not halt his sexual assault.

Other intimidatory tactics employed by rapists include the threat
of incarceration and attacks on the victim's social respectability.
Both these mechanisms were successfully utilised by a rapist against
a young woman:

> She had to give in, because she knew if she's not going to
> give in, then I'm not going to let her go home, because I'm
> going to keep her there the whole night. I just told her, 'if
> you not going to give it, I'm not going to let you go home.
> You'll sleep right here.'
>
> I wanted to rape her, but then I took on second thoughts
> and thought 'no'. I know her and she knows me, let me rather
> talk nicely . . . I told her, you must not come with your shit
> here. You must give me, otherwise it's bad and I'm going
> to tell everybody. You know, just making up stories.

The rapist's statement reveals his distorted conception of what it
means to rape or to 'talk nicely'. It also illustrates how society's
sexual double standards protect men and trap women. If anyone's
respectability should be endangered, it is the rapist's rather than
the rape victim's. Yet this rapist had such confidence in society's
prejudice against women who engage in sexual intimacy, that he
used the threat of social censure to gain further control over his
victim. Thus men's power to define women's social respectability
and worth was instrumental in this rape.

Research reveals that threats and overt intimidation are crucial
components of rape. Amir, for example, reports that in eighty-seven
percent of rape cases, the rapist either possesses a weapon or threatens the victim with death.[12] Those who deny that rape occurs,
and joke that 'a pencil cannot be inserted through a moving dough-
nut', fail to acknowledge that the victim faces menacing threats,
and that by the time sexual intercourse occurs, she 'has been ter-
rorized into co-operating with her assailant or is immobilized with
fear'.[13] The rape victim's failure to physically resist rape does not

indicate ambivalence towards her assailant, as some defence attorneys argue. Passivity reflects fear. That fear inhibits physical resistance is understood in relation to other crimes, such as mugging, but in the case of rape, primarily because of the prevalence of rape myths, failure to resist is repeatedly equated with acquiescence.

Use of physical violence

The majority of rapists do not stop at threats, and actually employ physical force. Amir has estimated that in over eighty-five percent of reported rapes, the victim endured some sort of physical violence.[14] Roughness was used in over twenty-eight percent of the cases; non-brutal beatings in just under twenty-five percent; brutal beatings in more than twenty percent; and choking in close to twelve percent. Van Ness reports that the majority of youthful rape offenders attacked their victims with guns or knives.[15] Clearly, if sadistic threats instil fear, then actual violence terrorises the victim even further.

One of the most common constituents of 'rough' behaviour is the forceful removal of the victim's clothes. For the victim, exposure of her naked body to a terrifying, hating attacker is a source of great humiliation. In addition to setting the tone for more gruesome violence, aggressive removal of the victim's clothes indicates the rapist's determination to accomplish his goal. Statements from two rapists substantiate this:

> I pulled off her trousers and gave her a smack. Then she started to lie there more still.

> I wanted to have sex – she didn't want to have sex with me. She was fighting back crossing her legs. And then I pulled off her boob tube and she pulls it up and I go and pull it off again. Eventually I got it down and then I struggle opening up her legs and all that.

In the second case, the woman had initially physically demonstrated her liking for the man. Yet he still found it necessary to use physical force. It appears that violence was used in order to guarantee completion of the sex act. This may be because the rapist, perhaps on the basis of previous experience, feared rejection. Alternatively, he may have believed that since the woman had consented to some sexual intimacy, he was entitled to her complete sexual submission.

As illustrated below, many of the rapists used moderate forms of violence. Rapists admitted to:

Holding her down with my hands.

Holding and opening up her legs.

Grabbing her by her tits.

Lay on top of her and forced her.

Use force – like keep her hand and pull down her panties.

There seems little doubt that if the victims in these cases had resisted more resolutely, moderate violence would have turned into brutal violence. In these instances, the process of rape had already begun, and the rapist was determined that no obstacle would prevent him from having sexual intercourse. One rapist reported that after threatening his victim and grabbing her by 'her tits', she continued to resist. He responded as follows:

How are you going to get that sexual excitement out of her, if she is not willing to have sex with you . . . You know how you get it, you become cross – I smacked her.

Some rapists do not even come close to the display of physical affection, and use violence immediately. A simple 'no' to sexual advances is sufficient to galvanise some rapists into brutalising their victims. Said one:

I was forced to do it because I couldn't control myself . . . Lots of times, I have used a lot of force. If I talk to a girl and she doesn't want to tell me the truth [that she wants to have sex with me], I smack her . . . if she still doesn't want to have sex with me . . . I would start hitting her.

Another rapist described one of his many violent rapes:

When I was seventeen, there was a girl that I used to like a lot. Now if there's a girl you like a lot and you make a date with her and she don't want to, you leave her — but she has to go out to the shop and so on. So you see her, and she still don't want to, so you grab her and pull her around, pull her in the dark, so she has to give in. You twist her hands and so on, and pull her to the ground. Actually I had to pull her to the ground with quite a lot of force and afterwards she had to give in.

The rapist's use of violence in response to female sexual rejection does not only serve to rid him of anger: it is also a declaration to his victim that no matter what she may do, he is still a 'man', still sexually and physically dominant. Through force he illustrates to her that she really does desire him — for despite her refusals, she is nevertheless having sex with him.

The rapist's impatience at not receiving instant sexual gratification further stimulates his violent behaviour. His socialised method of achieving instant solutions to problems is through violence (see Chapter 3). A rapist said:

A few kicks and smacks . . . is the quickest way. It's useless taking a cherry out and then sit the whole night and treat her nice. If you going to take her, what's the point, you are still going to be arrested.

Any discussion about mechanisms of coercion and physical violence in rape must examine the phenomenon of gang rape. Analagously to Amir's study, where close to forty-three percent of rape cases involved two or more offenders, the present study revealed that almost forty-five percent of rapists had engaged in gang rape.[16] The phenomenon of gang rape provides clues to men's brutal and deprecating treatment of women. Sketches of a few gang rapes described in this study will give the reader some sense of the ruthlessness of this crime:

One night, we saw two women standing at the gate. While we were talking with these two women, these fourteen ouens came up. We were all under the influence of liquor and we just decided at the same time that we are going to rape them. The one ran away, so there were about thirteen of us that rape the one woman . . . She was very 'dead'. They fucked her up, blue eyes and all . . . because she didn't want to take her pants off.

Another rapist stated:

> I was with the ouens [three or four] and we meet a cherry hiking . . . The big ous, they gave her a lift . . . We made her drink. From there she is in a hurry to get home and okay we are all deaf to that . . . It was a good fuck for a whole night . . . We were all standing around her. When one ou is finished, the next one comes.

The same rapist spoke of another of his gang rape experiences:

> We were eight ous riding around in Noordgesig. There were two cherries walking with some ous. And then this ou stopped and said let's rob of them. Then this lightie gripped this cherry and pushed her into the van . . and then we all got into her . . . We drove her to the veld and started fucking her. We gave her a few kicks and smacks . . . I gave her one or two kicks. Then we took her back to Noordgesig and dropped her on the highway.

What makes the gang rape unique is that even though it is a situation 'in which no brutality, no threat even, would be necessary to subdue the victim', sadistic violence occurs on a large scale.[17] Excessive force and debasement in rape point to other needs besides sexual gratification.[18] Thus in studying the gang rape syndrome, one discovers conformity pressure and the participant's need to prove his sexual competence and physical strength to the others involved in the rape. This desire stems from insecurities about masculinity and sexual prowess.

An example in the present study was the rapist who was concerned about the size of his penis during a gang rape: 'I was thinking about, I wonder whether she feels the difference inside her, you know, big and small.' Sexual anxiety of this sort may precipitate overcompensatory behaviour, resulting in intense degradation of the victim. Here the victim's feelings and responses may play a part in determining the degree of violence employed by the rapist.

The victim's behaviour and the rapist's response

More often than not, the victim does not passively accept her assailant's attack. She resists before or during the rape, or both. Her resistance may be related to her age, strength, her experience of violence and her confidence. According to Katz and Mazur, young girls are inclined to struggle less than adolescents and adults; working class women, who are often more familiar with violence, tend to resist physically more than their middle class counterparts, who are frequently strangers to violence and have been socialised to be 'ladies'; and women who are assertive and confident in day to day social situations resist the rapist more fiercely.[19] While these factors are of some significance, the primary factor determining the victim's resistance is the rapist's actions. In turn, his behaviour is influenced – to a lesser degree – by the victim's behaviour. From rapists' descriptions of their victims' resistance as described in this study, four broad categories of resistance have been identified: attention-seeking tactics; non-co-operation tactics; psychological tactics; and physical resistance.

Judging from an American study of victims' descriptions of resistance strategies during rape, rapists in this study have given a fairly consistent portrayal of their victims' resistance.[20] The American study published in *Psychiatric News* reported that

> eighteen percent [of victims] tried to determine possible alternatives, such as how to escape or wondering whether the assailant would panic; over half (fifty-seven percent) used a verbal tactic such as trying to talk themselves out of the situation, stalling for time, reasoning with the assailant by trying to change his mind, trying to gain sympathy from the assailant, using flattery, attempting to strike a bargain, feigning illness, threatening the assailant, trying to change the assailant's perception of the woman, joking and using sarcasm; and twenty-two percent employed the physical techniques of attempting to flee the scene, or fighting with the assailant. Naturally some victims used a combination of these strategies.[21]

Before delving into the four categories of victims' resistance, it must be stressed that resistance in this study has been discussed within the context of completed rapes. There are many accounts of successful resistance which have been documented elsewhere. One study, for example, claims that in one third of situations involving sexual aggression, the victim emerged victorious.[22] Successful resistance was primarily achieved through yelling (fifteen percent), physical resistance (eighteen percent) and fleeing (twenty-four percent).

Attention-seeking tactics

'She would shout oh no, no' was how a rapist characterised his victim's resistance. Shouting, screaming and yelling are the most common attention-seeking tactics. They are often the tactics first employed by the victim. In general, the rapist responds to his victim's verbal protestations either by verbally reassuring her that the situation is not as menacing as it seems, or by using physical force to silence her. In doing this, the rapist may also shift some responsibility for his act on to the victim. As one rapist stated:

> She did scream, but the way I was handling her was to say, you must not go on like this. You actually making me do it to you now.

Attention-seeking tactics appear to be successful only in public places. In other circumstances, they are largely ignored by the rapist. The development of hand-held gadgets which produce extremely loud sounds may be of use in scaring the rapist off. However, the high price of such technology makes it inaccessible to most working class women. Interestingly, none of the rapists in this study reported that any of their victims had protection gadgets.

Non-co-operation tactics

These tactics can involve refusing to remove clothing, or not assisting with the insertion of the penis into the vagina. Non-co-operation does not cause many difficulties for the rapist. He either tears the woman's clothes off or beats her up until she removes them. With regard to penetration, the rapist proceeds without the victim's assistance. He often makes penetration easier for himself by wetting his victim's vagina with his saliva, which he applies with his fingers.

Psychological tactics

Strategies that fall within this category include reasoning with the rapist, frightening or disgusting him, or trying to gain sympathy from him. The most assertive of these strategies is the victim's attempt to induce fear in the rapist through threats:

> She said she is going to tell her mother. She was still at school, she was seventeen. She said she will tell her friends. I said no man, what's she worried about her friends for.

In this example, the rapist went on to threaten her with physical assault and to rape her. Other rapists were similarly unmoved by the victim's endeavours to evoke sympathy. Said one rapist: 'She did it, but not willingly. She kept telling me she was a virgin and she is young and she is at school.' He did take some notice of her plea, however: 'I didn't want to do her harm, so I said she can keep my magazine [of the gun].' He proceeded to 'pomp her about three times'.

Begging and straightforward appeals for understanding also had little effect on the rapists studied. In one rape described to me, a woman was forcibly grabbed and pushed into a van by nine men. After they began physically assaulting her, she repeatedly requested that they release her. According to one of the rapists, she was saying, 'please guys, I don't know you. My mommy is going to shout and things like that. I can't go with you.' Her pleas fell on deaf ears. Six of the nine men brutally raped her.

A more sophisticated strategy employed by one victim was to attempt to evoke both sympathy and disgust in the rapist. Unfortunately, her gambit failed and the rapist responded even more aggressively.

> She came out with the story, she's sick and she has got a period. So I said to her, 'you mustn't speak shit with me'. I just wanted to have sex with her and she didn't have a period.

Although psychological tactics are clearly not always successful in preventing rape, Storaska believes they are the best method.[23] He believes women can almost always avert rape by adopting strategies based on a personality assessment of the rapist. Strategies including complimenting the rapist on his personality or physical build, engaging in lengthy conversations, being vulgar (burping, urinating, defecating, vomiting),[24] informing the rapist one has a venereal disease or Aids, or behaving in a bizarre fashion to defuse his sexual response.

Physical resistance

None of the rapists told of victims who maintained concerted physical resistance throughout the rape. However, fifty-five percent did report some form of physical rebuff from their victims. Two of the rapists spoke of victims who pushed their hands away or grabbed them so as to prevent being hit:

> So when I started pulling down her panties, she started pushing my hands away. So I asked her why she's doing that, doesn't she want to have sex with me. So she says no, she doesn't, she's not that kind of person, she only just fucks around. Like me, I got naar, so I forced her.

> She grabbed my hand because she thought I was going to hit her again, but I wasn't going to hit her.

Another form of resistance, which only temporarily bothered the rapists, entailed the victim crossing her legs and pushing her assailant away from her body. A rapist described his response to this tactic:

> We were laying there – I wanted to have sex, she didn't want to have sex with me. She was fighting back, crossing her legs . . . Then I struggled opening her legs . . . The clothes she had on were very loose and it was easy to get my hand up . . . her cunt. She was trying to take it out, I said no leave it there, I have felt it already; and I convinced her and she left it there. And then I pulled off her brooks . . . I screwed her.

The rapist sometimes meets the victim's attempt to push him away by lying on top of her with increased weight, and by using more violence. This response was also employed by a rapist who had to deal with biting and scratching – 'she started getting excited and biting . . . scratching too . . . I just stayed on top of her'. Of course, rapists do not always behave so calmly when confronted with this form of resistance. Said one rapist:

> They bite you, here on the chest, so you have to smack her and so on . . . After that she must be scared . . . she had to give in.

Physical resistance does not necessarily inhibit the rapist's will to continue with the act. In fact, it can have the opposite effect. Fifty-five percent of the rapists in this study said they became more 'excited' when their victims resisted. This may be because resistance provided the opportunity for heightened use of aggression and force. Answers to the question 'Did her struggling excite you?' took this form:

> You enjoy it more having to struggle first. When other girls just say okay just come, you don't enjoy yourself like that. You have to struggle first and she has to make you hot.

> It did, because now I was more determined to, now she must come, she must give.

> It did make me more excited. It made me feel I wanted it more.

> Yes . . . you want to have sex and so you think I must get it right.

The fact that rapists find resistance titillating again illustrates that the pleasure of raping lies in the assertion of power, and not merely in the achievement of sexual orgasm. During an interview, a rapist told Groth:

> You know, I could get all the sex I wanted because my brother ran a chain of massage parlours. But if they were giving it to me, I wasn't in control. I wanted to take it.[25]

However, rapists do not always enjoy continual resistance. Eighty-eight percent of rapists in this study wanted their victims to resist less. How is this apparent contradiction explained?

It appears that while the victim's resistance does increase the rapist's sexual excitement, this excitement does not match the gratification provided by a more co-operative victim. Ideally, the rapist craves a victim who resists slightly: her struggling enables him to conquer her and experience corresponding feelings of power and control. At the same time, he can interpret the weakness of her resistance as a signal that she really desires him sexually. Considering that none of the victims vigorously physically resisted rape, it was not surprising to discover that sixty-six percent of the rapists believed their victims were 'playing hard to get' or enjoyed the rape. One rapist stated:

> She didn't try and stop me, that's what surprised me. The way I see it, she just wanted to play hard to get.

Two other rapists said:

> She would try to resist . . . She was kind of playing hard to get, but if you were to check the scene like yourself, then you would have seen that she wanted it to happen. She wanted it to happen in a nice way.

> I was holding and opening her legs . . . but afterwards I don't think this could be rape . . . because she didn't really fight back. She did say, no she doesn't want to do it, but maybe she did.

For the rapist, slight resistance is part of the act. Some rapists believe women really enjoy rape. The majority of the rapists made comments such as:

> She did look scared – it was her first time. She wanted it also.

> She enjoyed it.

> This girl enjoyed the sex because she had a smile on her face.

With comments of this sort, rapists deny their own violence. In this study, most of the rapists used just sufficient violence to commit the offense, and then downplayed the existence of coercion. Because rapists do not see women as self-determining individuals, they often characterise their rape as a 'seduction'.[26] The idea of a sexually satisfied rape victim also helps the rapist minimise any guilt feelings he may experience after the rape (see Chapter 7). If apprehended, the rapist often conveys this perception by portraying himself as a benefactor and a sexually generous man – 'she wanted and I gave it to her'.

The question of whether women should be unco-operative and physically resist rape has been widely debated. Those favouring active revolt point to the many cases where potential victims have successfully resisted rape through attention-seeking tactics and physical resistance.[27] Those opposed to this position express concern that active resistance might provoke additional violence.[28] A gruesome illustration of the violence that resistance can provoke is given by Wood.[29] She quotes Lear, who tells of a thirty-seven year old woman who required one hundred and twenty stitches in her face and head after physically resisting a man who tried to rape her in New York's Central Park. A detective said of this case:

> We've been looking for this guy for a long time. Two years ago we picked him up for attempted rape, and it was a throwout in court; no corroboration. Now we have this poor woman, who fought like hell and didn't get raped. The guy has been indicted for assault in the first degree. She's scarred for life. And you know what she says now? She says she wishes she hadn't fought, and maybe he wouldn't have cut her up the horrible way he did.[30]

It is on the basis of such incidents that some researchers suggest that if resistance is to be employed, it should be done through manipulatory or psychological means rather than physical techniques.[31]

It emerges from this study that active resistance is unlikely to be effective in rape locations which are private, or with rapists who are extremely violent from the start of the rape. In these situations, psychological tactics may be more successful. However, in more public locations, active resistance may scare the rapist, who wishes to avoid detection. This is less the case in gang rapes, where there may be public support for the offence. *Time* detailed one such disturbing case:

Last March, a twenty-one year old mother of two walked into
Big Dan's tavern in New Bedford, Massachussetts, to buy
a pack of cigarettes. A man in the bar threw her to the floor,
stripped her and hoisted her onto a pool table, where he and
three companions took turns raping, sodomizing and beating the woman. Other patrons cheered the rapists on, screaming, Go for it! Go for it![32]

This was the rape on which the laudable film 'The Accused' was
largely based. The film emphasises the complicity of those men
who did not rape but cheered the rapists on. What is frightening
about this incident – and there are others like it – is that the rapists
felt they needn't employ any caution in concealing their rape. The
presumption was that all the men would support them. This incident, more than most, illustrates the meaning of a 'culture of rape'.

Resistance and consent

Lack of resistance does not imply consent. The police, courts and
many members of the public frequently fail to understand this.
For some courts, lack of consent must be supported by a great deal
of evidence. The victim must be able to prove that she 'actively
resisted the attack and attempted to prevent sexual intercourse from
occurring, regardless of the risk she ran doing so. If there is no
such evidence, then her consent will be assumed. Saying "no" is
apparently not enough, even in the face of physical violence.'[33]
    Rape is the only crime where insufficient resistance is equated
with consent. Taking into account the wide variety of coercive tactics employed by rapists, the law should view the victim's lack of
resistance not as consent, but as submission.[34]
    Inadequate acknowledgement of the coercion entailed in rape der-
ives partly from prevailing sexist ideology and rape myths. A woman must avoid being sexually tainted by a stranger at any cost. If
she values her sexuality above all else, she must be prepared to
defend it at all costs. Sometimes only this conduct will guarantee
some redress from the law. As Clark and Lewis put it, 'either she
must see her sexual organs as more important than anything else,
even her life, or we will not punish those who attack her sexual
organs'.[35]

The rapist's speech

Verbal abuse adds to the emotional damage created by physical abuse. The rapist's insulting language intensifies his victim's humiliation. In his eyes she is nothing more than 'cunt', 'pig meat', or a 'juicy little bitch'.

A rapist in this study reports an incident in which verbal abuse was used during a gang rape. He said, 'it was not talking – it was more like making fun of her':

> She was sitting in the van and five of us were laying there in the back, watching her and shouting about her body.

Demeaning comments were a feature of a rape perpetrated in the victim's house. Immediately prior to the rape, the victim was voluntarily having sex in her bedroom with one of the rapist's friends, while he and two other friends sat speaking in the lounge. The three then entered and proceeded to rape the woman. They were assisted by the man with whom she had been having sex who said to the victim as she was being raped: 'You can give my round to the others. I mean, it's still a cock.' This statement made the woman a sexual object. It presumed she was unaffected by whom the penis belonged to.

Earlier mention was made of verbal threats as a means of coercion. Occasionally this strategy leads to unexpected consequences. Instead of immobilising the victim, threats may engender hysteria. The rapist often alternates between physical aggression and verbal reassurance to control his victim's emotional protestations. In the cases described below, rapists tried to convince their victims that the rape wasn't so bad, or reassured them that their sexual encounter would soon be coming to an end:

> I would say isn't that nice and so on, or you see, we are nearly finished, why were you so scared? . . . She would say, no leave me, leave me . . . I would say okay just hold on, I will be finished now.

> One ou would touch her or tell her to have a cigarette while she is having sex to try and make her feel lekker.

> It was sore, you know how the first time a girl does it, she

can't take it. She started crying and I just kept it in and said,
it's going to be over now my dear.

She started to scream, and I just cuddle her and said, don't
be like that, it will be nice.

Ignorance of women's sexual responses and feelings is such that
the rapist can suggest to the victim that her rape experience 'will
be nice'. Rapists often confuse domination and sexual affection so
thoroughly that they see themselves as lovers. Rape is an act of
aggression and hatred, yet a rapist still called his victim 'my dear'.
For him the line between sex and violence is extremely thin.

The rapist's sexual behaviour during rape

The majority of rapists did not give any detailed account of their
sexual behaviour during the rape. Those that did appeared to have
incorporated a substantial amount of aggression and defilement into
their sexual activity. For instance, two rapists who participated in
a gang rape stated:

Then she gave in and we had sex. She was bleeding afterwards, I think it was because of the way I was forcing it in.
Also I think it was her first time.

We made her suck cocks. Sometimes we try and make it like
an orgy. There was one time with three or four of us and
everybody doesn't want to wait.

Yet it is the very use of aggression and physical force that often
inhibits the rapist's sexual enjoyment. To have their masculinity
validated, rapists have to believe that their victims wanted them
sexually. Thus when co-operation is lacking and force prevalent,
rapists may feel cheated and unsatisfied:

You don't enjoy it . . . because she is not willing to give you.

You can't get your satisfaction out of this woman lying there
like a piece of pole in front of you. A woman you rape will
never give you her best.

What does this mean for the rapist's sexual behaviour during the rape? In this study, none of the rapists made any mention of erections or orgasms. Consequently, all information on this issue is drawn from the work of other researchers. Literature on the subject is sparse, however.

Some rapists complain they have difficulty in achieving erection and orgasm. Levine and Koenig document the statement of one offender who spoke to Douglas Jackson in a filmed interview:

> She soon quit struggling. I pulled up her nightclothes and fondled her and caressed her and she cried and told me to leave her alone. Eventually I tried to rape her, I never did rape her. I tried a number of times to rape her, and this went on for three to four hours. I tried for a while to quit. She was lying on the floor and I told her not to move.
>
> During the time I was there I became more and more upset. I became more frightened that she would recognise me and I would be caught. Also I was upset that I couldn't rape her, that I couldn't maintain an erection, that I was impotent, and none of my fantasies were coming true. That really upset me.[36]

Some rapists have problems in maintaining an erection when they believe they are involved in a rape rather than a seduction.

Clark and Lewis have provided some statistics on the frequency of erection and orgasm among rapists.[37] In sixty-two percent of cases, no mention was made of orgasm. Only seven percent of rapists gave an unqualified confirmation of orgasm. Twenty-one percent admitted to not achieving orgasm, and just over ten percent to achieving orgasm with difficulty. Thus in thirty-three percent of reported rape cases, the rapist had problems with orgasm. According to Paske:

> Generally in psychiatric literature sexual dysfunction as a whole is correlated with psychological mood, states of anxiety, depression and anger as well as with conflicts regarding sex – viewed as negative or dirty, as dangerous, etc. These same factors are prominent characteristics of rapists.[38]

It should also be noted that in over half of the cases studied, problems with orgasm were associated with difficulties with erection.[39] From these figures, Clark and Lewis concluded that:

> A significant proportion of those who are labelled 'rapists'
> and, in the popular mythology, have excessive sexual appe-
> tites, are incapable of achieving orgasm in the rape situation.
> There is obviously a certain amount of irony in this
> paradox.[40]

Unfortunately, as the statement from the rapist interviewed by
Jackson illustrates, this paradox involves a bitter irony for the victim. It is precisely because the rapist is unable to achieve erection
or orgasm that the victim's forcible confinement is prolonged. In
this extended period, she has to endure further deprecation, and
sometimes degrading sexual acts. To compensate for his anxiety
about being impotent, and to demonstrate his sexual competence
and manhood, the rapist may ejaculate over the victim's face and
body; urinate on her; or insert into the victim's vagina bed legs,
broomsticks or bottles.[41] Thus instead of discouraging him from
raping his victim, the rapist's incompetent sexual behaviour often
results in more serious physical – and psychological – injury to
the victim.

Another irony of the rapist's sexual dysfunction is the legal consequences it may have after the offence. The rapist's defence team
may assert that since no sperm was found in the woman's vagina,
rape could not have occurred.[42] It is in the light of this that Paske
comments: 'The lack of sperm in the alleged victim's vagina does
not preclude the possibility that she was indeed raped.'[43]

Duration of the rape

No information was forthcoming regarding the exact duration of
rapes. Some rapists reported raping their victims for 'two hours'
and 'a whole night'. The length of these rapes could be the result
of problems with erection or orgasm, or prolonged desire to de-
base and humiliate the victim.

The rapist's feelings during the rape

The rapist's primary feelings during the rape have already been documented. Feelings of sexual enjoyment, sexual exasperation, power, control and insecurity have all emerged.

The four quotations cited below reveal rapists' principal feelings to be of power, control and strength. This bears out one of the central contentions of this study, namely that the primary motivation for rape is the offender's need for power, which he attains through sexual conquest:

I was kind of excited, not sexually, I just thought I am stronger than her and she has to do what I want.

I feel strong . . . It feels good to make a girl scared . . . It feels good because she is listening to you.

I felt . . . I was the best, I had put her down . . . It made me feel even better . . . to know I am a man because a woman is bowing down to you.

It was nice, she was a very young cherry [fifteen years old] . . . I scheme it's because they are inexperienced and it is more exciting because they don't know what is happening.

These feelings are not only a product of the rapist's sexual and emotional insecurities. They are also an extension of what society teaches to be appropriate male emotions. The offender's feelings during the rape support the contention that the rapist is engaged in a search for validation of his masculinity. This, as will be documented in Chapter 7, is partly achieved through the objectification of women. Greater insight into the rapist's attitude towards his victim and his crime will be gained by examining his behaviour and feelings after the rape has been committed.

Notes

1 Brownmiller, 1975; Connell and Wilson, 1974; Levett, 1981; Medea and Thompson, 1972; Russell, 1975.
2 Connell and Wilson, 1974.
3 Selkin, 1975.
4 According to Selkin (1975), older homes which have been transformed into 'flats' are the easiest residences for a rapist to enter. Basement or first floor flats are

also particularly dangerous. Selkin found that of all the rapes that occurred in buildings in Denver (United States), two thirds were committed in the basement or on the ground floor. He claims that large apartments with security guards are the most difficult residences for rapists to enter.

5 Amir, 1971; MacDonald, 1971; Medea and Thompson, 1974; Peters, Meyer and Carroll, 1976.
6 Amir, 1971; MacDonald, 1971; Peters, Meyer and Carroll, 1976; Svalasgota, 1962.
7 Medea and Thompson, 1974. Another popular location for rape is the hospital. MacDonald (1971) remarks that hospital rapes take place 'with more frequency than is generally recognised. Young children and unconscious patients in general hospitals and some psychotic, mentally retarded or senile patients in mental hospitals are particularly vulnerable to attack' (page 35).
8 1974, page 45.
9 Katz and Mazur, 1979.
10 Katz and Mazur, 1979, page 133.
11 Tedeschi, Schlenker and Bonoma, 1973.
12 Amir, 1971.
13 Selkin, 1975, page 71.
14 1971.
15 1984.
16 1971.
17 Medea and Thompson, 1974, page 36.
18 Deming and Eppy, 1981.
19 1979.
20 *Psychiatric News*, 1975.
21 *Psychiatric News*, 1975, no page number available.
22 Denver Anti-Crime Council Report, no date.
23 Storaska, 1975.
24 Storaska, 1975.
25 Cited in *Time*, 5 September 1983.
26 Clark and Lewis, 1977.
27 Finkelhor and Yllo, 1982; Medea and Thompson, 1974; Russell, 1975; Selkin, 1975.
28 Storaska, 1975.
29 Wood, 1974, page 150.
30 Lear, 1972, page 11.
31 Storaska, 1975.
32 5 September 1983, page 52.
33 Clark and Lewis, 1977, page 162.
34 Clark and Lewis, 1977; Robin, 1977.
35 Clark and Lewis, 1972, page 165.
36 Levine and Koenig, 1983, page 32.
37 Clark and Lewis, 1977.
38 1982, page 53.
39 Clark and Lewis, 1977.
40 1977, page 107.
41 Clark and Lewis, 1977; Herman, 1979.
42 Paske, 1982.
43 1982, page 57.

Chapter Seven

The aftermath of rape

Thus far we have investigated why men rape and how they feel while raping. But how does the rapist feel when the rape is over? An examination of the rapist's behaviour and feelings after the event, his rationalisation for raping and the way in which he is treated by the police and courts increases our understanding of the destructive consequences of men's objectification of women. This chapter will also illustrate some of the reasons why so few women report rape, and who so many rapists go undetected and rape again.

The rapist's behaviour after the rape

Most rapists in the present study were very calm immediately after the rape. They gave no indication of nervousness or panic and made no attempt to flee the scene of their crime. The only rapist motivated by some feelings of guilt remained with his victim and attempted to persuade her not to exaggerate the significance of what he had done to her:

> I was sobering up, the first thing I asked her is, are you cross with me? She said, very cross, so I start reacting, I start taming myself down. You know something is telling me, something I did is wrong, so I started to explain to her nicely . . . it's no use if you take it seriously, you know that I like you.

Another man who had raped several times felt sufficiently confident to escort his victim to a place of safety:

After I had finished with her, I walked with her back to the shop. On the way, she went into a house and I schemed it must be a friend's house because she was from Pretoria. When she got inside, she started crying, so I split.

The same confidence was shown by a third rapist who escorted his victim back to the discoteque they had come from. On arrival, however, he attempted to humiliate her by 'playfully' insinuating to his friends that she was a prostitute:

We went back to the disco. There was grass in my hair – I never knew – and I had on white pants and I had a few patches on my knee. At the entrance, it has bright lights. As I was about to go in, I saw my friends and they started laughing and asked, what's going on? I told them, no, I tried, but she didn't want to come down in price.

Another rapist's comments exemplify the rapist's denial of the pain he has inflicted on another person. His insensitivity was such that he decided not to tell his friends about the rape in case he wanted to rape the woman again:

Because I know if this woman don't send me to jail, then I can go to her tomorrow and I can ask her again for it. But if I tell someone else, then maybe she will put me in jail.

Rapists' behaviour immediately after the rape suggests that they are unaware of their victims' feelings towards them. Most of them do not acknowledge the brutality of their crime, and don't believe their behaviour is a violation of another human being. They tend to perceive their actions as being beyond reproach, or perhaps as a slight misdemeanour.

Rapists' inhumane attitudes and actions after raping are logical extensions of their attitudes and behaviours towards their victims during the offence and towards women in everyday life. A lack of respect for women invariably results in a lack of caring for them. The fact that a rapist can walk his victim home or take her back to a disco and laugh about the rape without extreme fear of legal and social reprisals exhibits confidence that the victim will not report the attack, and shows too the acceptability of rape in our society.

The rapist's feelings after the rape

The rapist's feelings after raping can be divided into three basic categories:

(a) The 'no guilt and indifferent' feelings;
(b) The 'slight regret' feelings; and
(c) The 'remorseful' feelings.

A man who rapes repeatedly does not necessarily feel the same way after every rape. Depending on where, whom and how he rapes, the rapist's feelings may fall into any of the three categories. Usually, however, they fall into the 'no guilt and indifferent' and the 'slight regret but indifferent' categories, largely because of the rapist's sexist attitudes and behaviour.

No guilt and indifferent feelings

The type of rapist who escapes guilt feelings entirely is one who objectifies women excessively. For such a rapist, the concept of rape is inconceivable because women are not self-determining individuals with the right and ability to choose. Clark and Lewis describe a rape incident involving such an offender:

> When the victim told the suspect to keep his hands to himself, the offender slapped her across the face several times and called her a bitch and a slut . . . When the offender put his penis into her, 'I told him I was menstruating and he said that was all right, that I was only a pig anyway'.[1]

If a woman is seen as a non-human designed to satisfy men's desires, then her resistance to sexual intercourse becomes irrelevant. It can be expected that rapists operating within such a conceptual framework will have little compassion for their victims. Said one rapist of his feelings when he saw his victim in court: 'I didn't feel anything. I didn't feel sorry for her.'

Other rapists' feelings about their victims were similar:

> That girl, I don't care about her.

> Once you have finished with that [sex], you feel nothing for
> that girl. Once you have come, you think nothing about her.

Some rapists identify the kind of women about whom they would
feel indifferent after raping. These men see rape as particularly permissible when the victim is sexually promiscuous or has been designated a 'whore':

> Girls are different, some of them are whores, that's why with
> them, I do it, but not with decent girls.

> I didn't feel bad because she was also a kind of whore.

Women categorised as 'whores' are more objectified than other
women. They are seen as disposable sexual objects to be used and
then discarded. It is extremely difficult for the 'whore' to evoke
the rapist's sense of pity, regardless of the amount of physical torture she endures.

Rapists' feelings after committing rape contrast sharply with their
feelings after assaulting men. They do not see the men they attacked as objects undeserving of compassion. Men are believed to
have feelings and to be worthy of respect. Physically assaulting a
man elicits feelings of regret and compassion. One rapist commented on his feelings after fighting with another man:

> I felt bad to think I am fighting with my own. The ou has
> got a family and all. But in hospital we lay next to each other,
> so we talked it over and settled it.

There is a second category of rapist who expresses 'no guilt' feelings. These rapists attempt to absolve themselves, consciously or
unconsciously, from their rape by calling it seduction. It has been
earlier documented that domination and submission are part of
many rapists' conceptualisation of ideal sexual activity. Rapists,
therefore, believe their victim is playing 'hard to get' or is enjoying the rape experience (see Chapter 6). An extract from an interview with an imprisoned rapist (who had received rehabilitative
therapy) conducted by Douglas Jackson illustrates the extent of
the rapist's misguided perception of his offence:

> I slapped her in the head and then I proceeded to have inter-

course with her. After that, I helped her get dressed and I got dressed and combed her hair and made sure she had everything.

We walked away . . . I didn't think I'd committed rape. I figured that maybe if anything, I'd get flak from her parents about slapping her or mistreating her or something along that line.

I put her in a taxi and kissed her good-night and I paid the taxi driver and that was it. Then I went home. I was picked up the next day. The police came to my house and as far as I was concerned, I thought they were coming for dope or something like that. Later on, I found I was charged with rape so I had to go to jail for that.

I didn't believe it. No I didn't. It's not that I didn't want to. It's just that I couldn't understand. It was shocking.[2]

The rapist's failure to recognise his own violence means he has little reason to feel remorseful. He believes his victim enjoyed herself, has no right to complain and he need not feel guilty.

Slight regret feelings

Rapists with 'slight regret' feelings recognise their use of coercion in the rape, and feel slightly perturbed by such coercive behaviour. This concern, however, is minimal and superficial. This is evident in one rapist's feelings and behaviour after his offense:

I felt shit and thought, hey, why did I do it? I went to her and we spoke about it but then I told her, 'it's your own fault and you know it's not the first time we are doing it and it won't be the last'.

The rapist indicated his awareness that intercourse achieved through coercion is morally reprehensible. But his insensitivity and superficial awareness prevent the development of a long-term sense of concern and guilt. This rapist preferred to escape responsibility for his actions by blaming the victim. Furthermore, the rapist repressed full recognition of the violence of his behaviour by suggesting that his conduct was not unusual — it had occurred often in the past and would continue in the future.

Within a rape culture, there are few people who encourage the rapist to recognise the seriousness of his actions or assist him to change his ways. Friends of the rapist may in fact congratulate him on his achievement. One rapist reported:

> I told my friends about it . . . they laughed and said, how did you get that right? . . . We were all the same. What they did, they would come and tell me.

This rapist's friends not only laughed encouragingly at his having raped a woman, but also appeared to have discussed their own rape experiences and given advice on refining their rape techniques. Their open discussion does not reflect unrepressed personalities. Rather, it reflects a lack of shame. Rape, in a subculture such as that which exists amongst many men in Riverlea or in a society where aggression and male domination are highly valued, is an act to be boasted about.

The rapist's slight regret (which soon turns into no regret) can be traced to a number of sources. Firstly, there is the rapist's desire to see his victim again. This applies particularly when his victim is his girlfriend or lover. Said one rapist about his apology to his girlfriend for raping her:

> She would swear and curse me. 'You know a guy is out for fun,' I keep on telling her. Then I told her to shut up and after that we didn't talk for two weeks. Only after two weeks I went to say I was sorry, then I knew she would make up.

The second reason for the rapist's self-condemnation and slight regret is his fear that his victim will report the crime to the authorities. He may apologise, or tell her that he did not mean to rape her, or explain to her that he meant her no harm but was just looking for some 'fun'.

Another motivating factor behind the rapist's unease is his social conscience. Even though his peer group or subculture may support his actions, the rapist is aware that a small section of his community (church officials, social workers) regard rape as wrong. For while many churches have conservative views about the role of women, all churches view rape as a sinful and loathsome act. But despite the fact that most of the Riverlea community and the subjects in this study belong to the church, the church's anti-rape influence is likely to be minimal in the face of the personality features of the rapist and general social acceptance of the partnership of sexuality and aggression. As is the case with religion, social workers and the few anti-rape articles that appear in the media cannot be expected to influence the rapist sufficiently to change his sexually aggressive behaviour.

Remorseful feelings

Only one of the rapists in the present study could be said to have shown any real remorse after the rape. It should be noted, however, that the rapist in this particular case had raped three times and his feelings subsequent to the rape on two of these occasions fell within the 'slight regret but indifferent' category. He said of his feelings after his first rape:

> I really felt guilty. I never saw her again after that until the day of the court. And then I saw her parents and I can see she's from a respectable family and I felt guilty about it and I couldn't do anything.

Here again the distinctive treatment accorded the 'respectable woman' and 'whore' is manifest. Unlike the sexually promiscuous woman, the respectable woman is perceived as having feelings and sensations. Thus the rapist felt guilty because he acknowledged his victim's capacity to feel pain, and therefore his capacity to hurt. The extent of his guilt was not sufficient, however, to end his sexually aggressive behaviour, since he went on to rape two other women who were less socially respectable.

Rationalisation of rape

The rapists in the present study behaved brutally towards their victims. Yet they believed their victims enjoyed being raped and felt no compassion for them. Despite their belief in rape myths, however, every rapist in the study claimed that rape, *excluding* his own, was damaging to women. Its damage, they said, was to the victim's sense of pride and her social status. Two rapists said:

Most women feel bad about it. Sex against her will, it's not nice for her. For a woman who is a virgin, maybe she thinks she is going to have a nice clean wedding and then she gets raped. It takes her pride away. I don't really like rape.

It's a shit move. Like my daughter [who was raped], she can't go no more to the school. We had to send her away. If she goes to the same school, what will the children tell her, that she was raped.

Other comments from rapists which referred to the victim's trauma were:

They must feel shit. I'm sure, because I knew a girl . . . she went . . . off her head.

I think they despise being raped and they despise the man that raped them too.

There is an obvious contradiction between the rapists' beliefs and their actions. The lack of remorse and guilt after the rape suggests that offenders do not classify their own behaviour as rape, are unaware of the devastating effects of their actions or are somehow able to rationalise their crime. This does not mean, however, that all rapists remain unperturbed by the incongruity between their attitudes and their behaviour. In fact, most rapists engage in a process of rationalisation in order to deal with their (slight) regret or feelings of guilt. It will be seen that this process of rationalisation further reflects rapists' prejudiced attitudes and feelings towards women.

Sexist beliefs

Sexist ideology and rape myths (see Chapter 4) are primary factors in assisting offenders to deny their responsibility for rape. For many rapists, rape is easily rationalised as seduction because they can draw upon the prevailing stereotype of male domination in lovemaking. Following on from this is the belief that men are often 'framed' as rapists. While the occurrence and possibility of false conviction does exist, the probability is low considering the nature of the legal system and the ordeal the victim experiences if she decides to report the crime.

Two of the nine rapists in the sample insisted they had been convicted for gang rape on fabricated evidence. Both used one or two 'technical' faults in the victim's evidence to prove their innocence on appeal. Judging from their own descriptions, it seemed clear that they were guilty of rape. One rapist explained his 'innocence' in this way:

> She mistook me for somebody else maybe. She definitely told the court that I was standing with a gun and keeping her steady on the ground. And she told the court that Kevin was the one that kept a panga, you know, a bush knife, here by her head and another one had a knife, keeping her so she could do nothing and she just had to lay still . . . That was really bullshit because that's the basic point that I brought up for the appeal case – she didn't have proof of who the real one is that kept it [the knife], because there was also people threatening her. But she just swopped it up, she didn't know who the right guy was.

Insistence on innocence and rationalisation for rape is also conducted on the assumption that the victim wanted to have sex but was playing hard to get. Along with this usually goes another justification for rape: that the victim was 'looking for rape' by being in an unsafe place (such as a street) alone or by engaging in certain activities such as necking or flirting. The idea that a woman must accept responsibility for whatever happens to her if she knowingly enters a precarious situation is argued by one rapist in his description of how he would respond if a member of his family were raped:

> Some of the cherries have asked us, how would you feel if it was your ma or your sister? – but it depends – if my sister goes around at night then it is what she looked for . . . If it was in my house, I would be cross because she didn't look for it. Then I would kill the person who did it. But if she looked for it, then I would just scheme it is not my problem. I would feel a little bit but there is nothing I can do.

Women's style of dress is another excuse used by the rapist to exonerate himself from his criminal behaviour:

In most cases, I'd say they are inclined to be tempting to
men . . I won't say they ask for it. They think they are just
treating themselves by dressing themselves up without thinking that they are doing a thing [tempting men] like that.

These examples expose the role played by sexist ideology and rape
myths in the social control of women, and the 'licence' to rape
which is given men (see Chapters 2 and 4). The perception is that
women who venture out unprotected or dress in a certain fashion
can be 'legitimately' raped. Women who are known to be sexually
licentious can expect no sympathy from the public if they are raped.
Because society is unmoved by the rape of sexually active women,
rapists can easily rationalise their rape of these women.

Alcohol and drugs

Rapists also vindicate their behaviour by claiming that alcohol and
drugs made them uncharacteristically aggressive and sexually uncontrollable. Said one rapist about the effect drugs had on him:

You become also sexually excited, especially when you take
Mandrax.

For another rapist, the heightened urge to rape was due to both
drugs and alcohol:

If you are under the influence of drugs and liquor, then the
idea of rape appeals more than when you are sober.

Alcohol or drugs alone do not cause rape (see Chapter 5) and in
no way do they render men violently or sexually uncontrollable.
At most, alcohol and drugs magnify the men's existing attitudes
and behaviours, some of which are primary in contributing to rape.

Since alcohol and drugs act as disinhibitors of behaviour, they
are contributing factors in the rapist's aggression. His choice of
women as a target for this aggression, however, is guided by his
attitudes – and those of his society – about women, sex and
violence.

Psychological mechanisms: Reducing cognitive dissonance

The theory of cognitive dissonance holds that inconsistent cognitions or conflicting motivations can produce tension, which people attempt to reduce.[3] According to Halloran, cognitive dissonance is an 'antecedent condition which leads to activity orientated towards dissonance reduction'.[4]

Cognitions are opinions about oneself, others or the situational context. In terms of cognitive dissonance theory, cognitions can be related to one another in three ways: consonant, dissonant or irrelevant.[5] For example, the cognition 'I enjoy rape' would be consonant with the belief 'the woman found the rape pleasurable'. When cognitions are inconsistent, they are dissonant. 'I rape' and 'rape is damaging to women' are dissonant cognitions. And if the cognition 'I rape' was paired with 'Pele was a great footballer', the relation between the two cognitions would be irrelevant.

Most cognitions are either related to the person's behaviour or to the environment. An alteration in these two variables can result in the changing cognitive elements. If a man stopped raping, his original cognition 'I rape' would change to 'I no longer rape'. Therefore, through behaviour change, he is able to transform a set of dissonant cognitions into a set of consonant cognitions – for example, 'I no longer rape' and 'rape is damaging to women'. In this instance, refraining from rape would be the clearest method of reducing cognitive dissonance. Unfortunately, the high degree of recidivism among rapists – as will be discussed later – indicates that this does not occur very often.

Zimbardo has listed other techniques of reducing dissonance.[6] These are probably more commonly used by rapists. They include de-emphasising the significance of the cognition; perceiving more common elements among the cognitions; and incorporating more consonant elements to alter the ratio of dissonant to consonant ones.

To make these dissonance reduction operations more explicit, let us look hypothetically at a man who, after much indecision, decides to rape a friend. By raping her, he loses much of the warmth that existed in the friendship and hurts her feelings. At the same time, the rape provides him with a feeling of power and strength. These two sets of cognitions are dissonant. Within the framework of Zimbardo's dissonance-reducing techniques, the rapist, in this example, may attempt to lessen his dissonance through a variety of means:

- By seeing his rape of his friend as highly unusual behaviour which he would never repeat again, and as an encounter which did not harm his good relationship with his friend;
- By de-emphasising the positive aspects of his friendship and emphasising his feelings of power and supremacy. His friend's warm and loving way of relating is seen as false and manipulative. It becomes irrelevant because rape provides him with a more satisfying way of relating;
- By minimising the distinction between his friend and all other women. He then believes that his friend, like all other women, wanted to be raped and is only good for sex; or
- By speaking to other rapists who do not feel guilty about their behaviour and gaining their support.

In a situation where a choice must be made, dissonance will occur. This is especially the case when two alternatives are equally appealing. As has been shown, virtually all the dissonance-reducing techniques involve making the chosen alternative more attractive. In the example above, sexual violence was therefore seen as a better option than a relationship of affection.

The social comparison technique

Social comparison is a further psychological mechanism used in legitimising rape. The theory of social comparison, as argued by Festinger, posits that it is imperative for people to compare themselves to others in order to evaluate their own attitudes and behaviours.[7] A man who rapes and is concerned about the acceptability of his behaviour must compare himself to other men. The rapist cannot conceptualise the acceptability or non-acceptability of behaviour if he has insufficient knowledge about how others behave.[8]

People do not compare themselves randomly to others: they tend to draw comparisons with people they see as roughly similar to themselves. A rapist who has doubts about his behaviour may therefore ask members of his peer group for their opinions and change his attitude in the direction of the norm. Because friendships are usually based on similarities, the rapist's peer group probably has sexist views and believes the common myths about rape. Consequently, after speaking to his peer group, it is likely that the rapist would be less conflict-ridden about his behaviour. As documented, peer group support for rape behaviour is part of our rape culture, and certainly a large part of Riverlea culture.

In the light of the fact that rapists believe strongly in rape myths and that they use psychological and sexist rationalisations for their behaviour, it is not wholly unexpected to find that approximately two thirds of rapists avoid admitting their guilt. According to McCaldon, thirty-three percent of rapists admit to their offence, twenty-seven percent deny it and thirty-three percent rationalise it.[9] This supports the hypothesis that the majority of rapists do not perceive their actions to be immoral or harmful.

To conclude: rape is seen as harmful to women by rapists in this study. However, for them sexual coercion does not necessarily constitute rape. They see rape as defined by extreme brutality – burning the victim with cigarettes, inserting objects into her vagina or killing her. Thus their own behaviour does not fall into the definition of rape. And when the possibility exists that what they have done was in fact rape, then sexist ideology, myths and various psychological mechanisms generally enable them to relieve themselves of regret and dissonance.

Police and courts

The next stage of the rapist's experience is probably slightly more harrowing than the rationalisation period, because there exists a threat to his freedom in the form of arrest and conviction. This knowledge determines at least some of his behaviours during and after the rape. While the majority of rapists were not particularly concerned about the consequences of their conduct, thirty-three percent were cautious about speaking openly about the rape in their community for fear of the police or the victim's family being alerted. As one rapist put it:

I won't go and talk to someone about it, but it may come up in conversation, but mostly I keep it quiet because maybe I tell someone and he knows the cherry or the family.

This rapist seems to have taken it for granted that his victim has not reported the rape. Some of the reasons for the victim's reluctance to report the offence will be made more explicit later in this section.

The considerable influence the police have in determining whether rape has taken place and in advising for or against prosecution sometimes puts the rapist at an advantage.[10] According to Robin, in Western countries the police's advice and behaviour towards the victim is often guided by the 'slum sex code', which is a moral appraisal of the victim.[11] For example, if the victim was alone or drunk, is black or has been suspected of sexual promiscuity, then her report is less likely to be believed. Police may also be less sympathetic to victims wanting to prosecute in cases where there has been little physical violence and where a prior sexual relationship has existed between her and the assailant.

In an interview with me in May 1989, Lieutenant Colonel Frans Malherbe, the Witwatersrand liaison police officer, commented that the police's attitude towards the complainant is irrelevant since they are obliged to investigate all complaints. It was only the public prosecutor, he said, through the Department of Justice, who could decide whether to charge someone or alter the charge to a lesser charge such as indecent assault.

While noting the obligations that police are under to investigate all complaints, the question is how much time they put into their investigations. While official policy does not determine which victims' complaints should receive more attention, policemen may be influenced by their political and social views when investigating certain complaints. One study conducted in the United States in the late 1960s suggested that the primary reason for the high number of dismissed cases of rape was the police and prosecutors' attitudes towards rape. According to the study, police believe eighty to ninety percent of the rapes reported to them are not really rapes.[12] There has been no local research done to establish whether this statistic holds true for South Africa, but if such official attitudes do exist, then the rapist need not be overly afraid of incarceration.

Police questioning, which reflects police attitudes, may equally provide the rapist with a measure of indirect protection. Insensitive questions asked of the victim – such as: 'Why were you walking alone at that time of night?', 'Did he get an erection?' and 'Did you enjoy it?' – serve to inhibit victims from reporting rape. Many South African women seem to be aware of the police's sometimes insensitive treatment of rape victims. *Darling*, a South African women's magazine published in the early 1980s, revealed in their Opinion Finder of 1981 that on the question of whether 'police are sufficiently sympathetic towards rape victims', eleven percent of their readers said yes, seventy-nine percent said no and ten percent were not sure. One of the respondents commented on her own case: 'The police were only sympathetic once they were satisfied that my case was genuine. I found their questioning harsh and I really had to convince them that I wasn't lying.'[13] This view of the police's attitude may help to explain why, in the same survey, fifty-eight percent of women said they would not go to the police if raped, while only thirty-two percent said they would.

Police sometimes argue that insensitive questioning is necessary in order to prepare the woman for aggressive cross-examination by the defence counsel and 'to make sure that the woman is not petrified, embarrassed or driven to tears on the stand'.[14] While there may be some logic to this, their heavy-handed manner of questioning may also reflect their own stereotyped views of rape. On the issue of insensitive police questioning, Robin quotes Cook, a gynaecologist, who addressed a seminar for police personnel in Philadelphia:

> Police brutalisation of the victim is responsible for the failure of women to report the crime of rape. You, with your inept questioning, rape the woman psychologically and, with your lack of understanding, are responsible for many instances of severe emotional damage and psychological trauma.[15]

Cook's comments seem to apply to some (although not all) quarters of the South African police. The treatment accorded to many victims in South Africa is characterised by the following examples given by Mayne and Levett. They write:

> Rape Crisis recently assisted a young woman who had been raped by six men for four hours. When the men had released her in the early hours of the morning, she went home, washed herself and went to bed, not wanting to disturb the rest of the household. In the morning she told her mother and together they went to the police. The policeman on duty told the young woman that she did not look like a rape victim. He told her that he would have to take her to the district surgeon for an examination. She stated that his attitude was one of impatience and disbelief. She told the policeman that she did not want to go to the district surgeon. She was told to

sign a paper stating that she was dropping the complaint. She
actually knew the names and addresses of two of her as-
sailants, but she was not questioned further.[16]

A middle class white women . . . was raped by a neighbour
when she was four months pregnant. He had offered to give
her a lift to town, but before reaching town, had driven to
an isolated area and, pushing down the back of her seat, raped
her. She went to the police to report the rape. They dissuad-
ed her from laying a charge on the grounds that the alleged
rapist was not really a bad chap, that he had probably just
got the 'wrong idea' about her, that he hadn't really hurt her,
and that to make a case of it would involve all concerned in
a great deal of unnecessary unpleasantness; so why should
she not just forget it?[17]

If the victim decides to proceed with the complaint after questioning, the insensitive treatment may continue. She will be taken to
the district surgeon or a hospital where she is often left alone for
lengthy periods. She often becomes nauseous as she is prohibited
from washing the semen or blood from her body. The medical examination she undergoes involves a gynaecological examination to
test for the presence of sperm and to ascertain whether sexual intercourse did occur.[18] The rape victim may also, according to
Levett, have to deal with an unsympathetic attitude from the district surgeon since 'there are some district surgeons [in South Afri-
ca] who readily express the belief that many women complain of
rape falsely'.[19]

After the examination, the victim can return to her home. She
is often assured by the police that she will be contacted by the investigating officer. While many investigating officers are dedicated to the arrest of the offender and may be sensitive in their deal-
ings with the victim, victims are frequently not told about preliminary hearings or what action has been taken concerning the rapist.
In order to gain any information, the victim must approach the
police herself. This uncertainty exacerbates the mental pressure
she experiences.[20]

It is the likelihood of insensitive handling and humiliation that
prevents many victims from reporting their rape. This means that
fewer rapists are brought to justice.

One consequence of the humiliation involved in informing the police about being raped is that victims may prefer to report the offence to other men such as fathers and friends. A rapist explained how he was apprehended because of the actions of other men:

> Then her father saw [she had been raped], then her father phoned the police . . . They came and locked me up.

In another case, the victim's woman friend, who managed to escape the rape, informed some of the victim's men friends about what was happening to her. These men then set out in pursuit of the rapists. This is how one rapist explained the incident:

> These okes knew us – gangsters from Riverlea. They came with a truck while we were raping this cherry. And this lightie that grabbed her, he got nervous because he had never done it before. He ran down to the houses and they rode after him and put him into the van and put him away.
>
> The cherry was still with us, they had only got him. This was on the Sunday and on the Monday I was arrested because they had this lightie and he gave them the addresses.

In contrast to the victim, the apprehended rapist may receive lenient and congenial treatment from the police. This occurs particularly when, according to the rapist quoted above, 'it's a policeman that knows you or likes you'. Familiarity with the local police is not unusual in the context of small communities like Riverlea, where residents and the police often consort and fraternise.

Of course, not all police treat rapists and victims in these ways. This point is important because police conduct may be stereotyped and distorted, so that understandings of rape, and particularly the non-reporting of the offence, may be incomplete or skewed. Numerous policemen act with care and concern for the victim and many work long hours in order to apprehend the rapist. Unfortunately, the treatment accorded by police to numerous rape victims and reports of policemen themselves raping negate much of this good work.

If the rapist is apprehended and charged, the law affords him good protection. South African criminal law rests on the notion that a person is innocent until proven guilty. There are also laws protecting the accused. Section 197 of the Criminal Procedure Act provides that: 'An accused who gives evidence at criminal proceed-

ings shall not be asked or required to answer any questions tend-
ing to show . . . that he is of bad character.' If the accused
challenges the complainant's character, then the accused may lose
the protection accorded him or her and questions may be put to
him or her which indicate that she or he is of bad character.[21]

This procedure changes substantially, however, when a person
is accused of perpetrating a crime of an 'indecent' nature. In a rape
situation, the accused is entitled to acquire information about the
complainant without endangering the protection granted to him
in terms of Section 197 (22). As Section 227 of the Act states: 'Evidence as to the character of any woman upon or regard to whom
any offence of an indecent nature has been committed, shall be
admissible.'

Thus complainants of sexual assault are placed in a different
category from any other complainant. The implication of this, says
Hoffman, is that testimony regarding sexual history cannot be used
against the alleged rapist, but can be used against the complainant
to demonstrate the probability of her consenting to sexual
intercourse.[23]

Satchwell uses statements from two rape cases to reflect this. The
headnote from the case *R v Van Tonder and Another* (1932 T.P.D.
30) reads:

> Impairment of the dignities of the complainant is an essen-
> tial of crimen injuria, and evidence relating to the mode of
> living and character of the complainant is a relevant evidence
> on whether the crime has been committed.[24]

The judgement refers to the case of *R v Curtis* which states that:

> Where the complainant is a woman it requires that she should
> be *honesta* – respectable, and the making of an immoral pur-
> pose to a prostitute would not be an injuria.[25]

In terms of the law, then, rape victims who are sexually promiscuous receive little protection against rape. Those women who are
not in an exclusive sexual relationship with a man, or have had
prior sexual relations with the accused, must often go to impossible lengths to prove they have been raped. In fact, it appears that
for the court to be persuaded that such a victim did not consent,
she would have to have engaged in enormous physical resistance.

In cases where a promiscuous woman does not physically withstand her assailant, the defence does not have a difficult task in obtaining an acquittal for the accused.

Thirty-three percent of the rapists in the present study were aware of the court's interest in the victim's 'contributory' behaviour and thus conducted themselves during and after the rape in a manner which would not mitigate against their testimony that the victim consented to sexual intercourse. One rapist, for example, assaulted his victim in such a way that he left no evidence to be used against him:

> If one or two smacks don't help, then you kick her in the ribs, so that she feels the pain inside and there are no marks or scars. That's why I'll never use a knife on a cherry.

Later in the interview, this rapist explained his other, more sophisticated methods for ensuring that he is not reported or convicted of rape:

> I will tell you my approach – I walk with her and talk with her. I always have an alibi and no one can see me dragging her and pulling her. We walk past the shopping centre, walking and talking, and everyone can see I'm not dragging her.

Another rapist used similar tactics:

> You see when I do a thing like that I always try and be romantic . . speak a few good words and things like that . . . so I don't have to worry that maybe I will go to jail.

The court's emphasis on consent seems rooted in the notion that women lay false charges of rape. This may derive from the belief that women do this to recover their lost pride and because they have little integrity. The prevalence of this belief is expressed by the fact that numerous legal commentaries on rape carry Lord Chief Justice Hale's observation that rape 'is an accusation easily to be made and hard to be proved, and harder to be defended by the party accused, though never so innocent'.[26]

To prevent unjust prosecution, courts demand corroboration of the victim's testimony. Corroboration is confirmation by additional evidence that the defendant is the rapist; that penetration took

place; and that the prosecutrix (the victim) did not give her consent.[27] Arguments for the necessity of corroboration are well illustrated by the magistrate's comments in the case of *R v M:*

> The statement that 'charges of immorality are easy for wom-
> en to formulate, difficult for men to refute' remains for me
> strictly valid . . . as a mode of obtaining vengeance for any
> affront to a woman's pride or dignity, and bringing of a charge
> of this kind is probably without equal. The very fact that the
> charge is brought at all is calculated to damage the man even
> if he is eventually acquitted.[28]

Corroboration, particularly with regard to identification, is seen
as crucial because of the possibility of erroneous identification
resulting from the woman's emotional and distraught state, the loss
of status the man may suffer and the heavy penalties attached to
the crime.[29]

The circumstances of most rapes make it likely that the victim
will be able to identify the rapist correctly: more frequently than
not, victim and rapist are not total strangers and the rape takes
place in the victim's home. In addition, the relatively long duration of rape gives the woman the opportunity to observe the rapist.
It takes time for the woman to undress or for the assailant to remove her clothes. The rapist may also decide to extend the rape
unduly, prelonging the period prior to, during and after sexual intercourse. Rape victims have a greater opportunity to take note
of the rapist's identity then do victims of other direct contact
crimes, such as mugging. Taking these factors into account, the
question arises as to why corroboration of identification in rape
cases is regarded as more essential than in other crimes, again such
as mugging.[30]

In the present study, two of the rapists who privately admitted
to the rape were acquitted as a result of lack of corroboration. This
rule was thus the direct reason for at least two criminals not being
punished.

It can be concluded that in the eyes of the law, a rape victim's
testimony is by itself often not sufficient to secure conviction. Her
reliability as a witness is evaluated, according to Connell and Wilson, within a context that in rape cases 'the defendant is innocent
until proven guilty, [and] the prosecutrix is guilty of making a false
accusation until proven innocent'.[31]

In defending the alleged rapist, the defense counsel tends to make maximum use of court laws and procedures. The job of any defense counsel is to prove the innocence of his or her client and to do this she or he will attempt to show the victim's consent, infer mis-identification of the accused and tarnish the image of the woman through insinuations of sexual promiscuity and immorality. Examples given by Mayne and Levett illustrate this, and also give clues as to why many rapists do not fear that their victims will report the rape:

In one case in the Cape Town Regional Court, the defence for the alleged rapist tried to show that a skinny teenage girl, who had been intercepted by five men on her way home from a coffee bar one night, had consented to intercourse with these five men for three hours on a filthy double bed mattress in a room in a semi-demolished house. He asked what she had been wearing at the time of the alleged rape . . . The defence counsel then asked her if she had worn her shirt unbuttoned low, whether she had struggled and fought against these five men, if she had screamed for help, and if her clothes were torn. To the last four questions, she answered 'no', the reason for not screaming or struggling being that her mouth and nose had been held closed and she had almost lost conscious-ness from suffocation. She was asked if she had met any of the men before the alleged rape. She had not. She was asked if she had any boyfriends and if she had any sex with them. This question was asked despite the fact that the district sur-geon had reported that she had been a virgin.[32]

In another case:

At the Wynberg Regional Court, the defence attorney tried to destroy the character of an 18 year old very introverted young woman. This young woman had been offered a lift in pouring rain by a well dressed, well spoken young man at 14h30. He did not stop at the shopping centre where she had asked him to drop her, but drove to an isolated spot, where he threatened her with a gun and raped her. The man even-tually took her back to the shopping centre where he let her go. The defence lawyer tried to suggest that she had lied about the rape, because she had arrived home late and had not cleaned the house or prepared supper as she was supposed to do, and intimated that she had been very afraid of her mother's anger. This led the extremely nervous, conscientious young woman to break down and cry uncontrollably. The rape had been psychologically terrifying and physically very painful. When the Rape Crisis counsellor saw her two days after the rape, she was in such a state of shock that she had not left her room or eaten for two days.[33]

When the harrowing ordeal of police questioning, medical examination and cross-examination is combined with the social embarrassment of being raped, the unofficial figure that only one in twenty rape victims reports the offence to the police becomes more understandable.[34]

The above figure is derived from estimates obtained from NICRO. This pattern of non-reporting was clearly visible in this study. By far the majority of rapists remained unreported.

From NICRO's estimates and figures provided by overseas researchers, it is apparent that rape is a crime which habitually escapes punishment.[35] According to Herman, in the United States in cases where police believed the complainant's accusation, only fifty percent of the suspected rapists were arrested.[36] Of those arrested, thirty-three percent were not prosecuted, forty-nine percent were acquitted and another nine percent were convicted of lesser crimes. After studying FBI statistics on rape, Legrand has concluded that:

A man who rapes a woman who reports the rape to the police has roughly seven chances out of eight of walking away without any conviction. Assuming only one woman in five reports the rape, his chances increase to thirty-nine out of forty. If these figures take into account the high percentage of those who receive probation or suspended sentences, his chances of escaping incarceration are in the vicinity of ninety-eight to ninety-nine out of a hundred. Forcible rape has a lower conviction rate than any other crime.[37]

There is also a strong likelihood of rapists receiving probation and having their sentences repealed in appeal cases. As one rapist explained:

We were discharged because she was lying. I can't tell everything but when we were arrested there were eight involved. Three of them went on the run and weren't arrested. Then they applied to start the case without them. Then we were sentenced, the one got seven years and the other four of us got eight years. About a month after we were sentenced, these ous were arrested and discharged. And then we made an appeal and it was easy to get a discharge – we had a lawyer, my mother paid a thousand rand, and the cherry contradicted herself. In our case she spoke one story and with these other three okes she said differently.

From the interview, it appears that the victim did not contradict herself substantially but went back on a statement about exactly which rapist was holding a gun and which was holding a knife. It seems, according to the rapist, that the defence inferred from this that she was an unreliable witness, and all eight accused were acquitted of the charge of gang rape.

It is inaccurate to assume that all courts evince identical attitudes and that police and judicial action are worthless in dealing with rape. Merely through their power to arrest and convict, these two law-enforcing institutions play a role in counteracting rape. The prospect of spending time in prison is sufficient to prevent many men, who might otherwise rape, from doing so. Furthermore, the rapist's awareness that excessive physical violence assists the prosecution in securing a conviction means he may refrain from inflicting substantial physical injury.

Recidivism among rapists

A final testimony to women's vulnerability to rape is the fact that rapists have a tendency to rape more than once. Groth, Longo and McFadin have examined this issue, using the concept of recidivism.[38] Recidivism is 'a critical variable for assessing the risk of an offender to the community and for measuring the success of efforts to rehabilitate him'.[39]

Groth and his colleagues, as well as the present study, reveal a high degree of recidivism among rapists.[40] In the former, rapists from two different areas of the United States of America were studied. Results showed that eighty-one percent of rapists in the one area and over forty-eight percent in the other admitted to one or more undetected rapes. The number of undetected rapes averaged about five per rapist.

Of the present study's sample of rapists, seventy-seven percent had raped more than once. One rapist, who had served a single prison sentence for rape, admitted (what is here defined as) raping fourteen times. Others admitted to raping five, six or seven times and some were more vague, saying they had raped 'a few times' or 'lots of times'. The failure of rehabilitation is borne out by the fact that forty-three percent of the seventy-seven percent of rapists who raped more than once had done time in prison for rape, but continued to rape after their release.

The figures for repeated rapes from both these studies could be even higher, due to rapists' misperceptions of their sexual behaviour at other times.[41]

Male socialisation, the pervasive influence of sexist institutions and the ease with which rapists rationalise their behaviour make it likely that they will rape repeatedly. The problem of recidivism is in some cases partially addressed through the conviction of the offender (as has been shown, this is an event that does not occur very frequently) and rehabilitation.

There are, however, many instances in which prison sentences, even when accompanied by harsh penalties and rehabilitation programmes, do not adequately address the problem of men raping repeatedly. In South Africa this was highlighted recently (1989) by the case of William van der Merwe. He had served a fifteen year prison sentence for four counts of attempted rape and five counts of rape, one of which included gagging, tying up and raping a menstruating fourteen year old. Upon his release, Van der Merwe raped two women, one of whom he killed with a screwdriver. Although some therapeutic programmes have achieved a measure of success, their long-term effects are questionable.[42] Said a rapist who had just completed therapeutic treatment in Miami, in the United States of America:

> When I see a light in the window, I start thinking about how I can do it and get away with it. That's a battle that will be with me for the rest of my life.[43]

This does not imply that rapists should not be imprisoned. As Clark and Lewis put it, 'we certainly do nothing for such men in convicting them, but we do nothing for women unless we convict them'.[44] While the failure of rehabilitation may be attributable to a number of factors (poor therapy, inadequate prison services), some of which have never been investigated, it is hypothesised that psychotherapy *alone* could never successfully treat those who rape and generally are insensitive to their victims after their crime. Firstly, from a clinical perspective, it appears that it would take a great deal of time before the offender would relinquish some of his psychological defences (denial, rationalisation), become aware of the brutality of his crime and finally resolve the particular psychological issues which led him to rape. Secondly, therapy, if it is to provide the rapist with a different perception of his offence, has to do battle with a powerful prevailing rape culture.

The failure of rehabilitation programmes, the police and the law to stem the tide of rape means that changes to the police, the courts and the prisons are necessary but insufficient. The social root of sexual violence must be unearthed and explored. Having done this, we must begin to transform these structures and relations so that we build a society in which the occurrence of rape – and ultimately men's desire to perpetrate it – is eradicated.

Notes

1 1977, page 101.
2 Cited in *Scope*, 2 April 1982, pages 33-34.
3 Festinger, 1957.
4 1970, page 99.
5 Zimbardo, 1977.
6 1977.
7 1954.
8 Festinger, 1954.
9 1967.
10 Herman, 1979.
11 1977, page 141.
12 *University of Pennsylvania Law Review*, 1968.
13 27 May 1981, page 36.
14 *American Criminal Law Review*, Winter, 1973.
15 Robin, 1977; Cook, 1977, page 141.
16 1977, page 167.
17 1977, page 167.
18 MASA, no date; Wood, 1974.
19 Levett, 1981, page 78.
20 MASA, no date; Mayne and Levett, 1972; Wood, 1974.
21 Criminal Procedure Act, 1977, Section 197 (a); cited in Satchwell, 1981.
22 Satchwell, 1981.

23 Hoffman, 1970.
24 Satchwell, 1981, page 44.
25 Satchwell, 1981, page 44.
26 1778, page 635.
27 Hibey, 1973.
28 Cited in Satchwell, 1981, page 45.
29 Legrand, 1973. No statistics could be found for 'unfounded complaints' of victims and wrongful arrests of rapists in South Africa.
30 Robin, 1977.
31 1974.
32 1977, pages 168-9.
33 1977, page 169.
34 MASA, no date.
35 Brownmiller, 1975; Herman, 1979; Legrand, 1973.
36 Herman, 1979.
37 1973, page 922.
38 1982.
39 1982, page 451.
40 1982.
41 Groth et. al., 1982.
42 *Time*, 5 September 1983. Two rehabilitation programmes which have reported short-term successes are those at Lino Lakes and Western State Hospital. At Lino Lakes, thirty rapists have group therapy sessions three times a week, read articles and books about their sexually violent behaviour and see films depicting the feeling of victims. The programme at Western State Hospital is markedly different. Rapists make tape recordings in which they speak about their deviant sexual fantasies. The tape is played back to them and when the moment of sexual gratification arrives, the script is changed so that something horrendous occurs.

   Besides these programmes, other popular rehabilitation techniques make use of the drug Depo-Provero, which reduces testosterone levels, and fantasy reconditioning whereby the rapist with deviant fantasies masturbates for an hour 'until it is physically painful' (*Time*, 5 September 1983).
43 *Time*, 5 September 1983, page 53.
44 Clark and Lewis, 1977, page 108.

Chapter Eight

Conclusion

One of the primary aims in writing and publishing this research was to engender greater discussion and thought about why men rape. It was not intended for the various viewpoints to be accepted unequivocally, or for the conclusion to draw the debate to a close. The intention was to investigate and expose an area which is under-researched and little discussed. In this conclusion, several issues relating to rape, research methodology and criticisms of the present study will be discussed.

A scientific study of rape has much to gain by incorporating into its methodology the feminist precept that 'the personal is political'. One important implication of this idea for home-grown and based researchers is that they are themselves products of the social, economic and political system which they are studying. Following on from this is the notion that there is a convergence between how one chooses to live and relate to people, what one writes about people and how one relates to the struggle for social change. For the socially concerned researcher, the implication is that it is incumbent to try and live out the ideals postulated in his/her work.

Litewka raises an important point about the personal vulnerabilities of the researcher and the psychologist, as well as the need for personal honesty. This is of significance in the rape researcher's personal life and experiences. Litewka comments:

> Have you seen much, written or spoken, about masturbation? I haven't. The psycho-healers, most of whom are men, always talk about the phenomenon of masturbation as if it was 'other', 'out there'. Have you heard a psycho-healer say,

'When I masturbate(d) . . .'? Of course not. They are incapable or terrified of dealing with their own experience. So I am attempting to deal with mine, with those of men I know, in an effort to help us begin to deal more honestly with one aspect of male socialisation.

Like the psycho-healers, like everyone, I am also damaged. I may be incapable of asking the right questions. I know I'm not able now to supply the answers that are needed. Desperately needed. But I'm going to try, and I hope that other men will also begin trying. Through persistence and honesty and perhaps by accident, we'll end up asking the right questions and be better able to answer them.[1]

Litewka's insights were significant to me in writing this study. I was aware of my need and desire for personal honesty, while, at the same time, cognisant of scholastic restrictions and fearful of revealing my own relevant experiences. I would like to believe that it was both these factors that impeded me from writing about my particular experiences. For now, I will continue to assist fellow researchers on sexuality by filling in questionnaires and giving interviews anonymously.

It should be noted that use of the notion that 'the personal is political' in research does not necessarily negate the scientific character of such research.[2] Discussion about personal experiences may provide extra knowledge about the topic under investigation, and so assist scientific enquiry.

For a 'science of rape' to emerge, every bit of information on the topic must be extracted and explored. Thus actual psychological practice must be examined alongside methods and findings of rape research. With this in mind, a number of ideas concerning the present study and further research will be explored.

Limitations of the present study and implications for future research

Methodologically, numerous improvements can be made upon this study. The use of a larger sample would improve the generalisability of assertions made and increase reliability. In categorising rapists according to certain traits, a sophisticated quantitative statistical analysis would be advantageous. However, if studies are to take an experimental form, findings must be accompanied by contextualised interpretation.

Rape, as has been pointed out, is one of the many mechanisms that reinforce the social control of women. However, instruments of female social control and women's oppression are not tacitly accepted by all. Feminists and the women's liberation movement are challenging male violence, women's second class status and prevailing sex stereotypes which inhibit both male and female development. But the increasing power and influence of feminist ideas might trigger sexist men, who are unwilling to alter their conduct, to resort to rape and other forms of violence in order to defend their domination of women. To find out whether this may indeed occur, it would be worth investigating whether sexist men in a more sexually egalitarian society have more potential of raping than sexist men in a sexist society. Findings from such an enquiry might shed more light on rape as an instrument of social control and the influence that social acceptance of rape has on its incidence.

Connected to research on men's potential for raping in different societies is the issue of what prevents men from raping. This study has attempted to show the link between the validation of masculinity and rape. To compensate for their demasculinisation, some men rape. Others do not rape, possibly because of a greater ability to self-reflect, a stronger superego or heightened fear of legal consequences. The exploratory nature of this study prevented further investigation into this hypothesis. Research into this area would be useful.

Longitudinal studies on convicted rapists released from prison would be another worthwhile area of research. Research of this kind would reveal the extent of recidivism among rapists and the effectiveness of rehabilitation programmes. Such programmes require urgent attention, and psychotherapists experienced in this field must begin to pool their knowledge so that a feminist psychotherapy appropriate to rapists can be developed and used both inside and outside prison.

Working within groups, whether in the form of consciousness-raising groups, group psychotherapy or support groups (such as Alcoholics Anonymous), may prove effective in curbing recidivism.[3] In general, such group situations are said to provide members with a sense that they are not alone in their problems, the opportunity to express their anxieties and the knowledge that alternatives are possible. Members may model their behaviour on that of the more successful members of the group and try out new forms of relating within the group. Through the process of sharing and giving, their self-absorption decreases, they discover the capacity to help others and come to the realisation that they are not inherently 'bad' human beings, or necessarily rapists for life. The group environment allows for a collective motivation to locate the root of the problem and to find mechanisms for overcoming it.[4] In terms of work with rapists, what requires exploration is how much feminist content can be inserted into these group processes and how far this will go in transforming the sadistic behaviour of rapists into more caring and sensitive behaviour.

Studies on rapists could also assess the potential of street psychotherapy.[5] Street therapy, as outlined by Kiley, is mainly directed at men who are unemployed and crisis-stricken and who spend much of their time on the streets, in bars, in parks and popular community meeting places. The street therapist concerned with sexual violence would attempt to assist men in despair and change their sexist attitudes to women, thereby decreasing their potential to rape. The technique comprises three stages: survival, modelling and teaching. In the survival stage, the street therapist must learn about life on the streets and the needs of the people who live there. The modelling stage requires the 'street shrink' to 'find a personally satisfying and professionally sound manner of modelling survival skills that are better than the ones street people possess'.[6] Demonstrating to 'street men' that they can have equal relationships with women without losing self-respect, self-esteem and confidence will earn the therapist the admiration of the street people. This admiration heralds the teaching stage, during which lonely and distressed men seek out the therapist's guidance so as to gain better coping skills and answers to their respective problems.

On the basis of findings from the present study, it would be of great benefit to society if researchers and psychotherapists were to assess and develop progressive sex education programmes. The aim of such programmes would be to assist both sexes in better understanding their own experiences and behaviour, their relationships with others and women's sexual oppression. Besides helping to explore more fulfilling modes of sexual behaviour, sex education, as well as psychotherapy, should inspire the sexes 'to respond to changing situations with whatever (humane) behaviour seems appropriate, regardless of the stereotyped expectations of either sex'.[7]

It should be noted that if these suggestions for future research and primary prevention are to contribute to a scientific understanding of the rapist, then biological reductionism must be avoided. A science of rape must focus on social context to unearth the particularities of the rapist's existence. Finally, while promoting human development, research must also concentrate on discovering different means of changing the societal conditions that nourish and perpetuate sexist attitudes and behaviour.

Findings and summary

Every day the pages of South African newspapers are filled with reports of rape. Sexual violence is common to every type of man, be he doctor, teacher, soldier, factory owner, factory worker, husband or lover. Women's vulnerability to rape increases as sexism continues to pervade virtually every area of our society. As time goes by, it is to be expected that the number of rapes will begin to far exceed the current (unofficial) figure of approximately three hundred and ninety thousand per annum. In South Africa we may well reach a situation analagous to that in the United States, where approximately one in four women can expect to be raped before they die.[8] If this is the future we stand to inherit, then concerted action must be taken by those progressive political and social organisations which are striving to make South Africa a better place for all to live. This is not the domain only of organisations primarily concerned with the problem of rape, such as People Opposed to Women Abuse and the Rape Crisis centres. The domain belongs to all organisations and individuals and demands actively working towards the establishment of an egalitarian and democratic society.

One of the central findings of this study is that men rape primarily to bolster their masculine pride and feed their desire for power. This is largely attributable to the rapist's need to live up to society's ideal of masculinity – to be aggressive, strong, virile, dominant and all-powerful; his need to compensate for feelings of powerlessness stemming from the family, alienation in the workplace and political and racial oppression; his socialised belief in rape myths; his objectification of women; his conditioning which leads him to believe that violence is the simplest means to solve problems and to get what he wants; his need to compensate for sexual and masculine inadequacy; and his strong association of sex with violence.

Wide-scale evidence points to the fact that men's wish to dominate is not instinctual (see Chapter 3). Men are not born to rape. The notion of instinctual male conduct, as suggested by radical feminists, conservatives and traditional psychologists, does not make sense in the light of changes in sex roles and attitudes from one generation to another.

The transformation of prevailing social patterns can only be achieved through a change in social relationships, structures and ideologies. In a transformed society where personal development is not defined by class, race or sex, the possibilities for egalitarian relationships abound. No longer would women be treated as sexual objects, or as human beings in the service of men. And no longer would their lives be restricted by discriminatory economic, social and sexual practices. In a society devoid of sexist conceptualisations of women and men, rape would be a strange phenomenon.

At present, however, rape is generally not considered a serious crime. The reasons for this lie both in the prevalence of sexist ideology and rape myths, and in the thin line separating sex and violence. Although not directly comparable, heterosexual intercourse and sexual conquest contain many of the same elements as rape – they fill men with a spirit of power, dominance and virility. But what distinguishes rapists from other men is that they often perceive sexually violent behaviour and seduction as one and the same thing. For them, sexual activity is closely linked to the attainment of feelings of power and domination (see Chapter 4).

Another distinguishing feature of rapists that has been proposed is that rapists may use more violence in long-term heterosexual relationships than do physically violent men. Thus it was suggested in Chapter 5 that if rapists use violence towards women with whom they are intimate, they will find it easy or easier to display violent behaviour towards women with whom they are less intimate. For many rapists, physical coercion and aggression have been significant components of their family's mode of communication. As adults, they are merely duplicating the behaviour they have learnt as children (see Chapter 5). This behaviour is often transformed into rape because they objectify women and because they associate sex and coercion.

Feelings of ascendancy achieved through sex help to relieve the fear of not being considered a 'real man'. Therefore, as this study has found, rape is the conquest not only of a woman, but of the offender's own fears about his virility. Tax throws some light on the existential dread a man suffers as a result of his attempt to live up to the masculine ideal:

> The ideal . . . male, in terms of the dominant values of our society, is a competitive machine, competent, hard-driving, achieving and soulless, with a sexual life, but no personal life. Fortunately, most men can't live up to this ideal; but the strain is considerable.[9]

Trying to fulfil the expectations of manhood keeps men separated from their feelings and incompetent in developing intimacy with others. Furthermore, their sexual activity is likely to be impoverished by its divorce from feelings of affection. Endearment in lovemaking and true sexual liberation require sex role liberation.[10] Only when men relinquish their perpetual quest for power and begin to perceive women as people will heterosexual relationships be truly sensual and rewarding for both partners. A change in men's beliefs and attitudes is a prerequisite for making sexual violence an aberration in our society.

However, the transformation of socialisation patterns is not sufficient to solve the problem of rape. What is required is a complete transfiguration of every structure and institution infected with sexism. This work must go together with the consolidation and promotion of gains made in the past. Any attempt to legalise sexist institutions should be viewed with extreme caution. With reference to this, the proposal that legalisation of pornography and prostitution is an extension of people's freedom of choice is obviously a strong argument, but needs to be weighed up against other considerations, primarily their social effect. Pornography and prostitution, by propogating and reinforcing stereotypes of women as passive sexual objects, help to reinforce the social control of women and increase sexual aggression directed against them (see Chapter 2). As previously stated, while individuals might gain freedom of choice, the rape victim certainly does not.

That our society is characterised by a culture of rape is evident not only in the fact that activities and institutions which deprecate women are tolerated; but also by the easy manner in which the rapist legitimises his behaviour, and the sometimes amicable treatment he receives from his social network and the state authorities. Of all categories of crime, rape is unique in that the offender is often cast as the victim and the victim as the criminal. While the rapist justifies his behaviour with social sanction, the victim may often be demeaned by the police, the law and in some instances her family. By 'having sex' with a stranger, even if it is against her will, she becomes vulnerable to accusations of losing her respectability and defiling her husband's and her family's reputation. On most occasions, the rapist is not open to these accusations since our society insists that men have uncontrollable sexual urges requiring immediate satisfaction, that women are often responsible for rape because of their sexually provocative behaviour or that women enjoy being raped.

Even with the revision of the norms of masculinity and femininity that are taking place presently, there is little indication that the relationships between men and women are changing substantially. Men wearing perfume, earrings and tight pants, doing the shopping or making the food does not radically change the older, inbred attitudes of dominance, possessiveness and competitiveness. As Hoch puts it:

> True, men no longer fight duels the way they did in the age of gallantry, and for the educated 'middle' classes, even fist-fights between rugged individualists have gone somewhat out of style. But competition for women and status is still with us; only now it tends to be fought out in terms of a consumption ethic of cars and clothes and credit cards. This kind of competition, this pressure to prove himself more of a man than the next fellow, will be with us as long as the present economic system with its hierarchical social classes and status.[12]

As long as the need to validate stereotypical masculinity exists, rape will probably remain a permanent feature of our society. The perpetuation of the masculine mystique makes the man brought up in squalid living conditions just as much a potential rapist as the academic, the intellectual theatre-goer, the politician and the business executive.

This finding is related to another: that membership of the working class, or living under poverty-stricken conditions, are not the causes of rape. Differences in emotional functioning, family socialisation patterns and perceptions of women help to account for why some working class men rape and others do not.

What of the changes in femininity? Even in the midst of greater

What of the changes in femininity? Even in the midst of greater economic opportunities which have provided women with a certain amount of autonomy and independence, powerful forces of socialisation still teach the feminine traits of acquiescence, passivity and submissiveness. There are many examples of women finding themselves in precarious situations because they did not assert themselves or were too dependent and trusting.[13]

Women's new-found autonomy and independence is far from complete. Social control mechanisms apart, many women remain hesitant to move towards an alternative lifestyle, as 'what will not be easily relinquished is the security derived from the folklore and customs that have traditionally defined sexuality and marriage'.[14] Therefore, despite the advances made by feminism, many women 'prefer' not to seek fulfilment in autonomy, but continue to rely on husband and family to give them their sense of identity and social respectability. Their dependence on a man means that in order to maintain a relationship with him, they must often yield to his authority and gratify his needs, even when unwillingly. The effect is that many men are unwilling to take 'no' for an answer in sexual encounters.

While we have discussed how men's objectification of women encourages rape, we have not touched on the ambivalence many women feek about being treated as sexual objects. The feeling of depersonalisation resulting from being sexually objectified is counterbalanced with women's experience that if they do not fulfil the role of object, they will receive less sexual affirmation from men. According to Russell, 'many women have internalised male notions of attractiveness, and so in order to feel good about their appearance, they have to pile on make-up, and display their breasts, legs or behinds. This need contributes to their own objectification, which in turn contributes to the rape problem.'[16]

The link between sexuality, sex roles, the politico-economic system and rape is a profound one. Rape, the violent face of sexism, will continue to exist as long as women are oppressed and as long as women's subjugation is anchored in the structure of our society. Anti-rape activities, ranging from psychotherapeutic and legal aid to self-defence and educational programmes, must therefore be conducted with the long-term vision of developing a society in which social, economic, political and sexual justice for all are the minimum standards.

Notes

1 1977, page 222.
2 Morgan, 1981.
3 For a valuable discussion on these groups refer to Rohrbaugh, 1980, page 456.
4 Rohrbaugh, 1981.
5 Kiley, 1980.
6 Kiley, 1980, page 638.
7 Hare-Mustin, 1978, page 181.
8 Shapiro and Shapiro (eds.), 1979.
9 Cited in Hoch, 1979, page 17.
10 Russell, 1975.
11 Hoch, 1979.
12 1979, page 144.
13 Russell, 1975, page 272.
14 Francoeur and Francoeur, 1974, page viii.
15 1975, page 272.

References

Abrahamsen, D. (1960). *The Psychology of Crime*. New York: Columbia University Press.

Alder, C. (June 1984). 'The Convicted Rapist: A Sexual or Violent Offender?', *Criminal Justice and Behaviour*, vol. 11(2), pp.157-177.

Amir, M. (1971). *Patterns in Forcible Rape*. Chicago: University of Chicago Press.

Amir, M. (December 1967). 'Victim-Precipitated Forcible Rape', *Journal of Criminal Law, Criminology and Police Science*, vol. 2, pp. 498-500.

Appignanesi, R. (1979). *Freud for Beginners*. London: Writers and Readers Publishing Co-operative.

Archer, I. (1976). 'Biological Explanations of Psychological Sex Differences', in B. Lloyd and I. Archer (eds), *Exploring Sex Differences*. London: Academic Press.

Arieti, S. and Bemporad, I. (1978). *Severe and Mild Depression: The Psychotherapeutic Approach*. New York: Basic Books.

Athanasiou, R., Shaver, P. and Tavis, C. (July 1972). 'Sex', *Psychology Today*, pp. 39-52.

Bandura, A. (1965). 'Influence of Models' Reinforcement Contingencies on the Acquisition of Imitative Responses', *Journal of Personality and Social Psychology*, 1, pp. 589-595.

Bandura, A. (1971). 'Analysis of Modeling Processes', in A. Bandura (ed.), *Psychological Modeling: Conflicting Theories*. Chicago: Aldine/Atherton.

Bandura, A. (ed.) (1971). *Psychological Modeling: Conflicting Theories*. Chicago: Aldine/Atherton.

Bardwick, J.M. (1971). *Psychology of Women: A Study of Bio-Cultural Conflicts*. New York: Harper and Row.

Barker, D.L. (no date). 'The Regulation of Marriage: Repressive Benevolence'. Cited in Littlejohn et. al. (1978).

Barrett, M. (1980) *Women's Oppression Today* London: Verso Editions.

Barry, H., Bacon, M.K. and Child, I.L. (1957). 'A Cross-Cultural Survey of Some Sex Differences in Socialization', *Journal of Abnormal and Social Psychology*, 55, pp. 327-332.

Bart, P.B. (1981). 'A Study of Women Who Both Were Raped and Avoided Rape', *Journal of Social Issues*, 37(4).

Bell, R.R. (1981). *Contemporary Social Problems*. Homewood: Dorsey Press.

Berger, P.L. and Berger, B. (1976). *Sociology: A Biographical Approach*. Harmondsworth: Penguin.

Berger, S. (1976). *Deliver us from Love*. New York: De la Corte.

Binney, V., Harkell, G. and Nixon, J. (1983). *Leaving Violent Men: A Study of Refugees and Housing for Battered Women*. London: Women's Aid Federation.

Bowker, L.H. (1978). *Women, Crime and the Criminal Justice System*. Lexington M.A.: D.C. Heath.

Bradbury, P. (1982). 'Sexuality and Male Violence', *Achilles Heel*, 5.

Briddell, D.W. and Wilson, G.T. (1976). 'Effects of Alcohol and Expectancy Set on Male Sexual Arousal', *Journal of Abnormal Psychology*, 85, pp. 225-234.

Broomberg, W. (1965). *Crime and the Mind*. New York (no publisher).

Brown, R., Galanter, E., Hess E. and Mandler, G. (eds). (1962). *New Directions in Psychology*. New York: Holt, Rinehart and Winston.

Brownmiller, S. (1975). *Against our Will: Men, Women and Rape*. New York: Bantam Books.

Burgess, A.W. and Holmstroom, L.L. (May-June 1975). 'Accountability: A Right of the Rape Victim', *Journal of Psychiatric Nursing*, 13(3), pp. 11-16. Cited in S. Katz and M. Mazur (1979).

Burt, M.R. (1980). 'Cultural Myths and Supports for Rape', *Journal of Personality and Social Psychology*, 38, pp. 217-230.

Burt, M.R. (January 10-12 1978). 'Attitudes Supportive of Rape in American Culture', *Hearing 95th Congress*, 2nd session. Washington: Government Printing Office. Cited in N.M. Malamuth (1981).

Business Day, 17 April 1989.

Carroll, J.C. 'The Intergenerational Transmission of Family Violence: The Long-Term Effects of Aggressive Behaviour', *Aggressive Behaviour*, 3 (Fall), pp. 289-299. Cited in M.A. Strauss (1979).

Carbary, L.J. (February 1974). Treating Terrified Victims', *The Journal of Practical Nursing*, pp. 20-22. Cited in S. Katz and M. Mazur (1979).

Cavell, M. (1974). *Since 1924: Toward a New Psychology of Women*. (No place and publisher.) Cited in J. Rohrbaugh (1981).

Chafe, W.H. (1977). *Women and Equality: Changing Patterns in American Culture*. New York: Oxford University Press.

Chappell, D., Geis, G., Schafer, S. and Siegel, L. (1977). 'A Comparative Study of Forcible Rape Offences Known to the Police in Boston and Los Angeles', in D. Chappell, R. Geis and G. Geis (eds), *Forcible Rape: The Crime and Victim and the Offender*. New York: Columbia University Press.

The Citizen, 29 May 1985. 'Changes in Sexual Offence Laws Planned', p.13.

Clark, L. and Lewis, D. (1977). *Rape: The Price of Coercive Sexuality*. Toronto: Women's Press.

Cleaver, E. (1968). *Soul on Ice*. New York: Dell-Delta/Ramparts.

Cody Wilson, W. (1977). 'Facts versus Fears: Why Should We Worry About Pornography?', in E.S. Morrison and V. Borasage (eds), (1977). *Human Sexuality*. Palo Alto: Mayfield.

Cohn, F. (1974). *Understanding Human Sexuality*. Englewood Cliffs: Prentice Hall.

Colaizzi, P.J. (1978). 'Psychological Research as the Phenomenologist Views It', in R.S. Valle and M. King (eds), (1978). *Existential—Phenomenological Alternatives for Psychology*. New York: Oxford University Press.

'Comment about Police Discretion and the Judgement that a Crime has been committed – Rape in Philadelphie', University of Pennsylvania Law Review (1968). 117 (2), p. 318. Cited in D. Herman (1979).

Concise Oxford Dictionary. (1976). Sixth edition. London: Oxford University Press.

Conn, J.H. and Kanner L. (1974). 'Children's Awareness of Sex Differences', *Journal of Child Psychiatry*, 1, pp. 3-57. Cited in J. Rohrbaugh (1981).

Connell, C.F. and Kahn, R.L. (1957). *The Dynamics of Interviewing*. New York: Wiley.

Connell, N. and Wilson, C. (1974). *Rape: The First Sourcebook for Women*. New York: Plume.

Conybeare, E. (1892). *Womanly Women and Social Purity*. Cape Town: Townsend.

Court, J.H. (October 1979). 'Pornography and Rape in South Africa', *De Jure*, pp. 236-241.

Coward, R. (June 1982). 'Pornography: Two Opposing Feminist Viewpoints', *Spare Rib*, p. 119.

Craft, M. (1966). 'The causation of psychopathic disorder', in M. Craft (ed), (1966). *Psychopathic Disorders*. Oxford: Pergamen.

Criminal Procedure Act No. 51 (1977). South Africa (Republic). Statutes.

Cronbach, L.J. (1970). *Essentials of Psychological Testing*, (third edition). New York: Harper and Row.

Crook, J.H. (1970). 'Introduction – Social Behaviour and Ethology', in J.H. Crook (ed), *Social behaviour in Birds and Mammals*. London: Academic Press.

Dahl, T.S. and Snare, A. (1978). 'The Coercion of Privacy', in C. Smart and E. Smart (eds), (1978). *Women, Sexuality and Social Control*. London: Routledge and Kegan Paul.

Darling, 27 May 1981, p. 36.

Davis, A.Y. (June 1975). 'Joanne Little: The Dialectics of Rape', *Ms*, 3 (12).

Davis, A.Y. (1979). 'Rape, Racism and the Capitalist Setting', in E. Shapiro and B.M. Shapiro (eds), *The Women Say, The Men Say*. New York: Dell Publishing.

Davis, A.Y. (1982). *Women, Race and Class*. London: Women's Press.

Davis, E.G. (1971). *The First Sex*. New York: Putnam.

Davison, G.C. and Neale, A.M. (1978). *Abnormal Psychology*, (second edition). New York: John Wiley.

Dawson, J.L.M. (1972). 'Effects of Sex Hormones on Cognitive Style in Rats and Men', *Behaviour Genetics*, 2, pp. 21-42. Cited in J. Archer (1976).

De Beauvoir, S. (1972). *The Second Sex*. Harmondsworth: Penguin Books.

Deming, M.B. and Eppy, A. (July 1981). 'The Sociology of Rape', *Sociology and Social Research*, 65(4), pp. 337-380.

Detention and Security Legislation in South Africa. Proceedings of a conference held at the University of Natal, September 1982.

Deutsch, H. (1944). *The Psychology of Women*. London: Grune and Stratton.

Dobash, R.E. and Dobash, R. (1977). 'Wives: The "Appropriate" Victims of Marital Violence', *Victimology*, 2. Cited in T. Hill (1982).

Dollard, J.L., Doob, L.W., Miller, N., Mower, O.H. and Sears, R.R. (1939). *Frustration and Aggression*. New Haven: Yale University Press. Cited in D.J. Schneider (1976).

Donnerstein, E. (1980). 'Aggressive Erotica and Violence Against Women', *Journal of Personality and Social Psychology*, 39(2), pp. 269-277.

Dublin Rape Crisis Centre. (1981). From the first report. In *Feminist Anthology Collective*. London: Women's Press.

Dugard, J. (1977). *Introduction to Criminal Procedure*. Cape Town: Juta.

Dworkin, A. (1981). *Pornography: Men Possessing Women*. London: Women's Press.

Eardley, T. (1982). 'Masculinity Acquitted: Implications of the Sutcliffe Trial', *Achilles Heel*, 5.

Edwards, S. (1981). *Female Sexuality and the Law*. Oxford: Martin Robertson.

Ehenreich, B. (1979). 'Toward Socialist Feminism', in E. Shapiro and B.M. Shapiro (eds), *The Women Say, The Men Say*. New York: Dell Publishing.

Eisenfeld, P. and Lazarsfeld, P.F. (1938). 'The Psychological Effects of Unemployment', *Psychological Bulletin*, vol. 35, pp. 358-90. Cited in P. Kelvin and J.E. Jarret, (1985). *Unemployment: Its Social Psychological Effects*. Cambridge: Cambridge University Press.

Eisenhower, M.S. (December 1969). 'To Establish Justice, To Ensure Domestic Tranquility', *Final Report of the National Commission on Causes and Prevention of Violence*. Washington D.C.: United States Government Printing Office. Cited in S. Katz and M. Mazur (1979).

Ember, C.R. (1973). 'Feminine Task Assignment and the Social Behaviour of Boys', *Ethos*, 1, pp. 424-439. Cited in P.C. Rosenblatt and M.R. Cunningham (1976).

Engels, F. (1972). *The Origin of the Family, Private Property and the State*. New York: Pathfinder Press.

Ennis, P.H. (May 1967). 'Criminal Victimization in the United States: A Report of a National Survey', *National Opinion Research Centre*. Washington D.C.: United States Government Printing Office. Cited in S. Katz and M. Mazur (1979).

Erikson, E. (1963). *Youth, Change and Challenge*. New York: Norton.

Erlanger, H.S. (December 1974). 'The Empirical Status of the Subculture of Violence Thesis', *Social Problems* (no volume number).

Evans, M. (ed). (1982). *The Woman Question*. Oxford: Fontana.

Faraday, A. (1982). 'On the Other Side of the Billboard . . .: Pornography, Male Fantasies and the Objectification of Women', in S. Friedman and E. Sarah (eds). *On the Problem of Men*. London: Women's Press.

Farkas, G. and Rosen, R.C. (1976). 'The Effects of Alcohol on Elicited Male Sexual Response', *Studies in Alcohol*, 37, pp. 265-272. Cited in G.C. Davison and J.M. Neale (1978).

Faust, B. (1980). *Women, Sex and Pornography*. Harmondsworth: Penguin.

Fay, B. (1975). *Social Theory and Political Practice*. London: Allen and Unwin.

Feldman-Summers, S., Gordon, P.E. and Meagher, J.R. (1979). 'The Impact of Rape on Sexual Satisfaction', *Journal of Abnormal Psychology*, 88(1), pp. 101-105.

Festinger, L. (1954). 'A Theory of Social Comparison Processes', *Human Relations*, 7.

Festinger, L. (1957). *A Theory of Cognitive Dissonance*. New York: Row Peterson.

Field, H.S. (1978). 'Attitudes Toward Rape: A Comparative Analysis of Police, Rapists, Crisis Counsellors and Citizens', *Journal of Personality and Social Psychology*, 36, pp. 156-179.

Finkelhor, D. and Yllo, K. (July 1982). 'Forced Sex in Marriage: A Preliminary Research Report', *Crime and Delinquency*, (no volume number).

Firestone, S. (1979). *The Dialectic of Sex*. London: The Women's Press.

Fischer, S. (1973). *The Female Orgasm: Psychology, Physiology, Fantasy*. New York: Basic Books.

Fisher, C.J. (1978). 'Personality and Assessment', in R.S. Valle and M. King (eds), *Existential-Phenomenological Alternatives for Psychology*. New York: Oxford University Press.

Francoeur, E.K. and Francoeur, R.T. (1974). *The Future of Sexual Relations*. New Jersey: Prentice Hall.

Frank, E., Turner, S.M. and Duffy, B. (1979). 'Depressive Symptoms in Rape Victims', *Journal of Affective Disorders*, 1, pp. 269-297.

Freeman, J. (ed). (1979). *Women: A Feminist Perspective*. (Place of publication unknown): Mayfield.

Fremont, J. *Rapists Speak for Themselves*. (Source unknown).

Freud, S. (1950). Letter to Fleiss, no. 71, in J. Strachey (ed. and trans.), *The Standard Edition of the Complete Psychological Works of Sigmund Freud*. London: Hogarth Press. (Originally published, 15 October 1897).

Freud, S. (1953). 'Three Essays on the Theory of Sexuality', in J. Strachey (ed. and trans.), *The Standard Edition of the Complete Psychological Works of Sigmund Freud*. London: Hogarth Press, vol. 7. (Originally published, 1905).

Freud, S. (1950). 'The Economic Problem in Masochism', in J. Riviere (ed. and trans.), *Sigmund Freud: Collected Papers*. London: Hogarth Press, vol. 2. (Originally published, 1924).

Freud, S. (1955). 'The Dissolution of the Oedipus Complex', in J. Strachey (ed. and trans.), *The Standard Edition of the Complete Psychological Works of Sigmund Freud*. London: Hogarth Press. (Originally published, 1924).

Freud, S. (1959). 'Some Psychological Consequences of the Anatomical Distinction Between the Sexes', in J. Strachey (ed. and trans.), *The Standard Edition of the Complete Psychological Works of Sigmund Freud*. London: Hogarth Press. (Originally published, 1925).

Freud, S. (1965). 'Femininity', in J. Strachey (ed. and trans.), *The Standard Edition of the Complete Psychological Works of Sigmund Freud*. London: Hogarth Press. (Originally published, 1933).

Freud, S. (1965). 'New Introductory Lectures on Psychoanalysis', in J. Strachey (ed. and trans.), *The Standard Edition of the Complete Psychological Works of Sigmund Freud*. New York: Norton. (Originally published, 1933).

Friedman, S. and Sarah, E. (eds). (1982). *On the Problem of Men*. London: Women's Press.

Gager, N. and Schurr, C. (1976). *Sexual Assault: Confronting Rape in America*. New York: Grossett and Dunlap.

Garai, J.E. and Scheinfeld, A. (1968). 'Sex Differences in Mental and Behavioural Traits', *Genetic Psychology Monographs*, 77, pp. 169-299. Cited in B. Lloyd and

I. Archer (eds) (1976).

Gebbard, P.H., Gagnon, J.H., Pomeroy, W.B. and Christenson, C.V. (1965). *Sex Offenders: An Analysis of Types*. New York: Heinemann. Cited in B. Faust (1980).

Gebbard, P.H. (1965). 'Situational Factors Affecting Human Sexual Behaviour', in F.A. Beach (ed.), (1977). *Sex and Behaviour*. New York: Wiley.

Geis, G. and Geis, R. 'Rape in Stockholm: Is Permissiveness Relevant?'. Paper presented at the annual meeting of the Pacific Sociological Association. Anaheim, California. Cited in M.B. Deming and A. Eppy (1981).

Gelles, R.J. (1972). *The Violent Home*. (Place of publication unknown): Sage.

Glueck, B. (1952-1955). *Final Report Research Project for the Study and Treatment of Crimes Involving Sexual Aberrations*. Minnesota. Cited in L. Melani and L. Fodaski (1974).

Goffman, E. (1963). *Stigma and Notes on the Management of Spoiled Identity*. Englewood Cliffs: Prentice Hall.

Goode, E. (1978). *Deviant Behaviour*. Englewood Cliffs: Prentice Hall.

Gordon, M.T., Riger, S., LeBailly, R.K. and Heath, L. (1980). 'Crime, Women and the Quality of Urban Life', *Signs: Journal of Women in Culture and Society*, 5, pp. 144-160.

Gornick, V. and Moran, B.K. (eds) (1971). *Women in Sexist Society*. New York: Basic Books.

Graser, R.R. (1980). 'Marxist Criminology: A Critical Consideration', *South African Journal of Criminal Law and Criminology*, 4.

Gray, I. (1971). 'Sex Differences in Emotional Behaviour in Mammals Including Man: Endocrine Bases', *Acta Psychologica*, 35, pp. 29-46. Cited in B. Lloyd and J. Archer (eds) (1976).

Greer, G. (1971). *The Female Eunuch*. London: Granada.

Gross, A. (1978). 'The Male Role and Heterosexual Behaviour', *Journal of Social Issues*, 34(1), pp. 87-107.

Groth, A.N., Longo, R.E. and McFadin, J.B. (July 1982). 'Undetected Recidivism Among Rapists and Child Molesters', *Crime and Delinquency*, (no volume), pp. 450-457.

Groth, A.N. (1979). *Men Who Rape: The Psychology of the Offender*. New York: Plenum Publishing.

Guttmacher, M. (1960). *The Mind of the Murderer*. Farrar, Straus and Cudahy. Cited in J. Renvoize (1979).

Gyermeck, L., Genther, G. and Fleming, N. 'Some Effects of Progesterone and Related Steroids on the Central Nervous System', *International Journal of Neuropharmacology*, 6, pp. 191-198. Cited in B. Lloyd and J. Archer (eds) (1976).

Hage, D. (26 July 1974). 'There's Glory for You', *Aphra: The Feminist Literary Supplement*. Cited in D. Spender (1980).

Hale, M. (1778). *Pleas of the Crown*. Cited in R.A. Hibey (1973).

Halloran, L. (1970). *Attitude Formation and Change*. Leicester: Leicester University Press.

Hallowell, A.J. (1955). *Culture and Experience*. Philadelphia: University of Pennsylvania Press.

Hampson, J.L. and Hampson J.G. (1961). 'The Ontogenesis of Sexual Behaviour in Man', in W.C. Young (ed.), *Sex and Internal Secretions*, vol. 2. Baltimore: Williams and Watkins.

Hanmer, J. (1981). 'Male Violence and the Social Control of Women', in Feminist Anthology Collective (ed.). (1981). *No Turning Back*. London: The Women's Press.

Hare-Mustin, R.T. (17 June 1978). 'A Feminist Approach to Family Therapy', *Family Process*, (no volume), p. 181.

Hartley, R.E. (1974). 'Sex-Role Pressures and the Socialisation of the Male Child', in J. Pleck and J. Sawyer (eds), *Men and Masculinity*. Englewood Cliffs: Prentice Hall.

Hartmann, H. (1981). 'The Unhappy Marriage of Marxism and Feminism: Towards a More Progressive Union', in Sargent (ed.), *Women and Revolution*. London: Pluto Press.

Heather, N. (1976). *Radical Perspectives in Psychology*. London: Meuthen and Co.

Hepburn, J.R. (Summer 1973). 'Violent Behaviour in Interpersonal Relationships', *The Sociological Quarterly*, p. 425.

Herink, R. (ed). (1980). *The Psychotherapy Handbook*. New York: Meridan.

Herman, D. (1979). 'The Rape Culture', in Freeman (ed.) (1979). *Women: A Feminist Perspective*. (Place of publication unknown): Mayfield.

Hibey, R.A. (Winter 1973). 'The Trial of a Rape Case: An Advocate's Analysis of Corroboration, Consent and Character', *American Law Review*, pp. 309-334.

Hill, T. (1982). 'Rape and Marital Violence in the Maintenance of Male Power', in S. Friedman and E. Sarah (eds) (1982). *On the Problem of Men*. London: Women's Press.

Hindelang, M.J. Gottfredson, M.R. and Garofalo, J. (1978). *Victims of Personal Crime: An Empirical Foundation for a Theory of Personal Victimization*. Cambridge: Ballinger.

Hite, S. (1976). *The Hite Report: A Nationwide Study of Female Sexuality*. New York: Dell.

Hjelle, L.A. and Ziegler, D.J. (1981). *Personality Theories*. New York: McGraw Hill.

Hoch, P. (1979). *White Hero, Black Beast*. London: Pluto Press.

Hoebel, E.A. (1960). *The Cheyennes*. New York: Holt, Rinehart and Winston. Cited in Reeves Sanday (1981).

Hoffman, C.H. (1970). *Law of Evidence*. Durban: Butterworth. Cited in K. Satchwell (1981).

Horney, K. (1967). 'The Problem of Feminine Masochism', in K. Horney (1967), *Feminine Psychology*. New York: Norton.

Horney, K. (1967). *Feminine Psychology*. New York: Norton.

Horos, C.V. (1974). *Rape*. Connecticut: Tobey Publishing.

Hunt (1982). *South African Criminal Law and Procedure*, second edition. Johannesburg: Juta.

Hutt, C. (1972). 'Sex Differences in Human Development', *Human Development*, 15, pp. 153-170.

Hutt, C. (1972). *Males and Females*. Harmondsworth: Penguin Books.

Hutter, B. and Williams, G. (1981). *Controlling Women: The Normal and the Deviant*. London: Croom Helm.

Huysamen, G.K. (1981). *Introductory Statistics and Research Design for the Behavioural Sciences*, vol. 2. Bloemfontein: (no publisher).

Hyman, H. *Interviewing in Social Research*. University of Chicago Press. Cited in Mayntz et al. (1976).

Jagger, A.M. and Rothenburg Struhl, R. (eds). (1978). *Feminist Frameworks*. New York: McGraw Hill.

Jersild, A.T. and Alpern, G.D. (1974). *The Psychology of Adolescence*. New York: Macmillan.

Josephson, W.L. and Colwill, N.L. (1978). 'Males, Females and Aggression', in H.M. Lips and N.L. Colwill, *The Psychology of Sex Differences*. Englewood Cliffs: Prentice Hall.

Kagan, J. and Moss, H.A. (1962). *Birth to Maturity*. New York: Wiley. Cited in B. Lloyd and J. Archer (eds) (1976).

Kanin, E.J. and Parcell, S.R. (1977). 'Sexual Aggression: A Second Look at the Offended Female', *Archives of Sexual Behaviour*, 1977, 6(1), pp. 67-76.

Kaplan, H.S. (1974). *The New Sex Therapy: Active Treatment of Sexual Dysfunctions*. New York: Bruner Mazel.

Kaplan, A.G. and Bean, J.P. (1976). *Beyond Sex-Role Stereotypes: Readings Toward* a *Psychology of Androgyny*. (Place of publication unknown): Little Brown.

Katcher, A. (1955). 'The Discrimination of Sex Differences by Young Children', *Journal of Genetic Psychology*, 87, pp. 131-143. Cited in J. Rohrbaugh (1981).

Katz, S. and Mazur, M. (1979). *Understanding the Rape Victim*. New York: John Wiley and Sons.

Kaye, H.E. (no date). 'Male Survival: Masculinity Without Myth'. (Place of publication and publisher unknown.) Cited in Hoch (1979).

Kerkhoff, A.C. (1972). *Socialisation and Social Class*. Englewood Cliffs: Prentice Hall.

Kiley, D. (1980). 'Street Psychotherapy', in R. Herink (ed.), *The Psychotheraphy Handbook*. New York: Meridan.

Kilpatrick, D.G., Resick, P.A. and Veronen, L.J. (1981). 'Effects of a Rape Experience. A Longitudinal Study', *Journal of Social Issues*, 37(4).

Kipnis, D. (1972). 'Does power corrupt?', *Journal of Personality and Social Psychology*, 24, pp. 33-41.

Klein, M. (no date). 'Our Adult World and its Roots in Infancy.' (Original source unknown.)

Koedt, A. (ed) (1972). *Radical Feminism*. New York: Quadrangle Press.

Koedt, A. (1974). 'The Myth of the Vaginal Orgasm', in *Radical Therapist Collective*, (volume and number unknown).

Komisar, L. (no date). *Violence and the Masculine Mystique*. Pittsburgh: Know Inc. Cited in D. Herman (1979).

Krech, D., Crutchfield, R.S. and Livson, N. (1974). *Elements of Psychology*, third edition. New York: Alfred Knopf.

Kristol, I. (1977). 'Pornography, Obscenity and the Case for Censorship', in E.S. Morrison and V. Borosage (eds), *Human Sexuality*. Palo Alto: Mayfield.

Lang, A.R., Goekner, D.J., Adessor, V.J. and Marlatt, G.A. (1975). 'Effects of Alcohol on Aggression in Male Social Drinkers', *Journal of Abnormal Psychology*, 84, pp. 508-518.

Lear, Q. (30 January 1972). 'If you Rape a Woman and Steal Her T.V., What Can They Get You For in New York? A. Stealing Her T.V.?' *New York Times*. Cited in P. Wood (1974).

Le Grand, C.E. (1973). 'Rape and Social Structure', *Psychological Report*, 35.

Levett, A. (1981). *Consideration in the Provision of Adequate Psychological Care for the Sexually Assaulted Woman*. University of Cape Town. Unpublished.

Levine, S. and Koenig, J. (eds). (1983). *Why Men Rape*. London: W.H. Allen.

Lips, H.M. (1981). *Women, Men and the Psychology of Power*. Englewood Cliffs: Prentice Hall.

Lips, H.M. and Colwill, N.L. (1978). *The Psychology of Sex Difference*. Englewood Cliffs: Prentice Hall.

Lipstein, B. (February 1975). 'In Defence of Small Samples', *Journal of Advertising Research*, 15(1).

Litewka, L. (1977). 'The Socialised Penis', in E.S. Morrison and V. Borosage (eds), *Human Sexuality*. Palo Alto: Mayfield.

Littlejohn, G., Wakeford, J., Smart, B. and Davis, Y. (1978). *Power and the State*. London: Croom Helm.

Lloyd, B. and Archer, J. (eds). (1976). *Exploring Sex Differences*. London: Academic Press.

London Action Rape Group. (1982). 'Towards a Revolutionary Feminist Analysis of Rape', in S. Friedman and E. Sarah (eds) (1982), *On the Problem of Men*. London: The Women's Press.

London, I. (1974). 'Frigidity, Sensitivity and Sexual Roles', in J. Pleck and J. Sawyer (eds) (1974), *Men and Masculinity*. Englewood Cliffs: Prentice Hall.

Lorenz, K. (1969). *On Aggression*. New York: Bantam.

Lunde, D. and Hamburg, D.A. (1974). 'Techniques for Assessing the Effects of

Sex Hormones on Affects, Arousal and Aggression in Humans', *Recent Progress in Hormone Research*, 28, pp. 627-663. Cited in J. Archer (1976).

Maccoby, E.E. and Jacklin, C.N. (1974). *The Psychology of Sex Differences*. Stanford: Stanford University Press.

MacDonald, J.M. (1971). *Rape Offenders and their Victims*. Springfield: Thomas.

MacKellar, J. (1975). *Rape: The Bait and the Trap*. New York: Crown Publishers. Cited in A. Davis (1979).

Malamuth, N.M. (1979). 'Rape Fantasies as a Function of Repeated Exposure to Sexual Violence'. Paper presented at the Second Annual Conference on the Treatment of Sexual Aggressiveness, New York. Cited in H. Lips (1981).

Malamuth, N.M. (1981). 'Rape Proclivity Among Males', *Journal of Social Issues*, 37(4).

Malamuth, N.M. and Check, J.V.P. (June 1979). 'Penile Tumescence and Perceptual Responses to Rape as a Function of Victim's Response'. Paper presented at the Canadian Psychological Association Meeting, Quebec City. Cited in H. Lips (1981).

Malamuth, N.M., Gaber, S. and Feshbach, S. (1980). 'Testing Hypotheses Regarding Rape: Exposure to Sexual Violence, Sex Differences and the "Normality" of Rapists', *Journal of Research in Personality*, 14(1), pp. 121-137.

Mandler, G. (1962). 'Emotion', in R.R. Brown et. al. (eds), *New Directions in Psychology*. New York: Holt, Rinehart and Winston.

Marsden, D. (1978). 'Sociological Perspectives on Family Violence', in Martin (ed.) (1978), *Violence and the Family*. Chichester: John Wiley and Sons.

Martin, J.P. (1978). *Violence and the Family*. Chichester: John Wiley.

MASA. *Rape, The Full Story*. (No publisher and date).

Maslow, A. (1966). 'Self Esteem (Dominance-Feeling) and Sexuality in Women', in H.M. Ruitenbeek (1966), *Psychoanalysis and Female Sexuality*. Haven: College and University Press.

Masters, W.H. and Johnsohn, V.E. (1966). *Human Sexual Response*. Boston: Little Brown.

Masters, W.H. and Johnsohn, V.E. (1970). *Human Sexual Inadequacy*. Boston: Little Brown.

Mayne, A.V. and Levett, A. (1977). 'The Traumas of Rape – Some Considerations', *South African Journal of Criminal Law and Criminology*, (2).

Mayntz, R., Holm, K. and Hoebner, P. (1976). *Introduction to Empirical Sociology*. Harmondsworth: Penguin.

McCaldon, R.J. (1967). 'Rape', *Canadian Journal of Corrections*, 9(1), pp. 37-57.

McCall, R.B. (1970). *Fundamental Statistics for Psychology*. New York: Harcourt.

McDonald, A. and Paitich, D. (1983). 'Psychological Profile of the Rapist', *American Journal of Forensic Psychiatry*, vol. 3(4), pp. 159-172.

McIntosh, M. (1978). 'The State and the Oppression of Women', in A. Kuhn and A.M. Wolpe (eds), *Feminism and Materialism*. London: Routledge and Kegan Paul.

McIntosh, M. (1978). 'Who Needs Prostitutes? The Ideology of Male Sexual Needs', in C. Smart and B. Smarts (eds) (1978), *Women, Sexuality and Social Control*. London: Routledge and Kegan Paul.

McNickle Rose, V. (1977). 'Rape as a Social Problem: A Byproduct of the Feminist Movement', *Social Problems*, pp. 75-85.

Mead, G.H. (1934). *Mind, Self and Society*. Chicago: University of Chicago Press.

Medea, A. and Thompson, K., (1972). *Against Rape*. London: Peter Owen.

Melani, L. and Fodaski, L. (1974). 'The Psychology of the Rapist and his Victim', in N. Connell and C. Wilson (eds) (1974), *Rape: The First Sourcebook for Women*. New York: Plume.

Miller, N.E. (1948). 'Theory and Experiment Relating Psychoanalytic Displacement to Stimulus Response Generalisation', *Journal of Abnormal and Social Psychology*, 43, pp. 155-178. Cited in D.J. Schneider (1976).

Miller, N.E. (1941). 'The Frustration-Aggression Hypothesis', *Psychological Review*, 48, pp. 337-342.

Millet, K. (1970). *Sexual Politics*. New York: Avon Books.

Mitchell, J. (1974). *Psychoanalysis and Feminism*. Harmondsworth: Penguin Books.

Mohr, J.W. (October 1965). 'Rape and Attempted Rape', *Sexual Behaviour and the Criminal Law*, part III. A Preliminary Report. Mimeographed, from the Forensic Clinic, Toronto Psychiatric Hospital.

Moll, I. (1982). Lecture Notes on Theories of Socialisation. Unpublished. University of the Witwatersrand.

Money, J. and Ehrhardt, A.A. (no date) *Man and Woman, Boy and Girl*. Baltimore: John Hopkins University Press. Cited in I. Archer (1976).

Morgan, D. (1981). 'Men, Masculinity and the Process of Sociological Enquiry', in H. Roberts (ed) (1981), *Doing Feminist Research*. London: Routledge and Kegan Paul.

Morris, D. (1967). *The Naked Ape*. London: Jonathan Cape.

Morrison, E.S. and Borasage, V. (eds), (1977), *Human Sexuality*. Palo Alto: Mayfield.

Moss, H.A. (1967). 'Sex, Age, and State as Determinants of Mother-Infant Interaction', *Merrill-Palmer Quarterly*, 13, pp. 19-36. Cited in J. Rohrbaugh (1981).

Mulvihill, D.J. and Tumin, M.M. (1969). 'Crimes of Violence', vol. 2, *A Staff Report to the National Commission on the Causes and the Prevention of Violence*. Washington: United States Government Printing Offices. Cited in V. McNickle Rose (1977).

News Report. (6 August 1975). 'Rape Victim's Copying Behaviour Examined at a Special Session', *Psychiatric News*, pp. 30-31. Cited in S. Katz and M. Mazur (1979).

Newsweek, 15 September 1975, p. 48. Cited in N.M. Malamuth (1981).

Nusas Women's Directive. (1982). *Nusas Conference on Women*. Rondebosch: University of Cape Town: Students' Representative Council Press.

Oakley, A. (1972). *Sex, Gender and Society*. Melbourne: Temple Smith.

Oakley, A. (1982).'The Politics of Sex Differences', in M. Evans (ed.), (1982), *The Woman Question*. Oxford: Fontana.

Paske, A.T. (1982). *Rape and Ritual*. Toronto: Inner City Books.

Peters, J.J. (May 1975). 'Social Psychiatric Study of Victims Reporting Rape'. A study presented at the American Psychiatric Association, 128th Annual Meeting, Anaheim. Cited in S. Katz and M. Mazur (1979).

Peters, J.J., Meyer, L.C. and Carroll, N.E. (30 June 1976). 'The Philadelphia Assault Victim Study', final report from the National Institute of Mental Health. Cited in S. Katz and M. Mazur (1979).

Phelps, L. (1979). 'Female Sexual Alienation', in J. Freeman (ed.) (1979), *Women: A Feminist Perspective*. (Place of publication unknown): Mayfield.

Pikunas, J. (1976). *Human Development*. Tokyo: McGraw-Hill.

Pizzey, E. (1974). *Scream Quietly or the Neighbours will Hear*. Harmondsworth: Penguin Books.

Pleck, J. (1979). 'Men's Power with Women, Other Men, and Society: A Men's Movement Analysis', in E. Shapiro and B.M. Shapiro (eds), *The Women Say, The Men Say*. New York: Dell.

Pleck, J. and Sawyer, J. (eds). (1974). *Men and Masculinity*. Englewood Cliffs: Prentice Hall.

Quick, P. (no date). *Women's Work. The Review of Radical Political Economics*, iv(3). Cited in Dahl and Snare (1978).

Rabkin, J.G. (1979). 'The Epidemiology of Forcible Rape', *American Journal of Orthopsychiatry*, 49(4), pp. 634-647.

Rada, R.J. (1978). *Clinical Aspects of the Rapist*. New York: Grune and Stratton.

Rada, R.T. (1983). 'Plasma Androgens in Violent and Non-Violent Sex Offenders', *Bulletin of the American Academy of Psychiatry and Law*, vol. 11(2), pp. 149-182.

Radical Therapist Collective. (1974). *The Radical Therapist*. Harmondsworth: Penguin.

Reeves Sanday, P. (1981). 'The Socio-Cultural Context of Rape: A Cross-Cultural Study', *Journal of Social Issues*, 37(4).

Renvoize, J. (1979). *Web of Violence*. Harmondsworth: Penguin.

Report of the Commission on Obscenity and Pornography. (1970). New York: Bantam. Cited in B. Faust (1980).

Riger, S. and Gordon, M. (1981). 'The Fear of Rape: A Study in Social Control', *Journal of Social Issues*, 37(4).

Roberts, H. (ed). (1981). *Doing Feminist Research*. London: Routledge and Kegan Paul.

Robin, G.D. (April 1977). 'Forcible Rape: Institutionalised Sexism in the Criminal Justice System', *Crime and Delinquency*, 23(2).

Robinson, D. and Rhode, S. (no date). 'Two Experiments with an Anti-Semitism Poll', *Journal of Abnormal Social Psychology*, 42(3), p. 146. Cited in Mayntz et. al. (1976).

Rogers, L. (1976). 'Male Hormones and Behaviour', in B. Lloyd and I. Archer (eds). (1976). *Exploring Sex Differences*. London: Academic Press.

Rohrbaugh, J.B. (1981). *Women: Psychology's Puzzle*. London: Abacus.

Roscoe, J.T. (1969). *Fundamental Research Statistics*. New York: Holt, Rinehart and Winston.

Rosenberg, B.G. and Sutton-Smith, B. (1972). *Sex and Identity*. New York: Holt, Rinehart and Winston.

Rosenberg, M. (1973). 'The Biological Basis for Sex Role Stereotypes', in A.G. Kaplan and J. Bean (eds) (1976), *Beyond Sex-Role Stereotypes: Readings Towards a Psychology of Androgyny*. (Place of publication unknown): Little Brown.

Rosenblatt, P.C. and Cunningham, M.R. (1976). 'Sex Differences in Cross-Cultural Perspective', in B. Lloyd and I. Archer (eds) (1976), *Exploring Sex Differences*. London: Academic Press.

Rosenblum, K.E. (1975). 'Female Deviance and the Female Sex Role', *British Journal of Sociology*, 26(2).

Rosenthal, R. (1966). *Experimenter Effects in Behavioural Research*. New York: Appleton-Century-Crofts.

Rosow, J. (ed). (1974). *The Worker and the Job*. Englewood Cliffs: Prentice Hall.

Rubin, J.Z., Provenzano, F.J. and Luria, Z. (1976). 'The Eye of the Beholder: Parents' View on Sex of Newborns', *American Journal of Orthopsychiatry*, 44(4), pp. 512-519.

Ruitenbeek, H.M. (1966). *Psychoanalysis and Female Sexuality*. New Haven: College and University Press.

Russell, D.E.H. (1975). *The Politics of Rape*. New York: Stein and Day.

Sailly, D. and Marolla, J. (June 1984). 'Convicted Rapists' Vocabulary of Motive: Excuses and Justifications', *Social Problems*, vol. 31(5), pp. 530-544.

Satchwell, K. (1981). 'Women and the Law', in Nusas Law Directive. University of Cape Town: Student's Representative Council Press.

Schachter, S. and Singer, J.E. (1976). 'Cognitive, Social and Physiological Determinants of Emotional State', *Psychological Review*, 69, pp. 379-399.

Schachter, S. and Wheeler, L. (1976). 'Epinephrine, Chloropromazine and Amusement', *Journal of Abnormal and Social Psychology*, 65, pp. 121-128. Cited in D.J. Schneider (1976).

Schiff, A.J. (January 1969). 'Statistical Features of Rape', *Journal of Forensic Science*, 14(1), pp. 102-111.

Schneider, D.J. (1976). *Social Psychology*. Phillipines: Addison-Wesley.

Schulz, M. (1975). 'Rape is a Four Letter Word', *Etc: A Review of General Semantics*, 32(1), pp. 65-69. Cited in D. Spender (1980).

Schulz, M. (1975). 'The Semantic Derogation of Women', in B. Thorne and N.

Henley (eds) (1975), *Language and Sex: Difference and Dominance*. Rowley: Newbury House.

Schwartz, B. (no date). 'The Effect in Philadelphia of Pennsylvania's Increased Penalties for Rape and Attempted Rape', *Journal of Criminal Law, Criminology, Police Science*, 59(4), pp. 509-515.

Scope, 2 April 1982. 'Why Men Rape'. p. 25.

Seaman, B. (1972). *Free and Female*. Greenwich Connecticut: Fawcett Crest Books.

Selkin, J. (5 January 1975). 'Rape', *Psychology Today*, 8.

Shapiro, E. and Shapiro B.M. (eds). (1979). *The Women Say, The Men Say*. New York: Dell Publishing.

Shapiro, L. (1979). 'Violence: The Most Obscene Fantasy', in J. Freeman (ed.) (1979), *Women: A Feminist Perspective*. (Place of publication unknown): Mayfield.

Simon, A.M. (1979). *A Guide to Practical Social Research for Students*. Johannesburg: University of the Witwatersrand Press.

Singer, M. (1976). 'Sexism and Male Sexuality', *Issues in Radical Therapy*, 3.

Skinner, B.J. (1975). 'The Steep and Thorny Way to a Science of Behaviour', *American Psychologist*, 30, pp. 42-49.

Smart, C. and Smart, B. (1978). *Women, Sexuality and Social Control*. London: Routledge and Kegan Paul.

Sorenson, R.C. (1973). *Adolescent Sexuality in Contemporary America*. New York: World Press.

Sowetan, 2 September 1983, p. 2.

Spender, D. (1980). *Man Made Language*. London: Routledge and Kegan Paul.

The Star, 5 January 1983.

The Star, 18 January 1984.

The Star, 29 May, 6 June, 1985.

Steinmetz, S.K. (January 1977a). 'The Use of Force for Resolving Family Conflict: The Training Ground for Abuse', *The Family Co-ordinator*, 19-26. Cited in M.A. Strauss.

Steinmetz, S.K. (1977b). *The Cycle of Violence: Assertive, Aggressive and Abusive Family Interaction*. New York: Praeger.

Storaska, F. (1975). *How to Say No to a Rapist . . . And Survive*. New York: Random House.

Sunday Express, 17 May 1981.

Svalastoga, K. (Spring 1962). 'Rape and Social Structure', *Pacific Sociological Review*, 5, pp. 48-53.

Tanay, E. (1969). 'Psychiatric Study of Homicide', *American Journal of Psychiatry*, 125(1), pp. 1252-1258. Cited in J. Renvoize (1979).

Tedeschi, J.T., Schlenker, B.R. and Bonoma, T.V. (1973). *Conflict, Power and Games: The Study of Interpersonal Relations*. Chicago: Aldine.

Thomas, K. 'The Double Standard', *Journal of the History of Ideas*, 20(2). Cited in M. McIntosh (1978b).

Thompson, C. (1943). 'Penis Envy in Women', *Psychiatry*, 6, pp. 123-125.

Thompson, E.P. (1978). *The Poverty of Theory*. London: Merlin Press.

Thorne, B. and Henley, N. (eds). (1975). *Language and Sex: Difference and Dominance*. Rowley: Newbury House.

Time, 5 September 1985. 36, p. 10.

Tolson, A. (1977). *The Limits of Masculinity*. London: Tavistock.

Turner, R. (1972). *The Eye of the Needle*. Johannesburg: Ravan.

Ullian D.Z. (1976). 'The Development of Conceptions of Masculinity and Femininity', in B. Lloyd and I. Archer (eds) (1976), *Exploring Sex Differences*. London: Academic Press.

Valle, R.S. and King, M. (1978). *Existential-Phenomenological Alternatives for Psychology*. New York: Oxford University Press.

Van Ness, S.R. (Fall-Winter 1984). 'Rape as Instrumental Violence. A Study of

214

Youth Offenders', *Journal of Offender Counselling, Services and Rehabilitation,* vol. 9(1-2), pp. 161-170.

Vernikes-Danellis, J. (1972). 'Effects of Hormones on the Central Nervous System', in S. Levine (ed.) (1972). *Hormones and Behaviour.* New York: Academic Press.

'The Victim in a Forcible Rape Case: A Feminist View'. (Winter 1973). *American Criminal Law Review* (editorial).

Vincent, S. (20 September 1980). 'No Immortal Longings?', *Observer,* (no volume). Cited in B. Hutter and G. Williams (eds) (1981).

Vogelman, L. (1981). *The Client: A Study of Sexism and Prostitution.* Unpublished Honours thesis, University of Witwatersrand.

Vogelman, L. (1982). 'Men and Feminism.' In Nusas Womens Directive, *Nusas Conference on Women.* University of Cape Town: Students' Representatives Council Press.

Vogelman, L. (1983). 'The Perpetrators of Sexual Abuse: An Appraisal of Contributing Societal Factors.' Paper presented at the Developmental Psychological Conference, Durban.

Wallace, D. and Wehmer, G. 'Contemporary Standards of Visual Erotica. *Technical Reports,* 6. Cited in Cody Wilson (1977).

Walters, D. (1975). *Physical and Sexual Abuse of Children.* Indiana University Press.

Warner, C.G. (ed). (1980). *Rape and Sexual Assault.* Germantown M.D.: Aspen Systems Co.

Webster, E. (ed). (1978). *Essays in Southern African Labour History.* Johannesburg: Ravan.

Weis, K. and Borge, S.S. (Fall). 'Victimology and Rape: The Case of the Legitimate Victim', *Issues in Criminology,* 8, pp. 71-115.

Weisstein, N. (1971). 'Psychology Constructs the Female', in V. Gornick and B. Moran (eds) (1971), *Women in Sexist Society.* New York: Basic Books.

West, L.J. (1985). 'Effects of Isolation on the Evidence of Detainees', in Bell, A.N. and Mackie, R.D.A. (eds) (1985) *Detention and Security Legislation in South Africa.* Durban: University of Natal.

Williams, M.G. (1977). *The New Executive Woman: A Guide to Business Success.* New York: New American Library. Cited in H. Lips (1981).

Wilson, E. (1983). *What is to be Done About Violence Against Women.* Harmondsworth: Penguin.

Wilson, P.R. (1978). *The Other Side of Rape.* (Place of publication unknown): University of Queensland Press.

Wolfe, J. and Baker, V. (1980). Characteristics of Imprisoned Rapists and Circumstances of the Rape', in C.G. Warner (ed.) (1980). *Rape and Sexual Assault.* Germantown M.D.: Aspen Systems Co.

Wollstonecraft, M. (1972). *A Vindication of the Rights of Women.* (No place or publisher). Cited in G. Greer (1971).

Wood, P.L. (1974). 'The Victim in a Forcible Rape Case: A Feminist View', in N. Connell and C. Wilson (eds) (1974), *Rape: The First Sourcebook for Women.* New York: Plume.

Yankelovich, D. (1974). 'The Meaning of the Work', in J. Rosow (ed.) (1974), *The Worker and the Job.* Englewood Cliffs: Prentice Hall.

Yawitch, J. (no date). 'Overcoming our Socialisation.' Unpublished paper.

Zimbardo, P.G., Ebbesen, E.B. and Maslach, C. (1977). *Influencing Attitudes and Changing Behaviour,* second edition. Phillipines: Addison-Wesley.

Zito, G.V. (1975). *Methodology and Meanings. Varieties of Sociological Inquiry.* New York: Praeger Publishers.